🚲

Mumbai
on Two
Wheels

GLOBAL
SOUTH
ASIA

Padma Kaimal

K. Sivaramakrishnan

Anand A. Yang

Series Editors

Jonathan Shapiro Anjaria

MUMBAI ON TWO WHEELS

Cycling, Urban Space,
and Sustainable Mobility

University of Washington Press / Seattle

Mumbai on Two Wheels was supported by a grant from the McLellan Endowment, established through the generosity of Martha McCleary McLellan and Mary McLellan Williams.

This book will be made open access within three years of publication thanks to Path to Open, a program developed to bring about equitable access and impact for the entire scholarly community, including authors, researchers, libraries, and university presses around the world. Learn more at https://about.jstor.org/path-to-open/

Design by Mindy Basinger Hill / Composed in Arno Pro

Photographs by the author unless otherwise noted.

UNIVERSITY OF WASHINGTON PRESS / uwapress.uw.edu

LIBRARY OF CONGRESS CATALOGING-IN-PUBLICATION DATA
Names: Anjaria, Jonathan Shapiro, author.
Title: Mumbai on two wheels : cycling, urban space, and sustainable
    mobility / Jonathan Shapiro Anjaria.
Description: Seattle : University of Washington Press, [2024] | Series:
    Global South Asia | Includes bibliographical references and index.
Identifiers: LCCN 2023050771 | ISBN 9780295752709 (hardcover) |
    ISBN 9780295752693 (paperback) | ISBN 9780295752716 (ebook)
Subjects: LCSH: Public spaces—India—Mumbai. | Cycling—
    India—Mumbai. | Transportation—India—Mumbai—
    Environmental aspects. | Sustainable urban development—
    India—Mumbai. | City and town life—India—Mumbai.
Classification: LCC HT169.I52 A65 2024 | DDC 307.121609544—
    dc23/eng/20240119
LC record available at https://lccn.loc.gov/2023050771

(∞) This paper meets the requirements
    of ANSI/NISO Z39.48-1992 (Permanence of Paper).

Contents

Acknowledgments

🚲   The vibrancy and creativity of Mumbai's diverse cycling communities are what inspired this book and what I hope to have captured in these pages. I thank the many people in Mumbai who invited me to join them as they cycled for work or fun and for their patience with my persistent questions and slow cycling.

Most of all, I thank Firoza Dadan, an enthusiastic supporter of this book project from the day we met in September 2015. I am incredibly grateful for her willingness to talk, collaborate, and cycle with me over these many years. Most importantly, I thank her for sharing with me her vision of cycling and bicycle advocacy in Mumbai. Her emphasis on action rather than words and her deep belief in the potential for cycling in Mumbai have profoundly shaped the arguments in this book.

This book also benefited immensely from many other people in Mumbai, as well as Pune, Delhi, and Bengaluru, some of whom I can name and others I cannot due to the need to keep them anonymous. In particular, I thank Ashish Agashe, Amit Bhatt, Mirza Saaib Bég, Mohammad Daud Chaudhari, Anuprita Dadi, Hansel D'Souza, Divyanshu Ganatra, Amin Hajee, Sanskriti Menon, Prashant Nanaware, Piyush Shah, Disha Srivastava, Divya Tate, Faisal Thakur, and Meera Velankar for their insights on cycling in India. I also thank Rishi Aggarwal, Mansi Jasani, and Ratoola Kundu, who provided essential assistance at the start of this project. I also thank Adwaita Banerjee, Ameen Hasan, Kalie Jamieson, Nupur Joshi, and Julia Karr for research assistance at various stages of this book project.

Multiple funding sources made the research and writing of this book possible. I am especially grateful for the Senior Research Fellowship from the American Institute for Indian Studies, which enabled me to do research in Mumbai in 2015 and 2016. I also thank Brandeis University for the Provost Research Grant and Theodore and Jane Norman Fund grants, which enabled multiple research trips to Mumbai between 2017 and 2022.

I am also grateful for a senior faculty semester leave from Brandeis in 2022, which enabled me to complete the writing for this book.

While this book is about Mumbai cycling cultures, my thinking on this topic has been profoundly shaped by my involvement in cycling-related issues in Cambridge, Massachusetts, my hometown. Thanks to a year-long Scholars and Society fellowship from the American Council of Learned Societies in 2019–20, I was able to work with staff at the City of Cambridge's Community Development Department, assisting on community outreach for the Cambridge Bicycle Plan 2020. I am also thankful to Cambridge City Council members and community activists for offering to meet with me during this time period. In Cambridge, special thanks to Joe Barr, Jan Devereux, Marian Darlington-Hope, Lonnell Wells-Roberts, Alanna Mallon, James Adius Pierre, Andrew Reker, Marc Roberts, Cara Seiderman, and Quinton Zondervan. Conversations during the period of this fellowship, as well as participating on the Cambridge Bicycle Committee and volunteering with the Cambridge Bike Give Back organization, founded by Lonnell Wells-Roberts, gave me greater clarity regarding the technical aspects of bicycle lane design, the limitations of seeing cycling only through the lens of infrastructure, and the larger stakes of focusing on the *context* of cycling in Mumbai. Moreover, my involvement with bicycle issues in Cambridge gave me greater clarity on what the ethnographic approach offers the world. In the years after the ACLS fellowship, in parallel with writing this book, I had conversations with over two dozen anthropologists doing applied work in industry and government settings as part of continued ACLS-funded work, as well as in my role as faculty director of professional development at the Brandeis Graduate School of Arts and Sciences. I hope the practical potential of ethnography I learned in those conversations is reflected in this text. I thank my interlocutors in Cambridge and career development work I've done since 2020 for all the insights they gave.

I thank Kalyanakrishnan (Shivi) Sivaramakrishnan for continued support, as well as the editors at University of Washington Press, who have guided me through the publication process. Special thanks go to the anonymous reviewers for their generous and productive comments. Their suggestions have helped me improve the book significantly.

This book has also benefited from conversations with numerous friends, colleagues, and current and former students, especially Sneha Annavarapu, Amita Baviskar, Tarini Bedi, Joshua Berman, Kavi Bhalla, Lisa Björkman, Namita Dharia, Gareth Doherty, Naresh Fernandes, Maura Finkelstein, Andrew Harris, Logan Hollarsmith, Asher Ghertner, Rahul Goel, Rutul Joshi, Moisés Lino e Silva, Adonia Lugo, Shilpa Phadke, Smruthi Bala Kannan, Divya Kannan, Nida Kirmani, Kareem Khubchandani, Rahul Mehrotra, Krishnendu Ray, Lucinda Ramberg, Nikhil Rao, Gowthaman Ranganathan, Parmesh Shahani, Naghmeh Sohrabi, Yana Stainova, and Malini Sur. I am also very grateful to my supportive colleagues in the Department of Anthropology at Brandeis. The book also benefited from audience comments, questions, and feedback after I presented my work at Boston University, Brandeis University, Indiana University, Northeastern University, the University of Pittsburgh, the Radcliffe Institute for Advanced Study, Harvard University, the Tata Institute of Social Sciences, Wellesley College, and Yale University.

Most of all, I thank Ulka, who truly made this book possible, and my sons Naseem and Rehaan for reminding me that everything isn't always about bicycles.

Portions of this book were originally published as "Surface Pleasures: Bicycling and the Limits of Infrastructural Thinking," *South Asia: Journal of South Asian Studies* 43, no. 2 (2020): 267–80; "Mumbai Has the Makings of a Great Cycling City—But It Needs to Set the Wheels in Motion," Scroll.in (2017); "'You Are a Mom, So Why Are You Cycling?' and Other Questions Pedaling Women Are Asked in Mumbai," Scroll.in (2016); and "Ethnography on the Move: Doing Fieldwork on a Bicycle," *Ethnographic Marginalia* (online, 2020).

⊕⊘

Mumbai
on Two
Wheels

Introduction

🚲   I once took a Kryptonite U-lock to Mumbai as a gift for a friend. She had seen me using one on a previous trip and asked me to bring one from the United States. U-locks are heavy, nearly indestructible steel locks that consists of two pieces—one shaped like a U and a short, straight section that goes over the top. Kryptonite U-locks are not common in India, where most people who don't ride affordable, Indian-made, roadster-style bicycles (which lock to themselves) lock their bicycles with a long, thin cable secured with a combination lock. But in places like Cambridge, Massachusetts, where I am while writing this, U-locks are the norm. Here, bicycle store clerks admonish customers eyeing the more affordable cable locks. They say it is quick and easy for thieves to cut cables, but cutting a U-lock requires a special tool called an angle grinder and some time. After using my gift for a week, my friend returned it to me and said she will go back to using a cable lock. She told me that the problem with U-locks is that they can only lock one bicycle at a time, whereas cable locks can be looped through three or four bicycles snuggly fitted together, securing them all at once. "Cable locks are more social," she said with a smile.

The small choice of what lock to carry as you ride through a city reflects many things: perceptions of security, the purpose of your trip, the physical features of the street edge, and with whom you will be riding. For instance, my friend found long cable locks to be useful at the end of group rides. At the end of one ride, as everyone dug into a small breakfast of keema pao, she joined their bicycles together with a single cable lock. Those bicycles will also likely be watched over by a nearby onlooker: perhaps a restaurant cashier sitting at a counter three feet away, a server handing off food to a stream of delivery workers, a paanwala under a nearby tree, or a friend who periodically goes outside to make a phone call. In that context, the biggest threat to the bicycles comes from passersby who might tinker with the gear shifts out of curiosity. In contrast, the Cambridge bicycle store clerk envisioned a different physical and social landscape of cycling: people commuting to work alone and leaving their bicycles locked in a desolate office garage, unattended throughout the day, or outside on a bicycle rack littered with cut cables and carcass-like bicycle frames that have been picked clean of their components by thieves.

Decisions regarding small things like what lock to use is a factor of the sociality of mobility and the physical environments in which we move. Indeed, embedded in the design of all bicycle-related objects and infrastructure are assumptions about what we do with a bicycle, who is cycling, and why they are doing so. This is true for all transportation modes. How we move through a city—whether walking or by bicycle, car, or electric scooter—is always shaped by context.

Cycling in Context

People's experience of cycling is determined by many factors. These include the physical layout or design of streets, the composition of traffic, the way the street edge is used, how public space is policed, and the history of urban development, as well as all the elements that shape our identity, including gender, race, ability, age, sexuality, caste, and class. However, most sustainable transportation planning, policy, and journalism in both the United States and India focuses on the first item of that list: the design of streets or the transportation policies that determine their design.[1] The anthropologist Adonia Lugo sees this as a reflection of the "bicycle infrastructure strategy" that has been planners' default thinking about sustainable transportation for two decades.[2] For instance, writing on the most "bicycle-friendly" cities in the world nearly always focuses on the bicycle infrastructure, such as networks of physically separated bicycle lanes.[3] Cities like Amsterdam and Copenhagen, which have made their city centers dramatically less car-centric through street redesign and policy changes since the 1970s, are considered the paradigm. Indian cities such as Mumbai are considered among the worst cities for cycling because they lack dedicated bicycle infrastructure, systematic planning for nonmotor-ized transportation, and a bicycle-friendly policy environment.[4]

But understanding cycling in context, as I do in this book, offers an al-ternative approach to sustainable transportation. It means taking the phys-ical layout of streets—that is, what they are officially planned for—as only one factor in people's experiences as they move through, and make claims on, a city. It also means focusing on the social, attitudinal, and behavioral factors that shape bicycle safety, as well as the urban histories and politics that have made those factors prominent and the personal motivations people have in choosing particular transportation modes. And it means looking at how the composition of traffic, the norms regarding the use of the street edge, how mobility is regulated, and the unspoken and unofficial rules of mobility shape people's cycling experiences. This "perspectival" and context-sensitive approach does not disregard the importance of street design but challenges street design as the only rubric through which bicycle safety and comfort might be understood and evaluated.[5]

This focus on the social environment of cycling in Mumbai follows the important work done by transportation equity researchers, writers, and activists since the early 2010s. In particular, the anthropologist Adonia Lugo's book *Bicycle/Race: Transportation, Culture, and Resistance*, on mo-bility and advocacy in Los Angeles, shows the problems with framing sustainable transportation issues primarily in technical or design-oriented terms. She shows how focusing on street design elements such as bicycle lanes ignores how people's experiences of bicycle safety are shaped by the racist history of urban planning in the United States and also how power implicitly shapes planners' imaginations of who will ride those "new street systems" in the future.[6] Lugo argues that rather than focus on street design alone, it is important to support the cycling cultures that already exist and the communities and networks that support them—what she calls the "human infrastructure."[7] At the same time, she argues that planners must also direct attention to the way "the social life of the street impacts the feeling of riding."[8] Moreover, by decentering the "bikes versus cars" narrative, this writing complements the important work of other US-based transportation equity activists and researchers, such as Julian Agyeman, Charles T. Brown, and Tamika Butler, who show that the singular focus on combating car-centric planning has ignored how people with marginalized racial, ethnic, and gender identities experience vulnerability on streets and restrictions on mobility.[9] For instance, through the 2010s, white bicycle advocates' focus on dangers from cars ignored the police violence perpetrated on Black and brown people on bicycles. Meanwhile, transportation researchers have shown how bicycle infrastructure can be co-opted by powerful real estate interests, especially when bicycle lanes are focused more on "help[ing] to brand place" than to equitably offer transportation options to city residents.[10] This literature shows that attempts to improve the comfort and safety of cycling, if they are going to be ethical and equitable, must move away from depoliticizing technical approaches and instead attend to the social and political contexts through which all people move.

In India, sustainable transportation discussions since the late 1990s have also de-emphasized context in favor of technically oriented universal design principles.[11] For progressive transportation professionals, creating segregated spaces for cycling has been the default solution to problems of safety or low ridership in Indian cities, with street upgrades in cities such as Copenhagen and New York City serving as aspirational models. But the dozens of bicycle lane projects implemented in Indian cities since the late 2000s (as I discuss in chapter 5), nearly all of which have failed, provide an important warning.[12] Recently built dedicated bicycle facilities now lie crumbling and abandoned on street edges in cities around India. Media reports have attributed these failures to corruption, government neglect, and encroachment by the poor, who use these spaces to sell food, build homes, or park their autorickshaws. But another explanation for these failures is that in India, as in the United States, the technocratic and design-oriented approach to bicycle safety has ignored the politics of street improvement projects, the way people cycle on and use the street edge, and the diverse relationships to bicycles that riders have. For instance, the anthropologist Malini Sur's important research on migrant bicycle delivery workers in Kolkata challenges the presumably apolitical nature of sustainable street design. She shows how the different identities of people cycling, and their different reasons for cycling, shape their "claims to road space ... [and] produce different sets of aspirations and demands."[13] Sur's point challenges universalizing discourses around street design, sustainability, and safety. Improving streets to address problems of bicycle safety and ridership is not just a technical issue. This goal must be accompanied by an analysis of what kinds of riders bicycle infrastructure projects invite, whose financial and political interests these projects potentially serve, and what relationship they have to larger changes in the urban environments to which they are connected.

Moreover, it is important to identify where the default solution to promoting sustainable transportation in India (i.e., creating separate spaces for cycling) comes from: cities in northern Europe and North America, whose mobility context is characterized by homogenous traffic, intensely regulated and monitored streets, and clearly defined street edges that are intended for car parking.[14] Of course, not all cities around the world have these characteristics, and so it follows that this street transformation will have different effects depending on mobility environments. Consider this question: if a city installs a bicycle lane, what is it replacing? In Cambridge, Massachusetts, it potentially replaces a row of privately owned cars stored on publicly owned land.[15] In Mumbai, a bicycle lane potentially replaces land with overlapping ownership claims and uses by a mix of the rich and poor; the same space might be used at night as a place to sleep, as a space for street vendors, or for what architects Rupali Gupte and Prasad Shetty call the "classic one-foot shops of Mumbai ... [that fold] in and out" throughout the day.[16] On a Cambridge street, the bicycle lane re-orders space, challenging decades of assumptions regarding what streets are for. On a Mumbai street, this hypothetical bicycle lane introduces a principle of homogenous use on a street previously characterized by fluidity and heterogeneity. This street design would potentially challenge decades of car owners' *and* poor people's spatial claims to the side of the road, while continuing a century-old elite desire to impose order on Indian streets.[17]

All cities have particular mobility contexts.[18] An argument of this book is that making physically separated bicycle facilities the default solution to the problem of urban transport has ignored the mobility contexts in which all street design is enmeshed. Certainly, most streets have the potential to be improved, and physically separated bicycle lanes can often be a successful way to do that. I am an anthropologist, so this book is not a critique of specific design principles. Instead, I use the tools of anthropology— long-term, immersive fieldwork, often involving talking with people while cycling—to show what Mumbai streets, traffic, and infrastructure look like from the perspective of people who ride bicycles on those streets. I argue that this perspective produces an embodied understanding, as well as an embodied expertise, of the city that can challenge professional planning norms. I hope readers such as transportation planners, architects, advocates, anthropologists, and anyone else who cares about how we move through cities will use this expertise to find more contextually sensitive and equitable ways of improving the comfort and safety of cycling.

An Embodied Understanding of the City

I started researching the contexts of cycling in Mumbai in 2015. This was fifteen years after I first visited the city and two years after my first bicycle ride as an adult. At the time, I was drawn to the city's eclectic and vibrant cycling activities.[19] Some of those activities—like bicycle-to-work rallies, neighborhood-based social group rides, and endurance events—did not exist in Mumbai when I first visited and lived there in the early 2000s, while other activities—such as the cycling done by people delivering bread, milk, eggs, and restaurant meals or going to work as security guards, electricians, and shop assistants, or by small-scale entrepreneurs who do door-to-door sales—had a longer history. I wanted to know how these bicycle communities existed despite Mumbai lacking the design elements transportation professionals associate with bicycle friendliness and having a government transport approach that is oriented toward cars. So rather than begin with the design and policy-oriented questions such as "What space is allotted for bicycles?" or "What government structures are in place to make cycling safer?" I started with an ethnographic question: "What do people do with bicycles?"[20]

I began this project by joining early-morning group rides organized in Chembur, the neighborhood where I lived in 2015–16.[21] These rides were casual and fun. They consisted of men and women, mostly middle-class professionals in their forties, who had turned to cycling as adults. I wanted to know why they chose to bicycle and how they understood their experience of cycling in Mumbai. Because most participants were new to cycling, the rides were slow paced. This appealed to me because I also had recently returned to cycling after a thirty-year gap. And I too was not particularly fit or athletic. My first group ride in Mumbai, in June 2015—a slow, completely flat, five-mile loop—left me so exhausted I couldn't get back on the saddle for a week. But gradually, distances that were once challenging became easy. Rides that were once painful became enjoyable. I noticed that people around me experienced similar transformations because they were as new to adult riding as I was. Then the group rides got longer. There was more laughter at the end and more talk of how cycling had become an important part of their lives. There was less talk about fitness and more talk about seeing, experiencing, and feeling the city, its roads, environments, and social worlds. While pedaling side-by-side with people on those group rides early on in this project, I found that one of the interesting things people told me was that cycling made them newly attentive to the city; for the first time they observed small features of streets, as well as the people and activities on and adjacent to them—all of which they missed while moving through the city in a car. It seemed that people were simultaneously discovering new parts of their own city as well as a new sense of what their bodies could do.[22]

On those initial group rides around Chembur, I noticed people were using bicycles to move through the city but also to reinvent themselves and their relationships to the surrounding environments and to the diversity of people cycling for work in Mumbai. It was clear that self-making processes were intertwined with city-making processes. Intimate and evolving notions of freedom; the good life; professional propriety; what it means to be a mother, father, wife, or husband; and how we move are connected with how we understand streets, traffic, and infrastructure.[23] In other words, I saw that "hard" topics such as street design and traffic safety might be linked to these intimate senses of our bodies and senses of self, pleasure, pain, desire, and responsibility.

Between 2017 and 2019 and again between 2021 and 2022, I switched focus to understand how people with a more utility-oriented approach to cycling sensed and understood the streets through which they move. During this period, I did over fifty hours of "ride-alongs" with food de-livery workers, small-scale entrepreneurs, and bicycle commuters, as well as dozens of additional interviews with bicycle mechanics, ride organizers, and bicycle advocates.[24] During this period of research, I saw that attentiveness to the microdetails of streets, traffic, and the everyday life of infrastructure was a commonality across Mumbai's socioeconomic spectrum. Cycling produced what Phil Jones calls an "embodied under-standing of the urban."[25] Simply put, cycling seemed to make people notice things: the condition, construction, and gradient of streets, as well as the seams, cracks, gravel, grease, drain grates, and utility covers on them and the nonverbal ways people in different vehicles communi-cate whether they are turning, stopping, or overtaking.[26] Cyclists could also notice the city's microclimates, the sounds and smells of streets, and how attempts to change street space (such as by installing bicycle lanes) work in practice.

Of course, not everyone observes these details of the city at all times, and cycling is not the only mode of transportation that compels people to sense and think about infrastructure. But put together, it seemed that the view of Mumbai from the bicycle could complement, if not challenge, the more commonly circulated and cited expertise of sustainable transporta-tion professionals.[27] In particular, people who cycle—whether for work, recreation, or some combination of the two—pay close attention to the small details, or microinfrastructures, of the city. And so, as I continued to do ride-alongs, as well as ethnographic interviews, conversations, and collaborations with people who cycle in Mumbai, I focused on how the bodily and sensorial experience of cycling can be "a way of knowing, a method of critical inquiry, [and] a mode of understanding" the city.[28]

At least since the 1880s, writers have noted that bicycles are remarkable because of two things: they enable autonomous travel and they offer an "intimacy" with the "immediate travel environment."[29] Bicycle riders don't just pass through landscapes but actively sense them. This is because on a bicycle, riders are "sensorily open to the environment."[30] As the anthropologist Luis Vivanco puts it, cycling exposes people "to certain kinds of interactions with their environments."[31] Most other forms of travel during the late nineteenth century, in both Europe and India, were not protected from the surrounding environment either, so this openness was not so significant then. The sense of openness became pronounced in the mid-twentieth century, when car technology evolved to make automobiles "a place of dwelling that insulates them from the environment that they pass through."[32] On a bicycle, without a boundary between the inner world of the passenger/driver and the outside world, people experience a greater sensation of exposure than they do in a car.[33] This exposure is double-edged; exposure makes people vulnerable and can also be pleasurable. Breaking a bone because of a pothole, getting hit by someone driving a car, feeling cold and wet, enjoying a refreshing cool breeze, seeing a beautiful sunset, and hearing a friend call your name as you pass by (and being able to stop without worrying about parking) are all effects of the bicycle's exposure. Another effect of exposure is attentiveness to the microinfrastructures of the city—what I see as central to people's "embodied understanding of the urban."[34] This can similarly be an effect of seemingly contradictory impulses: it can come from people desiring safety *and* fun in the city.

The experience of riding a bicycle also involves a particular relationship between bodies and objects.[35] As Luis Vivanco writes, "riding a bicycle has experiential, sensual, and social repercussions on one's life that are different from driving a car, riding on a train, or walking."[36] Moreover, in legal and regulatory discourse, bicycles are often referred to as vehicles, despite them being "a curious vehicle," as the professional cyclist John Howard said, because "its passenger is its engine."[37] But even this apt observation doesn't capture the particular way bicycles "work together with bodies."[38] Instead, it is more useful to think of bicycles in terms of assistance, or more specifically, "bodily augmentation."[39] Indeed, from the bicycle's earliest historical incarnation—the "velocipede," a device invented in 1817 that is similar to the pedal-less children's "balance bicycle" of today—the technology was conceived of as an "aid-to-walking," making it "feel like an extension of your body, a prosthesis rather than a vehicle."[40] In other words, the bicycle, like any tool or instrument, should be seen as a mobility assistive device that "extend[s] human bodies and capabilities . . . in specific ways."[41]

Why and how do these bicycle and body relationships matter? Answering this question requires looking at the contingent convergence of place, time, and technology. In this book, the technological and material features of the bicycle I focus on are its sensorial openness and its tool-like, or assistive, attributes.[42] The place and time where I show how and why these qualities matter is Mumbai in the 2010s and 2020s.

The Bicycle's Place in Mumbai

The bicycle has a contradictory set of associations in Mumbai. On one hand, it occupies a low symbolic place on the transportation hierarchy, as opposed to motorized two-wheeled vehicles (e.g., scooters) and four-wheeled vehicles (e.g., private cars).[43] This is because cycling is often associated with working-class occupations like bread, milk, and laundry delivery, which is a change from the 1950s and 1960s, when the bicycle was more associated with middle-class office workers. According to bicycle shop owners I interviewed in Dadar and Kalbadevi, Mumbai, bicycles lost their popularity among the middle class in the early 1980s, when affordable mopeds (usually called scooters or two-wheelers in Mumbai) arrived on the market.[44] This timeline is notable because it is before the economic liberalization of the 1990s, which many commentators blame for the decline in the popularity of cycling in India. Indeed, according to people I spoke with, in middle-class spaces of the 1980s, cycling was considered something embarrassing or shameful. For instance, screenwriter and director Amin Hajee told me that in the 1980s he was so worried friends would see him cycling that he would hide his bicycle behind bushes when visiting their homes. The BMX rider Rahul Mulani similarly said that in the 1980s "there was a sense that cycling wasn't cool—back then, there were either hard-core cyclists who have been doing it forever or the dudhwalas and paowalas [milk and bread guys]."[45]

On the other hand, there is a generalized fondness for cycling in the city. As a Mumbai bicycle commuter who also cycled in England (and whom I discuss in chapter 4) told me, "Cyclists aren't considered nuisances here." The levels of bicycle ownership, access to bicycles (for instance, being able to share or borrow a bicycle), riding knowledge, and experience are high relative to cities of equivalent size around the world.[46] Cycling is also lovingly depicted in popular Hindi films from the 1950s to the 1980s whose scenes, images, and songs continue to circulate widely. Movies such as *Padosan*, in which women's freedom and joy are expressed through cycling, and *Jo Jeeta Wohi Sikandar*, in which cycling represents young men's escape from pressure to succeed professionally, are central to the city's collective imaginary. Moreover, a bicycle race called Custom Point continues to take place annually.[47] This race was organized in 1981 by and for workers in the textile mills in neighborhoods adjacent to one of the first Indian bicycle factories, Hind Cycles, which opened in Worli, Mumbai, in 1939.[48] Although that factory, like most from that era, is now closed, the race celebrates the culture and history of the city's historic mill lands. As Harish Desai, one of the Custom Point founders, told me, "[In the 1970s] millworkers went to work on bicycles and all the mills had cycle stands. At that time, whoever had money, had a bicycle."[49]

The people who have carved out the largest space in Mumbai's bicycle landscape are dabbawalas, the five thousand men who do daily round-trip home-to-office lunch-box deliveries with famous efficiency and accuracy. Dabbawalas have an iconic presence in Mumbai. They are easily recognized because of their unofficial uniform that consists of a white kurta and a white cap with a sharp, folded peak. They often ride black roadster-style bicycles with spokes decked out with multicolored beads, and they transport dozens of bags containing lunch boxes (the dabbas, which is where their job title comes from) dangling from the handlebars. Dabbawalas do not work for anyone but do their labor as part of a collective. Raghunath Medge, president of the Mumbai Dabbawala Association, explained to me before a guest lecture he was giving to business students at Mumbai University that being part of this collective is central to what it means to be a dabbawala: "It is not a job but a share-holding system. Each dabbawala is a working partner. Whatever profit they get, they share. This is not a worker-boss relationship, this is a business."[50]

Before the COVID-19 pandemic—the first interruption of the dabbawala service in 125 years—a vast army of delivery workers, nearly all on bicycles, picked up and delivered 100,000 dabbas containing freshly cooked food every morning and then returned empty dabbas in the afternoon. This is a complicated endeavor that carefully links cycling trips with train schedules and a complex system of codes written on the dabbas to ensure none gets lost. After dabbawalas pick up homemade lunches from residents (and occasionally, restaurants and catering companies), they are brought to the nearest train station by bicycle, sorted according to the destination neighborhood and building, transported by train, then re-sorted by office building and floor, then taken by a separate bicycle to their final destination—which sometimes is a specific desk or cubicle. In the afternoon, the entire process is done in reverse order, taking the empty containers back to their owners' homes.

Dabbawalas are the most famous and well-documented element of Mumbai's vast and complex bicycle landscape. My attempt to understand what people do with bicycles led me to others who get less attention, like knife sharpeners, roof waterproofers, denture makers, jewelry polishers, and incense makers, as well as people who deliver restaurant meals, bread, milk, eggs, newspapers, laundry, cigarettes, and biscuits. How they incorporate cycling into their lives and what the bicycle means to them are central features of this book.

At the same time, a list of professions that make use of bicycles, while fine as shorthand, remains an inadequate way of capturing people's complex relationships to cycling.[51] Just because many people use bicycles for work does not mean that work encapsulates all that cycling means to them; the bicycle can be a source of pleasure or self-transformation *and* a practical tool to pay the bills. Similarly, the term "bicycle advocate," a phrase I sometimes use in this book, is also not ideal, since it conjures someone whose identity and practice are exclusively focused on this single object. For instance, I asked Harish, one of the Custom Point race founders mentioned above, if he bicycles now. He responded, "I used to. But now I use a motorcycle. It's easier to get around that way!" and laughed, fully recognizing the irony. In fact, I myself had taken a taxi to that interview with Harish because it was raining that evening; both bicycle advocates and bicycle researchers also use other forms of transportation.

Thus, this book is also about people who can afford the comforts of a motorcycle or taxi, like Harish, but at times choose to bicycle. When they do so, they consciously embrace exposure to rain and potholes, while also finding fulfillment in incorporating the assistive capacity of the bicycle into their lives. Middle-class professionals who participate in neighborhood group rides and endurance events or who commute to offices by bicycle are, as a percentage of the population, a small demographic. However, they represent a relationship to public spaces of the city that is at odds with the implicit assumptions of much social science writing on urban India. This writing maintains that in cities like Mumbai, Delhi, and Bengaluru, middle-class people primarily desire to distance themselves from the messy and uncomfortable realities of the street, which scholars attribute to the rise in consumerism following the early 1990s economic liberalization. For instance, the appeal of new shopping malls supposedly lies in their sanitized, consumer-oriented, semi-public spaces, which limit interaction with a diverse public.[52] But I noticed a small but significant counternarrative. Many middle-class people explained to me that the appeal of cycling is because it takes them out of sanitized spaces like shopping malls, corporate offices, and gyms and into the street and its mix of people and activities. People told me that cycling enables reconnection to the city that they feel has been severed; in a kind of flip side to their financial and professional success, the bicycle is for them a tool for a renewed intimacy with the urban.

"Nobody cycled recreationally in India before—it is hot and sweaty; why do it when you can be comfortable in a car?" Divya Tate once told me, tongue in cheek, while giving me an account of the recent history of recreational cycling in India at a Pune café one afternoon. The phrase "Why do it when you can be comfortable in a car?" echoed what academic writing on middle-class India also emphasizes: that wealth enables life in a climate-controlled bubble that keeps the discomforts of the city at bay. But the rise in recreational cycling indicates a potential change in attitudes. Divya said that that is because cycling reorients people's relationship to the "material world." For "all of us who cycle . . . you look at the rewards of that discomfort [and] you start enjoying [the] discomfort . . . and have fun and joy [in it]."[53] In other words, by choosing exposure to the public worlds of the city, by willingly embracing the sensory experience of being in the street and subject to the elements, new cyclists represent a small but significant alternative to the retreating middle-class narrative. Middle-class and elite people who choose to cycle in Mumbai challenge an aspirational norm that equates avoidance of physical effort in public, isolation from the street, and complete control of the physical climate (all encapsulated by the car) with financial and professional success.[54] Of course, not everyone who cycles feels this way, but Divya's comment suggests that there is a glimmer of hope and potential for change that is rooted in the sensory experiences of cycling.

Divya Tate is an astute observer of the changing significance of the bicycle in urban India because of her three-decade personal and professional involvement in cycling. She started cycling for practical purposes in the 1990s, as way to maintain financial independence as a single mother of two children. In the early 2000s she participated in the country's first timed long-distance rides. In 2011 she became the first woman in India to complete the full "brevet" series of continuous rides of two hundred, three hundred, four hundred, and six hundred kilometers under specific time limits in one year. Most importantly, as a ride organizer since the 2010s, she has had immense influence on the growth of recreational cycling in India. In 2010 she took over the fledgling Audax India Randonneurs—the India branch of Audax—and expanded it into an organization responsible for hundreds of endurance-oriented cycling events held annually in over forty-nine cities and towns in India.[55] Divya also organizes popular long-distance bicycle events under an entity she founded called Inspire India.

Divya believes that recreational cycling rapidly expanded in the early 2010s due to multiple factors, including the arrival of imported multigeared bicycles and new communities made possible by the internet.[56] As she later told me, when she started cycling for practical purposes in the 1990s, and then in the early 2000s doing long-distance rides, recreational cycling in India "was a like a desert—with just some plants coming up [that showed potential]." Yet now, when she sees cycling communities flourishing around the country—not just in the big cities but in smaller towns and villages as well—"it is a like a lush beautiful garden."

Versions of the question "But don't recreational riders in Mumbai and their expensive bicycles reflect class privilege?" were often posed to me when I presented this research at conferences or department colloquia. My answer is that they do, just like the expensive laptop I use to write talks and books reflects mine. I find it more useful to describe and understand what people are doing from within their class positions, as well as how they might be subtly challenging dominant and exclusionary ways of inhabiting a city. In a less lofty sense, my goal is to understand how people are experimenting with new ways of inhabiting and engaging with the city.

For middle-class professionals, choosing to cycle means embracing new, and not necessarily comfortable, sensory and material experiences. How should this be interpreted? On one hand, describing this activity in terms of class privilege fails to explain, on people's own terms, how they choose to engage with the city and experience things like sweatiness. But on the other hand, class and social status are certainly part of the equation. The anthropologist Julie Archambault's writing on sweat in urban Madagascar offers a useful way to navigate this tension. Like Divya Tate, who said that cycling got people to relate to discomfort differently, Archambault has observed that "new ways of sweating and thinking about sweat are inspiring alternative ways of becoming and relating, and offering women novel opportunities to access urban spaces."[57] In Archambault's ethnography, sweat matters in a material sense *and* symbolically, although she is careful not to reduce her analyses to either: "I aim to avoid reducing materiality to meaning while recognizing the role of the symbolic domain in shaping material efficacy."[58] I similarly recognize the importance of the symbolic—in other words, what sweating or doing a physical activity like cycling in public represents in particular social contexts—while emphasizing the significance of materiality and embodiment. I lean toward the material because this has been understudied in social science research on mobility and transportation; riding a bicycle could be about choosing to embrace the physicality and sociality of the street even as this choice is made possible by class privilege.

Indeed, while riding with some of the people Divya talked about, I saw them similarly grappling with the material and sensory aspects of cycling, as well as its social significance. I witnessed people using bicycles—sometimes new, imported, and shiny; sometimes old, rusty and domestically made—as a way to experiment with and remake themselves while having fun. I saw people struggling to give new value to physical exertion in public, often despite their families pushing them to stay at home or in an office. Some saw it primarily as a social activity, others saw it primarily as body work, while most saw cycling in a mix of practical, pleasurable, and symbolic terms, appreciating the ability to cycle alongside men carrying massive containers of milk or speeding past luxury cars trapped in traffic. These recreational riders did not have the meaning of cycling all figured out, and their relationships to cycling were and will be constantly changing. But what united them is that they were experimenting with new ways of inhabiting and moving through the city. For many, the meaning of cycling always returned to the embodied experiences it produces.

Cycling generates a valuable understanding of the city, its streets, traffic, and microinfrastructures. In other words, as people move through the city for fun or for work, they acquire a nuanced understanding of that city. This is why I focus on the idea of an embodied understanding of the city. This book is my attempt to represent this knowledge and communicate it in a way that is legible for transportation planners, sustainable transportation advocates, social scientists, and others interested in cycling in a context like Mumbai. This book is, however, my synthesis of a collection of other people's cycling experiences.[59] I draw from the conversations, observations, and ride-alongs I did with dozens of people in Mumbai from 2015 to 2022. I do not claim to represent the entirety of their cycling experiences, and I only share what they felt comfortable sharing with me, someone who is white, male, not disabled, rides a relatively expensive bicycle, and is not Indian and yet seems to have an intense interest in learning about why and how all people, rich and poor, cycle in Mumbai. Moreover, what people share with me about cycling is often a product of the research encounter itself. On one hand, people actively reflect on and interpret the cycling communities in which they participate. On the other hand, as with all embodied activities—like walking or sitting—sometimes being asked to talk about the activity will get you to see and understand it differently. And so I often saw this research not in terms of mining preexisting information that someone has but, at least in its best moments, in terms of working out the meaning of cycling in India together.

This book is about the understandings of streets and infrastructure that emerge from people's cycling experiences. The arguments I make are especially shaped by Firoza Dadan, a founder of the Smart Commute Foundation (a nonprofit advocacy organization) and the cycling campaign Cycle Chala, City Bacha. Firoza's bicycle advocacy began in 2010 with a few large group rides. These popular events caught the media's attention and grew in popularity each year. In 2016, she quit her job in ad sales to

Firoza Dadan (*in helmet*) with Shalini Dinesh Paswan, Snigdha Animesh Sarkar, and Sarita Shitaram Shelake, three participants in her cycling and bicycle education program.

focus on full-time bicycle advocacy. Since then, she has organized dozens of popular and inclusive community rides, promoted practical cycling for office workers and college students, given hundreds of free bicycles to underprivileged children and to women who are domestic workers, and worked with city officials to improve cycling conditions in Mumbai. In 2021, she started a unique program that appoints a "bicycle councilor" in each of the city's fifteen wards (important local-level administrative units in Mumbai); the persons occupying those posts organize group rides, identify local routes, and do outreach with new riders. This program, in addition to the dramatic increase in cycling during the COVID-19 pandemic, is why there was more cycling activity in Mumbai in 2021–22 than when I started research for this book in 2015. It is because of people like Firoza and her bicycle councilors that cycling is not just a remnant of Mumbai's past but an index to the city's future.

Firoza and I have cycled and collaborated together many times since

2015. During this period I observed that an important part of her work is cycling—simply being visible on the street on a bicycle—while also talking about cycling with people she encounters along the way. Her daily outreach does not get media attention, although she has received a lot of that too. In those many newspaper, magazine, and radio interviews, she narrates how she started cycling as a teenager growing up in a working-class neighborhood in Mulund.[60] Her initial impetus to bicycle was to save money as she visited people's homes giving after-school tutorials to children. In this way she discovered the freedoms and joy of cycling, despite hostility she faced from self-declared religious leaders who didn't like the idea of a teenage girl on a bicycle. Then, years later, she began to observe the public benefits to the city. Her changing relationship to cycling highlights her emphasis on the embodied practice of cycling. It also shows how it is futile to separate the intimate relationships people have with transportation from the public questions of design, policy, and infrastructure.

Since I started research for this book in 2015, my research goals and Firoza's outreach and advocacy goals have evolved to the point where they overlapped considerably. We saw that we were both interested in talking with, listening to, learning from, and riding with people who use bicycles for utility-oriented purposes in Mumbai. Many of the interactions with food delivery workers I include in this book occurred with Firoza. Some of these interactions were brief—such as when we flagged down people on bicycles, "intercept interview" style—while some included ride-alongs that lasted half a day or more, which enabled us to see how their work, daily life, and cycling were related. Other interactions turned into longer relationships that included numerous follow-ups over multiple years. So in some instances, Firoza acted as a research assistant, but more often our relationship was more like a team or collaboration, since this research was mutually beneficial. It gave me the material to write this book, and it helped her advocacy. For instance, she uses the data we collected to challenge radio and TV interviewers' uninformed questions about bicycle safety and to answer the skeptical government officials who invariably ask her, "Who cycles in Mumbai?" Throughout this collaboration, our understanding of cycling in Mumbai changed; throughout this project we were working through the meaning of cycling together.

Another part of the research for this book involved accompanying Firoza and her colleagues to many meetings—with human resource directors, municipal staff, elected officials, transportation planners, and journalists—in which they described their visions to expand cycling in Mumbai. After each pitch, I heard the same pushback along the lines of, "India isn't ready for this." Skeptical audiences implied that cycling won't flourish until certain conditions are met: *until* there is more traffic sense, *until* there are bicycle lanes, *until* there is better traffic enforcement, *until* there is a way to deal with the city's intense humidity and heat, *until* a cultural shift happens so physical activity is valued, and so forth. This reminded me of the "not yet" of postcoloniality described by Dipesh Chakrabarty, in which India's modernity is forever deferred.[61] In such a view it is as if everyday cycling is appropriate for European or North American cities now but for Mumbai only at some point in the distant future.

Mumbai on Two Wheels deliberately spotlights the people who are performing a cycling city now.[62] Whether it is people like Firoza Dadan, who explicitly articulates a theory of infrastructure that emerges from embodied experiences of cycling; Divya Tate, who has created a pan-Indian cycling community; Mohan, an incense maker who does door-to-door deliveries by bicycle; Kabir, who does food delivery for an app-based company; or Mohammad, a highly skilled bicycle mechanic, they all normalize the presence of the bicycle on Mumbai's streets. Although having different physical ability, access to power, and reasons for cycling, they are each a rejoinder to the "not yet" of sustainable transportation in urban India that dominates many technical analyses. This book is thus not about people making policy or development plans. It is about people enacting a cycling city now, like Mumbai's iconic dabbawalas whose daily movement across the city has shaped the traffic environment. As Firoza puts it at the end of her fundraising pitches: "They were the first people to cycle to work. They've been here for a hundred years. They are why we exist."

1 Starting with the Surface

On my very first ride for this project, I was cycling past Juhu Beach, in northwest Mumbai, as part of a group ride shortly after sunrise. We were headed to central Mumbai, where we would meet up with a thousand other people for an annual event celebrating cycling to work. Five minutes earlier, participants had gathered on the side of the road to listen to the ride leader's instructions. The ride leader was a skinny man with a carefully trimmed gray beard and round eyeglasses. He reminded us to be mindful of the many new cyclists and to be predictable to other road users. "Ride in a straight line—and it's not a race!" he said, and we pushed off.

It was a joy to ride through empty streets in the comfort of a group. We rolled around a bend in the road and passed Juhu Beach's shuttered food stalls, early-morning joggers, and municipal workers cleaning up the previous night's trash. A light, cooling mist fell. A gentle breeze came in off the ocean. Lulled into a sense of complacency during those first few moments, I did not notice that a rider in front of me, wearing a white T-shirt that had a thick spray of mud splattered on the back, had suddenly slowed. I panicked, squeezed my brakes, and fishtailed wildly. The mist and the previous night's rain—the first of the monsoon season—had mixed with engine oil, grease, and dust to produce a slippery film over the road's surface.

I regained control and avoided a crash, although my panicked shout got the man's attention. I introduced myself and we ended up talking while cycling side by side for the rest of the ride. He was in his late twenties, worked for a clothing manufacturing company, and, like many others riding with us that day, had recently returned to cycling after not having done it since childhood. This was his first group ride, which he had learned about through Twitter.

As we rode together that morning, he told me that the biggest challenge with cycling in Mumbai is typically the poor condition of the street surfaces. He pointed out the various features of the streets as we cycled—potholes, cracks, patches of sand, clumps of asphalt, open trenches where pipes were being laid, small mountains of concrete debris left by contractors, and raised edges of metal plates covering buried cables. There were also long stretches of smooth streets, although they too were interrupted with changes in surface materials and conditions. For much of the ride, the roadway on our left was paved with asphalt and, on our right, with cobblestone-like paver blocks. A thin seam separated the two types of surfaces. At one point, he lifted his hand off the handlebar, pointed down toward the road flowing beneath our wheels, and said, "Boston has one road surface, am I right? Here, there are two parts to the road."

Do Boston's roads have one surface type? I had no idea. I told him I never thought about street surfaces when I cycled back home. Prior to this conversation, I thought a lot about streets but primarily in terms of how they were designed, not how they looked and felt on the surface—a reflection of my own privilege and positionality within the United States, since I live in a well-serviced, wealthy city where street surfaces are generally fine. This is not the case in all US cities.[1] At the time, I thought what really mattered was how street space gets divided, such as whether or not there is a bicycle lane, a bus lane, and ample sidewalk space. Those street features matter because they give an indication of what modes of transportation city authorities care about, who cities are planned for, and what is considered the appropriate use of the street.

But seeing streets in terms of how spaces get divided is only one way of interpreting them—one that emphasizes the symbolic and ideological over the tactile and material. Seeing streets this way emphasizes who the road is implicitly designed for rather than who actually uses it. It assumes that deeper, structural phenomena such as car-centric planning, or automobility, are the fundamental safety and accessibility issues for people on bicycles. This view also reflects North American and European transportation advocacy that focuses on the "bikes versus cars" conflict above all others, sidelining other issues, such as equity.[2]

Indeed, conflict with motor vehicles is just one of the concerns of people who cycle in Mumbai. My interaction on that misty June morning was the first of many occasions in which people would direct my attention to the street surface. I heard people talk about variations in construction material; types of asphalt and concrete; potholes; the size, shape, and texture of precast paver blocks; the raised ridges between different types of surfaces; the age of surface material; the metal spikes joining sections of bridges; the seams between different types of road surfaces; and even the height and texture of the paint used for road markings.

Is all this surface talk superficial? During my first few months riding and talking with recreational cyclists in Mumbai, I thought it might be. I thought surface talk replaced more important critiques that get at structural issues such as the political economy of infrastructure—critiques that I was hearing at concurrent academic seminars in Mumbai on topics like the planned-for, and completely car-centric, Coastal Road project. I too was focused on how megaprojects disproportionately benefit a tiny elite in Mumbai who own cars and ignore, and often actively exclude, all non–car users. Those critiques seemed deeper, structural, and more politically engaged, whereas talk of the surface seemed apolitical and somehow supportive of the status quo.

But I soon realized that I was ignoring the attention to surfaces because of an assumption about what political critique looks like. Attention to surfaces does not appear to constitute cultural or political critique because it is commentary on the parts of infrastructure that we can see and feel. Social scientists trained in the hermeneutics of suspicion—myself included—are trained to question readily apparent social phenomena and look for deeper realities instead.[3] Thus, while the surface-attention of people who cycle is focused on what is "evident, perceptible [and] apprehensible," the critical social scientist digs beneath the superfice of the "apprehensible" to find the true politics of a text, sign, or utterance.[4] Even our language devalues the word *surface*, which connotes superficiality and shallowness of thought. So the duty of the anthropologist is often assumed to go beyond a surface that supposedly can only hide, rather than "to figure out how things mean and how they matter" on their own terms.[5]

Indeed, early on in this project I saw a tension between the surface-attention of people who cycle and the writing on infrastructure that I read prior to doing this research.[6] Since the 2010s, anthropologists, historians, and geographers have produced nuanced studies of the everyday life and politics of infrastructures such as electricity, water, waste, and roads. As both Dominic Boyer and Brian Larkin have noted, following an anthropological tradition of critique, these ethnographies emphasize the "surfacing of hidden relations" that "reveal forms of political rationality that underlie technological projects."[7] While there are important exceptions to this focus on the "technopolitics" of infrastructure—notably, Doreen Lee's writing on traffic socialities in Jakarta and Hannah Appel's writing on oil extraction—most writings on this topic have tended to emphasize how political power flows alongside the substances that support city life.[8] For example, trains and electricity are not just technical interventions on the landscape but also expressions of colonial ideology.[9] And roads are not just "a means of circulation" but also "can be interpreted as a manifestation of linear modes of power."[10]

This scholarship has a particular relationship to surfaces and depth; it often involves revealing structures of power that are concealed. This is not necessarily a bad thing, but it is a particular approach necessitated by a specific kind of critique. For instance, anthropological and geographical studies of infrastructure are often invested in challenging widespread assumptions, such as the idea that infrastructure provision is only about the application of apolitical technological expertise; as Boyer notes, anthropologists often document "the failure of the technocracy to continue to deliver on its promises of an ever-intensifying, -perfecting [sic] modernity."[11] While revealing hidden meaning and going beneath the surface to expose power relations that structure the city are important, they are not the only ways to challenge the status quo.

The cyclist's relationship to roads at first could seem inner directed, as if only motivated by self-preservation.[12] But I argue that regardless of why

people cycle—whether primarily for utilitarian or recreational purposes—
the embodied experience of cycling produces knowledge of the road that
has "outward" potential as well.[13] In her ethnography of blind-sighted
tandem cycling, the anthropologist Gili Hammer shows that touching,
hearing, and seeing the landscape while cycling "draws the gaze outwards,
creating intimate relations with other people."[14] I also saw how attention to
the surface of the roads enabled an emergent politics of infrastructure. In
other words, the small details of the road that people notice while cycling,
either via sight or feel, shape how riders understand, and sometimes hope
to improve, infrastructure in a more equitable way. People see road infrastructure very differently after cycling, writes Zach Furness: "Whether one
chooses to ride a bicycle or does so out of necessity, daily mobility quickly
becomes an issue when some of the most mundane, routine experiences
one has as a bicyclist are fraught with a degree of hassle that one rarely
experiences as a driver."[15] The effect of being "sensorially open" to the environment while cycling is an accidental, contingent, and sometimes fleeting
activism rather than a sustained ideological critique.[16] And sometimes,
what emerges after cycling is not quite activism at all but an enactment of
an ethical understanding of governance, transportation development, and
urban planning that challenges the professional status quo.

Noticing the Surface

"As a cyclist, we are always on the left side of the road. What is in store for
us?" said Faisal Thakur, a bicycle shop owner and technician with three
decades of Mumbai cycling experience. He was speaking into a lav mic,
which I had earlier attached to his shirt collar to record him while walking
along the edge of a heavily trafficked road, and describing what he saw.
"There are gutter lids on the left side of the road. The road is sloping to
the left-hand side because they want the water to drain to the left side.
Then there are interlocking tiles, which creates a very uneven condition
to ride. And there are joints between the concrete and the interlocking
tiles due to which you end up slipping on the road." He paused as he

tried to maneuver around a pile of dirt from a trench recently dug up by a telecommunications company. "Sorry, it is a bit chaotic out here," he mumbled. He hopped over a mound of rubble, momentarily stepped into the roadway, and then found an open space to continue talking.

I had asked Faisal to do this walk-through-style monologue on camera after a conversation in his bicycle shop in which he emphasized the importance of road surfaces. In his shop that day we had been discussing a proposed—and ultimately never implemented—bicycle track called "Green Wheels along Blue Lines" (which I discuss in chapter 5) to be installed on land that was home to thousands of families. He observed that in a recent public meeting, the architects did not provide information about the material they would use for the surface. To him, their inattention to surfaces was a sign of a larger problem: the architects and project leaders had ignored the expertise of people who cycle in Mumbai. If they listened to people who cycle, Faisal said, then they would have paid more attention to details like the material and texture of the surface. Moreover, neglecting the surface revealed the true goal of the project: to use environmentally friendly–sounding infrastructure to fight encroachment and remove poor people from the land on which the project was proposed.

Outside his bicycle shop, Faisal stood on the road edge facing the street's slow-moving early-evening traffic, pointed downward, and described the first problem with the road's surface. "You can see that the joints are not right," he said. "There is an issue between the joints and the interlocking tiles. That is where the problem is. That is where [bicycle] tires are getting stuck—between the concrete and the interlocking tiles. Cyclists are crashing because they can't move left—there is just a very small patch of space on the left—and you can't go right because cars and autos will honk at you." He directed my attention to an intermediate zone where two types of surfaces meet—the street space that cyclists are expected to occupy. On the right, the road surface consists of smooth concrete, while on the left, the surface consists of small interlocking tiles, or paver blocks, separated by countless thin ridges. In between these surfaces are the two joints. These are half-inch wide seams that form a double line along the

Faisal Thakur pointing out the various elements of the road surface over which cyclists have to maneuver.

length of the road. In some sections, the seams are a half inch deep. In other sections, they have been smoothed over with sand, dirt, or gravel.

Faisal walked a few feet to show me a joint that had been fixed. He pointed at a dark gray patch of asphalt that stood out from the light gray concrete surrounding it. "You can see at this point, the joint is not there anymore," he said. "This was a big issue. They've tarred it over. This patch was repaired last year. It is more safe now to move [by bicycle] from the concrete part of the road to the tarred road."

Noticing seams and their depth, location, and evolution over time reflected an intimacy with street surfaces that many other cyclists shared. For instance, on a ride with Firoza Dadan one morning two years after this conversation with Faisal, she slowed down and showed me a space between two types of road surfaces where a seam would usually be. She said maintenance work had been done here that greatly improved the riding experience. I asked how she knew, and she told me there was fresh tar that "covered the gaps" between the asphalt and concrete road surfaces.

This tar was visible only because it was a shade of black slightly deeper and with more shine and smoothness than the adjacent asphalt.

Every year at the start of the monsoon, when the street surface starts washing away, there is a stream of social media commentary, articles, video clips, and memes about streets in Mumbai and other Indian cities. They show streets so full of potholes that they look like lunar landscapes—potholes that seem to swallow scooter tires, potholes so wide that it looks like the road no longer exists. But even among those who talk about Mumbai's street conditions, the thin lines Faisal and Firoza say are important safety issues get ignored. Potholes are the attention grabbers because they are dramatic instances of road infrastructure failure. They make driving slow, uncomfortable, and dangerous—especially for people on scooters and motorcycles, who crash with devastating consequences when the wheel of their vehicle gets stuck.[17] Thin seams, on the other hand, are a subtle interruption of a road's texture that only someone who rolls over them on a bicycle would notice.

Faisal, continuing his walk-through, pointed out some more obvious surface dangers on the road. He stopped by a metal utility cover, three by three feet square, on the road edge. The cover was a few inches off the ground and surrounded by jagged metal edges. "Let's talk about these lids that belong to different telecommunication companies, Reliance, and so on," he said. "The problem is that they have a metal frame around these things. They aren't done properly. The metal is coming up. It cuts into the tires. There are punctures. People lose their balance. This is very dangerous." At that moment, a large truck carrying dirt made a wide U-turn in front of him. It rolled over the cover. We watched the metal depress slightly and then spring back up after the truck passed—a troubling sign of wear on the material.

A bicycle commuter who worked for Reliance Industries warned me that these utility covers can be located anywhere—near the street edge or even in the center lanes—as a result of previous road widening. Most utility covers were installed before 2001, he said; however, many Mumbai streets have been widened since then. As a result, utility covers once safely located on the street edge become dangerously located right in the middle of traffic. Moreover, they are ubiquitous because each telecommunications company has its own utility cover through which they access fiber optic cables. This is the source of the "trenching problem," as an official in the BMC (Brihanmumbai Municipal Corporation, which is Mumbai's municipal government) roads department once put it to me, referring to street sides being perpetually dug up as companies search for the source of connectivity problems. On many street edges, companies like Reliance have installed large, empty pipes to function as containers for cables to be installed in the future. On these roads, the side has to be paved with asphalt or tar and cannot be concretized, which is often a longer-lasting solution. The communications infrastructure below the road is thus directly related to the feel and condition of the surface on top.

Faisal crossed the road, passing stacks of tiles, mounds of gravel, and a small group of workers taking a break. Pickaxes and shovels lay at their feet. He passed an autorickshaw inching through traffic. A bicycle wheel stuck out the side. A young man sat in the back, clutching the frame. "Where are you going with that cycle?!" Faisal shouted. "Turn it the other way. Move that wheel inside!"

Faisal stopped, pointed down once more, and said, "This is causing accidents." At his feet was a square drain grate with six metal slats separated by two-inch gaps. He said that that year there were multiple bicycle crashes on this road because of these grates. In each case, a wheel got caught between the slats. The crashes could have been prevented simply by rotating the grates 90 degrees. That way, the slats would be perpendicular to the roadway, rather than dangerously parallel to it. After those crashes, Faisal took some photos of the grates and sent them to his local corporator, who got the municipality to rotate them.[18] This success was widely shared on social media among Mumbai cycling groups. He showed me one of those rotated grates. "Look at this one. The previous grate was parallel to the road. This one is perpendicular to it. Now, when a cycle passes over this one there is no way for the wheels to get stuck. This is one good thing that is happening out here!"

A food delivery worker cycles past a drainage grate whose bars are dangerously aligned parallel to the roadway and the flow of traffic. Unevenly spaced and broken paver blocks shown in this photo are another source of danger.

The effect of small features of street infrastructure on cycling safety was a theme that I heard in many different contexts. For instance, one evening while sitting at a street corner with Kamal, a food delivery worker, I asked what worried him the most while cycling. Since he was waiting for an order to come in on his app, he had time to explain his evolving understanding of traffic and risk. When he started cycling in Mumbai three years earlier, he had worried most about the fast-moving cars and autorickshaws. Compared to his previous home in Bihar, in Mumbai "there were a lot of vehicles, so I cycled with a lot of fear. I was scared about crashes. Everybody feels scared in the beginning, but after two to three weeks that fear goes away," he said. While still wary of erratic drivers, especially in the early morning, when empty roads invite excessive speeds, what concerns even the most experienced cyclists are the road surface conditions. After three years of cycling in Mumbai, Kamal said, "if the street is good then there is no problem. If there are potholes, then it becomes a problem."

Traffic, he said, he can manage, but rough streets and the municipality's lack of attention to microinfrastructural details create the most danger. He blames Mumbai's rough street surfaces for the knee pains he gets after a long day of work. Indeed, his one major crash occurred because of a carelessly installed drainage grate. While out on a delivery one evening, he was cycling downhill on a street that lacked lights and caught a drainage grate aligned parallel to the road. His front wheel slipped through the metal slats, and he got thrown to the ground. He extends his fingers and flattens his palm to show me how the grates are dangerously positioned parallel to the road. "They are kept like this. Our tire is thin, so we can get caught in the gap. I'd like to tell them [the BMC] to make it like this"—he rotates his fingers 90 degrees, showing a grate alignment people can cycle over—"to avoid accidents and injuries."

The next morning I was chatting with Hansel, a tall, thin, clean-shaven man in his fifties who rides a high-end road bicycle. We were riding side by side at the end of a fifteen-mile group ride. I asked him versions of the question I had asked Kamal: What problems do you experience on the road? What do you worry about while cycling? Like Kamal, the first things he mentioned were microinfrastructures such as grates, potholes, and paver blocks. He told me a similar story about crashing while going downhill on a poorly lit road at night. "I hit a paver block, panicked, and crashed. I broke my wrist and had to have two surgeries. Those paver blocks are a nuisance!" he said.

As Hansel and I cycled together through narrow Bandra roads looking for a breakfast spot, he explained the importance of infrastructure details: "The biggest problem is the smallest, most nonsensical issue. It is those grate things on the side of the road. The way they are aligned. For ten years I've been telling the BMC to fix this issue. Just realign it 90 degrees so tires don't fall in!" Hansel is an athletic cycler who rides a road bicycle with very narrow tires, which makes the grates especially dangerous. He also cycles for practical reasons—to visit friends and to do small errands like shopping—and told me he wishes more people saw cycling as a practical mode of transport, as it once commonly was in Mumbai. "My father would cycle to work every day from JJ Hospital to Mahim, wearing a white cap and tie," he recalled fondly. "But the politicians are constantly looking at cycling as only a recreational thing!"

Mumbai's rough street surfaces, and speculation on the cause of this roughness, are often a topic of social media and discussions about the city. These discussions highlight the "small things" that have a big impact on people's everyday lives, as well as the everyday processes of maintenance, repair, and materials acquisition. For instance, an X/Twitter account called @RoadsOfMumbai provides a regular log of potholes, street surface conditions, and speculation about the corruption and BMC mismanagement that produce them. While corruption is likely a major cause of the city's rough streets, the journalist Jeet Mashru provides a more precise explanation. He shows that potholes are the effect of confusingly overlapping jurisdictions over the city's streets; Mumbai's street maintenance is the responsibility of many local and state agencies, and some important streets have multiple agencies responsible for repairing potholes. As a result, the authorities do not always have a clear idea of where their responsibility starts and where it ends. Mashru adds that intersections are especially generative of interagency confusion. Moreover, the lack of clarity over which agency is responsible for each section of a street enables authorities to deny responsibility for particularly rough streets.[19]

There are multiple, and sometimes contradictory, explanations for why paver blocks (also called interlocking concrete blocks) are a common street surface material in Mumbai. Streets paved with blocks first appeared in Mumbai in 1999.[20] At the time, they were used only at intersections on account of turning-related friction; intersections are the parts of streets that get the most wear. In 2008, the BMC started paving long, straight stretches of road with paver blocks, in many cases replacing concrete road surfaces to do so. In one report, an officer in the roads department stated that the city switched to paver blocks because they are quicker to install and therefore contractors can get paid faster.[21] According to other writers, paver blocks make access to belowground utilities easier. However, the most widely held view—and what numerous people who cycle in Mumbai told me—is that paver blocks are used because of extralegal arrangements between BMC corporators and paver block manufacturers. Finally, in 2016 the BMC stopped the use of paver blocks as a surface material in new street reconstruction; however, as of 2022, many streets continue to have paver block surfaces.[22]

According to Hansel, fixing microinfrastructural problems like paver blocks, potholes, and poorly aligned grates helps everyone who cycles, as opposed to projects like the Green Wheels along Blue Lines bicycle track that Faisal mentioned. Like Faisal, he criticized these projects because designers assume that cycling should happen away from the hubbub of the city, "as if you are going on a picnic." Indeed, projects like bicycle tracks, or physically separated paths, that the government periodically comes up with are almost always located away from the dense parts of the city and seem to be intended only for recreational riding. But attention to street surface detail benefits everyone.

According to Hansel, realigning the drainage grates creates more space to cycle. And so for the past decade he has been pushing this issue. Like Faisal, he wrote about the grate alignment problem to the municipal commission and the chief engineer of roads. When he sees road contractors, he tells them about the problem as well. "I said put it in the manual. It should be laid like this—but they haven't thought about it. It's a little thing. It's not the Sea Link," he said, referring to a costly restricted-access bridge built in Mumbai over the course of a decade. He tells me that the problem is the authorities' approach to infrastructure. Details do not matter to them. What matters are big projects like the Sea Link that make a dramatic visual impact on the urban landscape.

All this surface attention—attention to seams, paver blocks, and the alignment of drain grates, for instance—is not articulated as a challenge to car-centric planning, or automobility, but it does promote bicycle comfort and safety. In other words, surface talk does not sound like ideological critique, or a critique of underlying conditions, and yet its benefits are potentially egalitarian. All bicycle riders are vulnerable to the dangers of poorly aligned drain grates, missing paver blocks, ridges, and potholes, even if the financial consequences of crashes are experienced differently. And beyond the rotated grates or smoothed surfaces, this surface talk is about getting city officials to look at the road differently. It means getting people in power to focus not just on headline-grabbing projects like the Sea Link, or even sweeping changes like bans on certain road construction materials, but to focus on the importance of maintenance and attention to the small details and features of the road—the microinfrastructures that impact everyday life.[23] While not framed in terms of spatial claims, surface talk also represents a politics of infrastructure. And it means sensitizing those in power to the actual experiences of people as they move through the city, whatever their mode of transport.

Surface Encounters

Perhaps all this attention to surfaces shouldn't come as a surprise. While riding a bicycle, you often look down and ahead, constantly scanning the road for potential dangers (pebbles, sand, glass shards, chunks of concrete, crushed bottle caps, nails), while factoring in weather and time of day (Has it rained recently? Has the sun dried the road? Are the leaves still wet?) and evaluating the potential for new potholes, bumps, cracks, and gaps to appear on a previously smooth street. As you cycle, ridges, cracks, and gaps create vibrations that travel through the wheels, fork, head tube, seat tube, seat post, and saddle, which you sense in the palms of your hands, back, neck, and head. Sometimes you can even hear the changes in the road surface—for instance, in the clatter of bicycle components as you ride over rough terrain. Of course, all modes of transportation make people sense the road surface in some way. In Mumbai, pedestrians also navigate uneven sides of the road, potholes, high curbs, and open trenches where cables are being laid. And scooter and motorcycle riders are even more vulnerable than people on bicycles to crashes that result from poorly maintained streets.[24]

And yet, the combination of exposure, the rolling sensation, and self-propulsion make the embodied experience of cycling inseparable from the street surface. Some of the earliest writing on the experience of cycling emphasized the connection to the surrounding environment that this technology produced. As historian Kenneth Helphand writes, "The bicyclist, perhaps more than any other vehicular traveler, has an intimacy with his route."[25] This "intimacy" with roads was reflected in guides to cycle touring in the United States written in the 1880s, which included extensive information on the textures, materials, and microdesign elements of roads. Notably, in these guides, while "directional information was secondary, the primary information was specific road data," such as accounts of the materials used in road construction—accounts that demonstrated a "detailed, intimate knowledge of the road."[26] This knowledge of road surface was important so cyclists knew where they could ride safely, what roads were navigable, what kind of equipment was needed, and how long a ride would take. But cyclists also noted that this surface attention had an effect on how they experienced and enjoyed the landscape. For instance, Jean Rudd wrote in 1895, "Gradually I began to get intimate with the roads and to know all their little ups and downs, like wrinkles, or like a family disposition."[27] For this writer, cycling produced a new way of sensing the landscape and a new "intima[cy]" with her surroundings and with experiencing the pleasures of place. While knowing the surface condition can help people cycle safely, the attention to street surfaces cannot be explained by practical considerations alone. Embodied experiences of the street can be fun too.[28]

Indeed, in Mumbai I initially learned about the significance of surfaces from participants in fun, leisure-oriented social group rides comprising middle-class professionals who had returned to cycling as adults. Sometimes people explicitly told me the importance of surfaces when I asked why they cycle: "When you are in a car, you don't even know if the road goes up or down, but when you are on a bicycle, you know the road. You know its surface," said one recreational ride organizer as I chatted with him in his home office, echoing Jean Rudd, quoted above, who enjoyed gaining a new "intima[cy] with the roads." But more often, people showed the importance of surfaces in more indirect ways. When I asked why they cycle, people would often describe a sequence of events: initially motivated by a desire to start a healthy activity, lose weight, or meet new people, after cycling frequently they became attracted to something they did not expect—the unique engagement with the city the activity offered. Group ride participants mentioned appealing things such as the sensation of subtle surface undulations, the detailed knowledge of a road's microtextures, the feel of the wind on one's back, the smells from roadside food vendors, or the smiles from busloads of schoolchildren rooting for them as they cycle by.

The group rides that directed my attention to street surfaces usually started before dawn. One morning, I woke up at 5:00 a.m., well before my alarm went off, because I had spent the night worrying about missing the group. As I waited for my stovetop coffee to boil, I checked WhatsApp. It was forty-five minutes before our meeting time, but people were already writing messages:

"Who's up?"

"Good morning."

"Who's late?"

"I'm coming."

"Good morning."

"Where do we meet?"

All the "good mornings," thumbs-ups, and high-fives gave the organizer an informal count of how many people to expect. Eight people said they were coming. I added another "good morning" message, filled a water bottle, checked my tire pressure, ate a banana, and slipped out of my apartment.

The creaking gate woke the sleeping security guard of my building. I turned on my lights and pedaled slowly to our agreed-upon spot—an underpass beneath a highway leading to Navi Mumbai. As I descended another overpass, I saw a few small red lights blinking in the dark. I then caught sight of helmets, some bright yellow vests, reflector lights, and the metal glint of bicycle frames. The participants were all in their thirties and forties and worked in industries like real estate, banking, and IT; many were married, some had children, and all were relatively new to cycling as adults. This ride, like many others, was deliberately slow and fun in order to be more inclusive of people with less cycling experience. The participants deliberately referred to themselves as a cycling group rather than a club, to convey a sense of informality and to show that this was not a space for intense training rides.

That morning our destination was the Sewri jetty, a beautiful spot on the eastern coast of Mumbai visited by few other than oil tank drivers and bird-watchers.[29] We followed up our ride with breakfast at a unique wood-fired vada pao stall. We started out in the predawn darkness on the smooth roads of a semiprivate residential colony. We passed a fertilizer factory humming in the darkness, felt a fine mist emanating from the huge cooling plant, then rode under the monorail and the Eastern Freeway to arrive at the smooth, bucolic Mahul Road, a narrow road that runs through the Mahul-Sewri mudflats on the fringes of the city. The traffic was light. A flock of white herons took flight as we cycled by. Just before a turn onto the flats, Shiv, one of the ride participants, told me that it was going to get cold. We made the turn, and, as predicted, it felt like the temperature dropped a few degrees. A cool breeze blew in from the sea. Mist and fog covered the salt pans, which looked like squares etched into the mud. Men were squatting on the embankments shitting, and flocks of white cranes lifted into the sky. I turned to my left and saw Sonam, an accountant in her thirties who participated in group rides before going to work; a scarf was wrapped around her neck and head under her helmet to fight the early-morning chill. She also wore an antipollution mask, arm coverings, and gloves. We made a left turn down a wide dirt road lined with dozens of fuel trucks waiting for their day's deliveries to start. The road was muddy and slick with a black sludge. Men bathed and smoked beedis on the side. And at the end, we reached a jetty lined with rusty fishing boats. The bay swept around us in a broad expanse. The Trombay hills were on the left, covered in mist. Birds dove into the rippling water as the sun slowly rose.

We silently parked our bicycles, drank water, took photos, and took in the view. A large rusty boat was parked at the jetty. A skinny man wearing a white kurta sat by the water's edge listening to music from a small speaker. Ranbir, one of my riding companions, said, "Hello, Uncle," then told us that this man comes here each morning. His friend Shiv looked off into the distance, admiring the view of the water in the early-morning sunlight. He moved his bicycle toward the edge of the jetty, leaned it against the wooden railing, stepped back, adjusted the bicycle, took a moment to get the framing right, and then clicked a photo with his phone. The picture is beautifully composed—the bicycle against the glassy water, diving birds, mist-covered hills, and the sunrise. Ranbir, standing behind him, said to no one in particular, "Shiv and his love."

In these moments, I saw how the intimate knowledge of streets and landscape is mediated by the materiality of the bicycle. Bicycle intimacies manifest in a variety of ways: in a photo shared among cycling friends on a WhatsApp group showing a man giving up his bed for his bicycle, a statue of Ganesha made of bicycle parts, a bicycle puja, or a lovingly composed bicycle portrait set against images of the sublime. Friends joke about choosing their bicycle over a partner or having a bicycle wedding complete with an officiating priest riding a bicycle, and they share stories about bicycle addiction, dreams, nightmares, and anxieties of cycle-related sexual betrayal—in which a bicycle is ridden by someone else.[30] Of course, these are just some possible relationships with bicycles; not everyone has these kinds of attachments to them. Meera Velankar, whom I discuss in chapter 3, categorically rejected the idea that the bicycle is a "vibrant" object when I suggested that possibility.[31] To her, the bicycle is and should remain an inert tool; nevertheless, embodied experiences of bicycles and cycling abound.

Ranbir and Shiv told me that their attachment to bicycles, their commitment to waking up at dawn, and their appreciation of the city and its unexpected beauty are all interconnected. On our way back that morning, Ranbir described the group's genesis. It had started a year earlier and was meant to provide an opportunity for adults to return to cycling. We were cycling together as he explained this. At one point, after we passed a small toll booth, he told me, "In the beginning, getting to this toll both was a huge accomplishment. Twenty kilometers. We thought, wow!" Shiv, overhearing this comment, chimed in: "And then we thought fifty kilometers was huge!" Sonam added later, "When we got to that toll booth, I thought, 'We've really arrived!' But then we thought, let's keep it fun, get people who want to stop and eat and chat with friends." The group rapidly got more popular. They added new destinations—the Gateway, Worli Sea Face, Sewri Fort—and found new places with delicious tea and vada pao. However, participation in the rides slowed during the monsoon. "People stopped riding then," said Ranbir. "I stopped too. With the road conditions and all—with the paver blocks and with so much water on the road you couldn't see the potholes." This ride was an attempt to generate new interest after that lull.

Certainly, not all encounters with street surfaces are pleasurable, such as when people ride on bumpy, potholed roads, or roads with missing cobblestones, or rain-slicked roads with cracks hidden beneath puddles, or roads with gravel and construction debris that vibrate through the palms of your hands, jarring your teeth and rattling your head. Crashes, like the ones Kamal and Hansel mentioned, are of course a very different feeling of the surface. Those moments, when the surface seems to rush up to tear through skin and flesh, constitute an encounter with street surfaces people obviously try to avoid. And certainly, deriving pleasure from sensing the landscape is not universal; identity and experience powerfully shape the meaning and content of this desire for bodily encounters with the built environment. For Ranbir, Shiv, and the other recreational riders mentioned above, their relatively privileged background shaped the sense of novelty they expressed; feeling and sensing the city's surfaces was new and fun because prior to cycling, they had the option to move through the city by car, taxi, or autorickshaw—that is, in ways that involved little feeling of the surface.

Sonam later told me that what motivates her to go out at dawn, before her children wake up, is the new intimacy with the city's surfaces: "Now

I have a feel of the road." It is not just that sensing the road is pleasurable in itself, but there is joy in knowing the city through *feeling* it in a way that was otherwise not possible.[32] Sonam elaborated on this idea:

> Earlier, before riding, I just saw left and right [out of a car or autorickshaw]. Now I am thinking, "That's where the potholes are, that part is paved, that part has paver blocks that make riding difficult." You aren't only looking but you are *feeling*. On a bicycle, you can feel every bump, you feel the terrain and you hear the cycle beneath you. When you are on a cycle, you smell the area that you go through, you can feel the road, you know what's cobbled, you know what's tarred road. You know where someone fell down. . . . You can hear the sounds—early in the morning, someone reading out namaaz. The woman out washing utensils. It is a four-dimensional experience. You experience the same place you are living in in a whole different way!

To Sonam, the appeal of cycling was that it enabled a fuller engagement with the city. That engagement included a mix of sensory and social encounters. It meant feeling the road, or sensing the small nuances of the surfaces, and seeing mundane, intimate acts—like "someone reading out namaaz" or "washing utensils." To her, like Shiv and Ranbir, cycling involved novel encounters with the overlapping physical and social surfaces of the city.

Knowing the Surface

Not everyone spoke so explicitly about surfaces as Sonam. More often, people showed me the significance of surfaces by inadvertently redirecting my gaze downward, challenging my instinct to look only at how traffic was arranged or how cycling was accommodated in transportation projects. Once, this redirection happened at the home of Mirza Saaib Bég, a lawyer, bicycle commuter, and endurance racer. His two-room apartment in northern Mumbai felt like a bicycle shop; frames and bicycles in various states of disrepair hung on the walls. The floor was lined with pumps, parts, saddles, and helmets. On the bookshelves, wedged between dozens of books on political economy published by academic presses and multivolume sets on Indian law, were folded tires, boxes of cycle parts, accessories, and trophies from the various bicycle races he placed in or won.

One evening, we had just finished a chicken biryani dinner in Mirza's bedroom, where four young men had joined us after stopping by to get racing advice. While some of us sat on the floor and the others lay on his bed chatting, Mirza instructed me to show some video clips of him cycling that I had taken and stored on my portable hard drive. He clicked on the first file, a low-angle shot of the highway traffic I took while sitting on a grassy median as I waited for him to show up. That morning I was tired, bored, and new to videography. I experimented with different angles, like this one with the camera a few inches from the ground. For the first twenty seconds, the shot just showed cars and trucks passing by, then two men on bicycles roll by, and finally Mirza enters the frame in a blaze of bright green, black, and yellow, the colors of his jersey, shorts, and cycle.

The clip ended. I sat embarrassed by this unexpected screening of my raw and amateurish effort. I urged him to click on another that was filmed more deliberately. In this shot, I had meant to focus on the traffic but accidentally focused on the road surface. But Mirza and his friends saw things differently: "All I see is the broken glass on the road. Look at all that!" exclaimed one of his friends. Mirza agreed, shocked by all the debris. They played the clip again and paused the footage of what I thought was meaningless traffic. Beneath the blurred traffic were shards of glass, like from a car window, mixed with small bits of gravel, sticks, and some rocks, scattered over the white lane. The debris stretched from the edge where I was sitting halfway into the lane. I had ignored that at the time. But they taught me to look at this footage differently. At first, I was looking at the top of the frame, focusing on the traffic interactions. But Mirza and his friends were looking elsewhere—at the bottom of the frame, at the road's surface.

Mirza and his friends showed me how their cycling experience is shaped by the road surface. As we continued watching footage of him cycling down the Eastern Express Highway amid fast-moving heavy vehicles, I mentioned that there is a seemingly safer option than riding on the highway—a service lane that is physically separated from the highway by a low concrete wall, trees, and bushes. Traffic in that lane is relatively light and slow. "That looks like a good place to cycle, why don't you ride there?" I asked. "The service road has too much trash, rubble, and potholes," Mirza replied. "That's why I ride on the main part—it has the relatively smoother spots. Of course that puts you amidst the fastest-moving traffic." Indeed, in the clip we watched together, he was going at an incredibly fast speed. At one point he was cycling 30 miles an hour, faster than many scooters and trucks. In part, this was possible because he was on an unusually wide and flat highway for Mumbai. But there was an additional reason. He said speeds like that are only possible because he was confident about what to expect on the surface. "I don't speed like that unless I know the road," he said. "You really need to know what is coming ahead. There can be speed breakers and massive potholes. And in the monsoon, you never really know. Sometimes holes can just pop up!" It was the height of the monsoon that day, and so some roads were particularly rough with potholes. Mirza asked if I had been on the Andheri-Kurla Road recently, an important thoroughfare connecting the eastern and western sides of the city. "You know Paris-Roubaix," he said, referring to a race in northern France deliberately held on rough, cobblestoned roads whose route changes year to year to avoid smoother, newly paved roads in the region. "If they really want a challenging race, they should just come to Mumbai and do it! The race could be called Kurla-Roubaix!"

Racing on the Surface

Mirza's joke was especially apt because it was the day before the Custom Point race, held annually on August 15—Independence Day in India—in the neighborhood of Prabhadevi. Like Paris-Roubaix, the Custom Point takes riders on streets that are often cracked, potholed, muddy, and cobblestoned, although of course without the quaint aesthetic intention of Paris-Roubaix. But like Paris-Roubaix, success in this race hinges on one's ability to navigate these rough surfaces.

Custom Point was founded in 1981 by a neighborhood welfare association at a time when Prabhadevi and surrounding areas—Parel, Sewri, and Lalbaug—were dominated by the working-class culture of the historic textile mills. This was a bicycle race initially organized by and for textile workers and their families. To ensure that the children of millworkers could compete, until recently participants were allowed to use only afford-able, Indian-made, single-speed bicycles. Organizers have recently relaxed that rule by adding a separate race category for people with imported bicycles, though the two groups still do not race together. Encouraging the use of Indian-made bicycles also connects with the race's name. According to one of the founders, "Custom" was chosen to highlight the race's connection with the neighborhood's customs—he described the name using the Hindi words riwaj and parampara, which can also be translated as "traditions."[33] "Point" referred to the neighborhood or the place itself as the locus of those traditions. "We start here because we are staying here. All millworkers were staying here. This is all a millworker area. So we decided to start from here," said one of the original race organizers. In this quote, he switched between the past and present tense because of the influx of high-end apartment complexes and malls that have changed the area. However, despite these changes, the neighborhood still maintains a strong sense of its millworker history.[34]

Custom Point is a short, frenetic race with four sharp turns and start and finish points in a narrow lane that has a buzzing mix of homes, shops, temples, and markets. Although the route goes through thoroughfares that are wider, smoother, and better constructed, those streets are lined with new, tall apartment buildings set back from the street, large banks, showrooms for expensive cars, and office buildings—with no connection to the neighborhood's heritage. So part of the "custom" of this race is to take riders through the social heart of the neighborhood, which means cycling on roads with varying surface textures, materials, and quality and

Participants in the annual Custom Point race, including Mirza Saaib Bég (*center*), navigating a street with uneven, cracked, and missing paver blocks.

where people are used to living adjacent to "streets that doubled as festival spaces."[35] On these multipurpose streets, cyclists must navigate streets with dirt, gravel, and debris, as well as patches of uneven and missing paving blocks. There are also utility hole covers surrounded by metal ridges covered in asphalt. Moreover, the race is always held in August, during the monsoon, so participants often have to navigate large puddles on the side of the road, potholes filled with water, mud, and a wet sheen over the road.

To start the race, a cop smashed a coconut on the pavement. Coconut water spread on the asphalt and the crowd cheered. The ride organizer sat on a stage decorated with bright red banners above the starting line and announced the heats. Lining a table next to the organizer were two dozen gold trophies ranging in size from something like a soda bottle to a towering wedding cake, along with a large gold bust of Chhatrapati Shivaji Maharaj. The event attracted an eclectic group of cyclists—a mix of amateurs and semiprofessionals, people from Mumbai and small towns in Maharashtra, some in expensive jerseys and cleats, as well as a handful of people riding barefoot. Most of the participants were young men, although roughly two dozen women also participated. After the casual kids' races were the main events—races for the amateurs and semiprofessionals. Every twenty minutes or so a dozen riders completed the circuit, which went through active streets. Six men on scooters—three in front and three on the left side—alerted pedestrians and drivers with shouts, whistles, and horns that bicycle riders were about to pass through the area at breakneck speeds. However, these were busy roads, and the race organizers' attempts to keep people away were never 100 percent successful. As Mirza explained, "Anyone can still come in—pedestrians, cars, stray animals—they all can come in at some point. It is a cutthroat, dangerous, and a bit of a chaotic race. But it is fun too."

The morning of the race, I am sitting with Mirza at his small dining table eating eggs he prepared for me. A wrench lies next to my plate as if it were part of the place setting. A half dozen tires and wheels lean against the wall. He takes a series of phone calls from friends who are going to be in the race. They report to him on the route conditions and the schedule for the day. He hangs up and tells me about his strategy. "The first thing you need to do for a race is to familiarize yourself with the route. This is a choppy route, a lot of potholes, manholes, very sharp turns, and it has been raining," he said. The combination of rough streets, slick surfaces, and sharp turns onto narrow lanes requires a different racing strategy than if the route were on smooth roads, he said. Whereas a typical racing strategy is to focus on reducing drag by drafting close behind someone, this does not work during Custom Point. Mirza explained that during this race, to avoid a crash he needs to focus on the road and have a sense of who else knows the road well. For instance, if he drafts behind someone, he needs to be confident that person knows the road well enough to avoid the metal utility covers and potholes "that can be anywhere," he said. And because of the "small crevices and lines created by paver blocks," he needs to avoid the temptation to just focus on pedaling hard, otherwise "with tires so thin, any imbalance will just throw you off." To compete successfully, and safely, in Custom Point requires intimate knowledge of the surfaces.

Surface Activism

Where does this embodied knowledge of the street lead? Can it translate to a more equitable city? Or, because it focuses on the surface, is it merely superficial? It was not until I cycled and collaborated with Firoza Dadan, the founder of the Smart Commute Foundation, that I had answers to these questions; she showed me that a surface-oriented approach does not mean absence of critique but can point to an alternative way of approaching the problem of automobility.

One ride with Firoza started at dawn in Juhu and took us north to Madh Island, in the northwest corner of the city. We passed by fishing boats docked along the beach, nets laid out to dry, and small bungalows with large signs in front advertising the space for film shoots. At that time of day, the only traffic was an occasional bus, autorickshaws packed with children going to school, and a few Lycra-clad men cycling, who nearly crashed into each other when Firoza waved hello as they passed by. As we cycled side by side and chatted, the early-morning sun created a beautiful dappling effect through the trees. At one point she turned to me and said, "In a car, you miss all this. People don't see this morning sunlight." We took in the scene in silence as we pushed our way up a hill. And then, as if worried I would get the wrong impression about what cycling means to her, she said, "I don't often do leisure rides like this. I stick to commuting." Practical riding on busy streets, not leisure riding, is her regular routine, "rather than being out in the countryside on leisure rides just for fun."

We reached the busy pier at Marvé Beach, where the ferry from Gorai docks, and stopped for tea at small stall. As children in crisp gray uniforms and women wearing bright orange and green saris and carrying baskets of fish walked past us, I returned to the conversational threads that Firoza dropped during our ride. I asked her to talk more about what motivates her to cycle. "The big reason I cycle is that I hate the crowds at stations and on the trains. I cycle because there is no touching. It gives freedom—." She paused there and added, "freedom for women." Later on, she described how her personal experiences cycling as a teenager informed what she meant by "freedom." As a teenager, she said, cycling meant autonomy. Cycling enabled her to travel around the neighborhood without having to ask her parents for money. It enabled her to make money because with a bicycle she could give private math lessons to local children. Cycling was a practical mode of transportation, a source of economic independence, something pleasurable in its own right, and a marker of her identity. She acquired the nickname "Mulund ki Cyclewali" (the Cycling Girl of Mulund) because she was seen so often with her bicycle. But as she grew older, the visibility of her cycling was increasingly treated by others as a problem. Neighbors pressured her parents to prevent her from riding and propagated an old myth that cycling ruins women's fertility. Her parents were supportive of her, but the pressure on them built up until one day, as Firoza put it, "the bearded so-called clergy, they went to my mom and said, 'She won't have any kids.'" To them, her gender nonconforming clothing was also part of the problem. "I didn't wear salwar kameez. So they said, 'She'll never behave like a lady' if I continued like this." Her mother knew that forbidding cycling was not an option, so they struck a compromise: "I invented a solution. I would wear a long kurta with jeans underneath. I said, 'Okay, fine, I'll wear a kurta on top.' And no one bothered me after that."

As we sipped tea with our bicycles at our sides near the Marvé jetty that morning, I asked about her cycling advocacy work and how she hoped to make changes in the city. She explained that she does not see herself as someone who claims to make structural change or is explicitly political.

"Don't call me an activist—that word has been murdered in India," she said. At the time, I struggled to make sense of the comment. Three months earlier, I had seen her on stage speaking about cycling in front of thousands while wearing a helmet, black fingerless gloves, and a turquoise T-shirt depicting a chain, pedal, and gears arranged to look like a heart. Nothing seemed more activist-y than that.

"So, what should I call you?" I asked.

"Call me a cyclist. People ask me, what do you do? My answer is that I am a cyclist—being an activist means talking against the government, intimidating them, being seen as a threat. . . . That's not me. I started cycling when I was young to save my parents money. I had no idea it would lead to this. Now it is my life."

I realized that her personal story of discovering the pleasures and practicality of cycling mattered because it was reflected in how she approached advocacy: she focuses on everyday acts of cycling more than on making big symbolic gestures. In other words, she focuses on doing, on *enacting* a cycling city rather than only *talking about* it. As she later told me, "I cycle to show people that you can cycle. At every light, every intersection, dozens of people see me. I want to show them, in their cars, that you can cycle. That's the main—the primary—reason that I cycle every day. I want people to see me on the road."

Cycling daily, being physically present on the road, also enables Firoza to form connections with the diversity of people who cycle in Mumbai. These encounters are often brief, but they do important work strengthening a "latent commons."[36] They also forge momentary and unexpected alliances among cyclists of different class backgrounds. For instance, a few months later Firoza and I were cycling from Bandra to Worli to meet a colleague. We crossed the Mithi River, which separates north Mumbai from the central part of the city, and immersed ourselves in a street festival surrounding a famous shrine in Mahim. It was 11:00 p.m., but the roads were lively with families and decorated with a canopy of colorful lights. Through the honking and engine noise of dozens of vehicles, I heard music blasting from sidewalk speakers, as well as the chatter of cheerful crowds weaving toward the shrine. Through all this, I struggled to keep up with Firoza as she slipped through small gaps between the stopped cars. At one point, she picked up her bicycle to maneuver between a truck and a scooter. An opening finally appeared; she took the lane and pedaled furiously. Headlights made her yellow reflective vest glow. An autorickshaw cut her off, and she quickly stopped; she looked left and looped around, cutting diagonally across the road toward a middle-aged man in a baggy red T-shirt casually pedaling on the side.

"Helmet!" Firoza shouted as she reached him. "Where is your helmet?" Smiling, he replied, "My head is too big for a helmet!" Her comment was meant as a way to make a connection and start a conversation. She motioned for the man to pull over. On a side lane, away from the activity near the shrine, he told us that he was returning home from his family-run bookshop five miles away, which he rides to daily. "Cycling is my passion. I only ride this cycle—an old, hand-me-down, single-speed ghoda cycle. My family has a car, but I hate it. There is a fire inside me . . . sometimes I feel paralyzed if I don't ride," he said.

Firoza and I have encounters like this nearly every time we ride to-gether—at intersections, while stopped in traffic, at tea stalls, on a ferry, or in a restaurant. Sometimes phone numbers are exchanged and a lon-ger relationship ensues. But more often, they are brief encounters that offer moments of hopeful alliance—of meaningful connection—across difference. There is no clearly articulated political position or fantasy of a collectivity of people with a shared perspective—she has no illusions that all Mumbai cyclists have the same vulnerabilities, problems, access to power or aspirations. She knows that encounters start off on very unequal terms—people read her clothes (often T-shirt and spandex or jeans), or-ange bicycle, sporty-looking helmet, and, when she is with me, her foreign riding partner—as a sign of closeness to power and privilege. But her ethical practice is to identify potential connections across differences and recognize moments of hope. This encounter inspired an alliance over the refusal to separate the practical from the pleasurable. Firoza, like the book-shop owner, shares a "passion" for cycle commuting—which means im-mersion in the dense sensory experiences, dangers, and pleasures of traffic.

While riding together one day, I told Firoza that she seemed more comfortable cycling on loud, gritty, traffic-jammed Mumbai streets than participating in recreational rides to quiet and conventionally beautiful spots outside the city. She smiled and said, "Of course! I try to stick to commuting—it's my natural habitat!" To her, bicycle commuting means embracing the sensory experiences and encounters with eclectic sociali-

The bicycle advocate and organizer Firoza Dadan cycling in Mumbai.

ties of the street. Cycling allows her to move through the city on her own terms—as she said earlier, separate from the train station crowds and the associated risk of unwanted touching—while also immersed in the public life of the city. This is a vision of cycling that enables autonomy and mobility outside the logic of the enclave, which suggests that separation from the eclectic mix of people, forms of transportation, objects, and textures of public space is the solution to the city's problems.

The surface attention I saw as central to Firoza's and others' understanding of cycling reflects an alternative to technocratic approaches to infrastructure. By focusing on encounters with physical surfaces as well as street socialities, this vision of mobility highlights the unintended politics of separation implicit in street design. I saw this in action during the meetings with Mumbai city officials I attended with Firoza to discuss cycling. In one instance, I accompanied her to a meeting with Harish, a local BMC corporator. She was invited to his office because a bicycle lane project had been proposed in his neighborhood. In the exchange that ensued, I saw how Firoza's focus on surface conditions and surface social encounters challenged the exclusionary nature of a seemingly progressive transportation project.

Harish was an interesting elected official because he had participated in rides organized by neighborhood cycling groups, supported bicycle and pedestrian-friendly initiatives, and was known to push back against wealthy residents of his neighborhood who felt entitled to on-street parking. At the same time, he was skeptical of the possibility of increasing ridership in Mumbai without a dramatic change to its streets and traffic environment. As he later told us, his enthusiasm for cycling "fizzled out" after a few scary encounters with drivers. "There's no road sense," he said. "The last thing people think about are cyclists!"

When Firoza and I entered his small office, Harish was simultaneously texting on his phone and talking to a constituent on a landline. Six chairs were arranged in a semicircle around his desk. He used his one free hand to beckon us to sit. While still talking he handed us a glossy proposal for a street redesign with a new bicycle lane, and he told us to take a look. It had been made for Harish and the BMC free of charge by a local architecture firm known for creatively remaking public spaces in Mumbai. The central part of the proposal consisted of two architectural renderings of street cross sections. One cross section was labeled "existing" and the other "proposed," referring to the street before and after the redesign. What I immediately noticed was that the representation of the "existing" street was as imaginative and as ideologically loaded as that of the "proposed" street. The proposal—and Harish's seeming endorsement of it—reflected not only how professionals understand street improvements but also how they see the city as it is now.

The proposed street design included many of the features of complete streets seen in progressive sustainable transportation-oriented design guidebooks such as NACTO's *Urban Bikeway Design Guide* and Janette Sadik-Khan and Seth Solomonow's *Streetfight*: prominent zebra crossings or crosswalks and wide, bright-green cycle lanes running adjacent to uninterrupted curbs and wide sidewalks. In this rendering, the road edges were clean and orderly. Pedestrians—represented abstractly with thin black lines—occupied an otherwise empty sidewalk flanked by the outline of trees and a turquoise-colored sea. The proposed street was juxtaposed with the drawing of the existing street. The aesthetic of that drawing was similarly minimalist except lacking in the proposed design details such as the cycle lane. It showed a largely blank sidewalk populated by pedestrians. The curb was clearly delineated from the street with a long, thin, continuous black line. Like the proposed street drawing, the road was flanked with trees but without the space reserved for people to cycle.

The drawing of the "existing" street and the proposed street looked nothing like real-life Mumbai streets, such as the street outside Harish's office. The drawing of the existing street was calm and orderly. It lacked the usual mix of people and activities usually found on streets in this neighborhood, such as the couples whispering with their backs to the road, the people grilling vegetable sandwiches in small stalls, the men pushing handcarts, the joggers, pedestrians, and men sitting on their motorcycles parked on the street edge while chatting on the phone. Moreover, *both* street renderings showed public space that was strictly segregated according to use. They also showed public spaces that were largely empty and homogenous. Indeed, in this architectural rendering, the proposed street seemed to be improving on a street that did not actually exist.

After giving us a few minutes to look through the proposal, Harish hung up the phone. I expected him to ask Firoza her opinion, but instead he jumped into a debate with her on bicycle safety and ridership in Mumbai. While he emphasized projects like the proposed street redesign as the solution, at the time Firoza was focusing on increasing ridership through organizing group rides and working with businesses to encourage bicycle commuting. Picking up on that theme, he said, "Cycling to work, it's difficult. The pollution and the crowds—." He paused and then turned to me, adding, "She has the passion, so she does it. But personally, I feel there is no traffic sense here. Things like right of way are not highlighted when we learn driving, unlike abroad. Until we have road sense and proper civic sense, then we will have respect for cyclists, then cycling to work will be common."

Firoza interjected, "But Harish, seriously, I've never had any of those problems with traffic." She smiled nervously, knowing how counterintuitive this defense of Mumbai traffic sounded. "When I walk, I get more scared than when I cycle," she said. "Sometimes I hold someone's hand just to cross the road!" And indeed, the same drivers who are hostile to pedestrians might also, however reluctantly, accommodate people on bicycles; this reflects both the unacknowledged privilege people on bicycles have over people walking in Mumbai (and certainly, people experience this privilege to a greater and lesser degree depending on the visual appearance of their bicycle), as well as the figurative space for cycling that exists in the city.

Harish, fresh off of unpleasant personal experiences with erratic drivers, argued that cycling in Mumbai is not realistic without dedicated space for it. "Cyclists like Firoza and others have been asking for a cycling track," he said. "As youngsters, we just fell, [picked ourselves up,] and learned [on our own]. Today, there's no space for kids to cycle. In those days, traffic was so different." He explained that he was attempting to address this problem by backing a small cycle lane project. This project, which I discuss in chapter 5, was a short bicycle lane that briefly appeared on Carter Road in Bandra, Mumbai, in 2019. However, even this modest transformation of street space was generating backlash from the police, various government entities that deal with roads, and local neighborhood associations. Harish explained, "When I show police this plan, they immediately say, 'What about parking?' When I show residents, they also say, 'You can't sacrifice our parking!'"

Despite what Harish implied, Firoza had not actually asked for a cycling track. Instead, when asked how cycling could be made safer, in that meeting and in others, she emphasized surfaces. "The problem is the road," she often said in response to skeptics who argued that, without bicycle lanes, cycling in Mumbai is not possible. "When it is totally smooth—like butter—then it is safe. The danger comes from uneven surfaces, potholes, bumps, ridges, and paver blocks," she said. She similarly tried to get Harish to focus on road conditions when, during a break in the conversation, she described her most recent experience cycling with her son: "Yesterday, I tried cycling to Versova with my son. If the roads were good and there weren't any potholes, then it would have been fine, but those paver blocks made it dangerous. The paver blocks need to be removed and the potholes filled, then cycling would be easy. Then I would allow my son to cycle to school. Frankly speaking, for a cyclist it is only good roads that matter."

Throughout this meeting, it was notable that Harish, the official, emphasized the need for street redesign and reconstruction—such as the design depicted in the proposal on his desk—while Firoza focused on fixing the existing infrastructure. In particular, Firoza proposed to shift focus from infrastructure *projects* to surface conditions, or the small details like the ridges, cracks, gravel, and paver blocks that cyclists sense as they move through the city on a bicycle.

This conversation revealed the political stakes of a surface-oriented approach to sustainable transportation and the particular ways bicycle infrastructure plays out in different cities. In this meeting, Firoza underlined the need for better surfaces, whereas the official argued for a complete transformation of Mumbai's street and traffic system. These represent two different approaches to the city and its future. The official suggested that cycling will only be possible after fundamental changes in the city—better traffic sense, driver education, street design, and so on, whereas Firoza insisted that cycling can happen now, on the infrastructure and in the traffic conditions that already exist. In this way, like so many other cyclists discussed in this book, Firoza rejected the official's view of the inherent disorder of Mumbai's roads and the sense of deferral (the "*until* we have . . . ," as he put it) this view produces. Moreover, the juxtaposition of a supposedly Indian propensity for disorder (e.g., "right of way . . . those things naturally don't come to *us*" and "there is no traffic sense *here*") with an orderly "abroad" is an old trope. Government authorities "seeing" the city as an out-of-control space that needs to be made more homogenous, more orderly, and more in line with an imagined modern urban landscape elsewhere is a state vision that has characterized colonial and postcolonial urban Indian governance for at least a century.[37]

Even though the bicycle lane Harish was supporting included taking away space usually occupied by parked private vehicles owned by the elites of the city—a seeming challenge to power structures—it also coincided with a statist vision preoccupied with imposing order over a disorderly city. Indeed, as I discuss in chapter 5, many city officials in Mumbai find bicycle lanes appealing, ironically, because they promise to impose order on a supposedly disordered urban space. Moreover, design proposals for bicycle infrastructure that get the most attention are located away from mixed-use areas of the city or, as in the case of a bicycle track project along a water pipeline proposed in 2017, located off the streets altogether and literally intended to act as a security device that keeps poor people from accessing land.[38]

Surface attention challenges the status quo because it is not based on a logic of reorganizing urban space or the dramatic megaproject. Instead, cyclists who focus on surface often see infrastructure in a way that emphasizes process and detail—a better street maintenance system, for instance—and enhances what already exists, whereas the singular focus on new bicycle infrastructure as the answer to cyclists' vulnerability is premised on spatial segregation, re-ordering, and sometimes sanitizing space. In this way, and in the context of Mumbai, dedicated bicycle infrastructure can ironically function like infrastructures of automobility, such as a multilane bridge over a bay or a tunnel beneath a mountain. The singular focus on the bicycle lane can even echo elitist discourses, which suggests that separation from the eclectic mix of people, forms of transportation, and objects and textures of public space is the solution to the city's problems.

Traditionally, critique and surface have been at odds. As Stephen Best and Sharon Marcus argue, academics often see the surface as something "that conceals, as clothing does skin, or encloses, as a building's façade does its interior."[39] Surface supposedly lacks analytic rigor because it is what we immediately sense. And, because it supposedly "conceals," it is politically suspect. But this chapter has offered a critique of infrastructural thinking that doesn't hinge on showing an underlying system but instead emphasizes—and finds transformative political value in—what is immediately "apprehensible."[40] People who cycle in Mumbai demonstrate a mode of engagement with infrastructure that is characterized not by revealing hidden power arrangements but by building an ethical vocabulary from practices, emotions, and sensations that are felt and apparent.[41] Sticking to the surface does not just normalize the status quo but can challenge it as well.

Perhaps this tension between surface-as-feeling and depth-as-abstraction is why Firoza told me to call her a "cyclist" and not an "activist" when we first met. She sees a futurity in the embodied experiences of the road and rejects nostalgia for a mythic, ordered city of the past and the impulse to retreat behind walls that this nostalgia produces. Similarly, many other people use their embodied cycling experiences in Mumbai to create an alternative, surface-oriented approach to infrastructure: they see world-making possibilities in immersion in the city and its problems. So, in this way, surface matters literally and metaphorically. The "cyclist" rolls across the surface, and her imagination of the city and its possibilities are animated by the bumps and textures of the road, whereas the "activist," and often the academic as well, goes below to reveal what is hidden.[42] Sometimes, however, in doing so the activist and the academic miss out on the pleasures and political possibilities that lie on top.

2 Mumbai's Cycling Landscape

When I first met Dinesh, he was casually checking his phone on the side of the road while leaning over the handlebars of his bicycle. He was wearing dark jeans, a black backpack, and a curved-brim hat that sat low on his forehead. He seemed to have a moment to spare, so I introduced myself and asked what work he does.

"I make deliveries."

"What kind of deliveries?"

"Teeth," he said. With the constant din of honking from cars, trucks, and autorickshaws behind me, I thought I had misheard him. He pronounced it again slowly: "Daanth." Seeing my confused look, he pulled his black backpack from his slight shoulders and extracted a pair of dentures. The dentures were freshly made, with bright pink gums, and wrapped in plastic. "After making teeth, I deliver them to dentists. From Andheri to Bandra. From morning until night." Again, smiling, he said, "Teeth," and I understood.

"Why do these deliveries by bicycle? What challenges do you encounter on the road?" I asked. He shook his head and said, "There aren't any problems. I know the road; on a cycle, there's no need to stop in traffic. In the evening I easily maneuver around the huge traffic jams or I can just get on the footpath and go." He then added that cycling keeps him lean and feeling energetic.

During subsequent conversations and ride-alongs, Dinesh described his work and how cycling fits into it. He told me that after three years of working as a denture technician in an unlicensed workshop, his boss decided to leave Mumbai and sold the business to Dinesh and two other employees. After becoming an owner, Dinesh took on multiple roles: he became a delivery person and a salesperson, while continuing to manufacture dentures by hand. When business is good, his workday is hectic: he makes dentures first thing in the morning, does a round of deliveries by bicycle, then returns to his workshop after lunch to work on more dentures, then does a second round of deliveries in the early evening. However, despite being technically skilled, having access to their former boss's customer list, and being adept at fulfilling the demand for low-cost dentures that the big labs ignore, his sales fluctuate because their workshop is unlicensed. Occasional government crackdowns scare off dentists from buying Dinesh's products. During the months when sales are unsustainably low, he has to shut the workshop and wait until the authorities loosen their oversight or until dentists are once again driven to buy his popular and cheaper product.

I met Mohan, another small-scale entrepreneur, under similar circumstances. He was standing next to his bicycle after making a delivery. I learned that he too is a small-scale entrepreneur who delivers products he makes—in this case, homemade incense. When we first met, he was standing in front of a small shrine in an Andheri East basti, near where he had just delivered packets of incense, having used old inner tubes to secure a black leather bag to his bicycle's rear rack. On that afternoon and subsequent days, I rode along with him as he made deliveries, and I observed him making incense at his workshop and interacting with customers outside their homes. I saw how he uses a bicycle to wind his way through lanes that are too narrow to traverse in a motorized vehicle.[1] Like Dinesh, he told me that he appreciates being able to fly past cars stuck in traffic and not be bothered by the police (compared to people who use motorcycles). For him, a bicycle has clear, practical advantages: it is a cheap form of transportation but also allows him to access parts of the city that would be impossible to get to on a motorcycle. But at his home and workshop one afternoon, he offered reflections on cycling that exceeded these utilitarian explanations. While I watched him wrap bundles of incense in bright blue cellophane, he told me, "People who are connected to the cycle, only they know the joy of cycling. Those who don't cycle, they will feel it is just a toy. But if they start riding, they will see the transformation in their body. Then they will appreciate what the bicycle does to them."

I begin with these two vignettes because they reflect how Mumbai's cycling landscape does not cohere into a single narrative. Dinesh's and Mohan's stories of cycling represent a mix of practicality *and* pleasure, compulsion *and* autonomy. On the street, they are delivery workers, but at home they are also entrepreneurs and business owners. Their profits are small, and they live in precarious housing conditions, but they also have choices. For many, cycling is an economic decision, but Dinesh and Mohan describe benefits that are not always financial, such as looking good, feeling energetic, having a good night's sleep, enjoying the feeling of wind on one's face, and easily maneuvering in narrow, pedestrian-only lanes. They use bicycles primarily for work but also describe their pleasures and possibilities; as Mohan, who claims to both *need* and *enjoy* cycling, told me, the "joy" of cycling comes from the embodied experiences associated with it. To him, the practical and utilitarian aspects of cycling are inextricable from its materiality.[2]

This overlapping mix of motivations, meanings, and practices associated with Mumbai's cycling landscape is often not reflected in transportation writing. When I read planning reports, academic articles, and social media, I see India's cycling landscape divided into two distinct categories, with each category presumably having clear and mutually exclusive sets of experiences, practices, and motivations. In the literature, people who ride bicycles are described as being either "captive" or "choice" cyclists. If they are captive cyclists, their cycling is presumably all about utility and functionality. If they are "choice" riders, their cycling is presumably all about leisure and symbolism. As one report on cycling in India puts it, "Bicycle users in India are either captive or choice users. Captive users, who belong to low-income households, are dependent on cycling as their primary means of mobility."[3] Another report states, "Cyclists can also be classified into two categories—one who cycles by choice and the other a 'captive' cyclist who is bound by economic constraints and does not have a choice."[4] Another author describes a cycling landscape consisting of people "atop high-end bicycles, wearing helmets, and in some cases, bicycle shorts, gloves, and other gear[;] these riders represented a new brand of cyclist. Not poor—cycling out of choice—these cyclists belonged to the new middle classes of India."[5]

Certainly, people who rely on bicycles to make deliveries and people who ride for exercise with neighborhood groups have very different access to power, choice, and opportunity. Considerable differences in status are reflected in tangible ways—in how drivers react to their presence on the street, how police interact with them after crashes, and how media outlets represent their injuries and deaths. Highlighting this power differential is one reason writers use the "captive" and "choice" binary in the first place. The binary also serves as a reminder of how the neoliberal city is increasingly unwelcoming to the poor. But in this reading of the city, meaning and experience are often inferred from people's class position, which is often seen to contain all that might be known about a person.[6] Writing on a similar problem of "the seemingly self-evident explanation" of "necessity" in social science writing, the anthropologist Kathleen Millar observes that understanding work—even in demanding physical environments—as a "product of scarcity or a last resort leave[s] little room to ask why this work is *taken up* by those who pursue it, how it emerges from and fashions particular social and political relations, and how it expresses different visions of what life is for."[7]

The vignettes presented in this chapter highlight the multiple possible meanings of cycling in Mumbai. The individual stories are not meant to be illustrative of a single point; nor is the analysis, or theory, distinct from the story at all instances. As Olga Demetriou argues in "Reconsidering the Vignette as Method," whereas "the vignette distills analysis in one moment . . . it always gestures to its multiples."[8] Indeed, the vignettes I present in this chapter—about Dinesh, a denture entrepreneur; Mohan, an incense maker and door-to-door salesman; Prakash, an ice warehouse owner; Sunil, a knife sharpener; and Shweta, an administrative assistant, for instance—contain bicycle stories that are shaped by power but are nevertheless irreducible to taken-for-granted assumptions about autonomy, choice, and pleasure. Moreover, focusing on what people do with bicycles allows me to show the practical ways people incorporate cycling into their lives, how cycling is an interface between the physical and social landscape of the city, as well as what cycling means to people in various contexts. This simple question—what do people do with bicycles?—allows for the development of an understanding of how class affects mobility while also accounting for multiplicity and overlap.

What People Do with Bicycles

The most common bicycle in Mumbai is the black, Indian-made roadster style used by tens of thousands of people who deliver milk, bread, and laundry, as well as by the five thousand dabbawalas who deliver lunches. These bicycles are nicknamed ghoda cycles—"ghoda" means horse in Hindi—reflecting their sturdiness and reliability. These bicycles have big pedals and wide handlebars, which give riders an upright posture; a wide, padded seat supported by thick springs; and wide, often deliberately underinflated tires—design elements that emphasize stability and comfort rather than speed. They also have a heavy frame, cable-less brakes made of metal, extra-large rear racks, and rear axle kickstands. Ghoda cycles are often modified by their owners. For instance, dabbawalas often attach vertical metal bars to the front fork to prevent bags from hitting the spokes during rides, while bakery delivery workers add multiple metal supports for heavy loads in the rear and milk delivery workers attach thick hooks to the rear rack to carry heavy canisters. Other modifications include reinforced fenders or seat posts, extra hooks, extra-large rear racks, and bottle-cleaning brushes attached to keep the axles clean.

Because of their ubiquity and connection with the city's historic dabbawala community, these ghoda cycles have become the iconic working-class bicycle of Mumbai. For example, a bicycle advocate once posted an image on social media that showed a low-angle shot of a shiny black ghoda cycle parked in front of a busy train station. The accompanying caption reflects an emotional connection many have with these cycles: "#cyclesofmumbai: Amid the morning rush, a roadster in full glory at Lower Parel station, hours before she helps deliver tiffin boxes." Indeed, because they are parked by the dozen in front of train stations, bakeries, and general stores, these bicycles form an important part of the visual and auditory landscape of the city. As the journalist Prashant Nanaware told me, "They make an interesting sound. Once you hear this bell, *tring*, you know a ghoda cycle is there—the most commonly seen bicycle in India."

Ghoda cycles in Mumbai are pushed, pulled, and used as workbenches; they can display goods or serve as a support on which to sit and relax while reading a newspaper—they are not just used to get from place to place. For instance, vendors tie mesh bags of apples between the seat post and front fork of their bicycles and dangle a scale from the handlebars. They keep the tires underinflated in order to provide sturdier support for the extra weight. Pickle and spice vendors display their goods on the rear rack of bicycles parked in busy market areas; these vendors make their bicycles part of a street market infrastructure that changes throughout the day. Men working in teams of two can often be seen pushing bicycles that carry long metal tubes to construction sites. Meanwhile, workers from a car repair shop sometimes carry tires by stacking them on the rear rack, tying four more to the side, draping two tires around each side of the handlebars, and securing each to the fork with a cable.

In a study of ghoda cycles in Mumbai, Logan Hollarsmith describes some of the ways people adapt them to suit their needs.[9] He calls them "cargo bicycles," although the ghoda cycle's design does not announce them as such; instead, ghoda cycles are transformed into cargo cycles by their owners.[10] Hollarsmith writes, "The pedals have multiple uses . . . oversized loads such as plywood . . . are held by a pedal and the cycle becomes a pushcart"; the "thick rear axle kickstand allows people to load bulky items like eggs stacked four feet high without tipping. When hazards are too great, egg couriers prefer walking the cycle [with one hand on the handlebar and the other on the stack of eggs]"; dabbawalas transport lunches by attaching "hooks on the rear rack"; knife sharpeners "convert their cycle into a knife sharpening stall" with the help of the sturdy kickstand and sharpening stone attached to the top tube; and, finally, "the combination of the durable rack and upright [rear axle] kickstand"

Indian-made bicycles (often referred to as ghoda cycles) parked near a commuter train station in Mumbai.

Bicycles being used for bread delivery.

enables people to sit on the cycle while doing things like drinking tea or reading a newspaper. In these cases, the cycle becomes a "mobile bench that transforms an object associated with functionality and movement into one of leisure." These multiple uses and modifications on the ghoda cycle show how "entire professions are centered on this simple vehicle which people adapt to make the cycle work in ways beyond just transportation."

Some of the most complex modifications to bicycles are done by mobile knife sharpeners. Consider Sohail, who sharpens knives by sitting on the rear rack and spinning a heavy, double-sided sharpening stone by pedaling while his bicycle is parked on an upright-style kickstand. This style of kickstand lifts the bicycle's rear wheel off the ground, which allows Sohail to pedal freely while sitting. When he pedals in a stationary position, his power spins the sharpening stone rather than propelling his bicycle forward. This happens with the help of a thin cord that he temporarily loops around the rim of a small extra wheel attached to the rear axle and a small nob attached to the sharpening stone. Moreover, he places a large wooden display board in front of his bicycle's handlebars. This board has multiple functions: it displays knives for sale, provides a place to temporarily store customers' knives while he works, and, because it is so distinctive, implicitly advertises his knife-sharpening services.

While wiping away sweat with the thin towel that he always keeps on his shoulder, Sohail explains how he started this work: "I arrived in Mumbai twelve years ago from Haryana. I am uneducated, so I can't get a job with a salary. From spending time with some guys from Rajasthan I learned about this. I am fond of cycling. But I do this because at first I couldn't find another job." He paused to take a puff of the lit beedi in his hand and continued: "Now I have 150 regular customers and I have a different route every day. Today I'll be in Lokhandwala, tomorrow in Juhu, the next day in Powai."

The eclecticism, adaptation, and reuse seen in Sohail's knife-sharpening setup is similar to the "cultures of repair" seen in most Indian cities.[11] These characteristics are especially applicable to people who have recently migrated to the city and, due to their having little access to capital or

A bicycle-based knife sharpener riding to his next customer.

social support networks, have restricted occupational choice. As Malini Sur documents, the adaptations cargo bicycle operators make in Kolkata, like Sohail's, are shaped by multiple forms of marginalization, while also constituting an infrastructure that makes "life sustainable" in the city.[12] This is part of an infrastructure that centers on "repair, metal welding, and the use of cheap ordinary objects to generate a distinctive assemblage."[13] For instance, Sohail added an extra fork to the front of his bicycle to support the heavy wooden board displaying knives for sale. This board slants slightly backward so it rests on the handlebars and front fender (the extra fork connects the front axle to the stem). Moreover, he asked a friend who makes window grilles to weld two metal supports to the fender to prevent it from getting crushed. Sohail explained that these parts come from multiple sources: from bicycle shops in Andheri, from Null Bazaar in south Mumbai, and from friends in his village in Haryana. And they are almost all reused: the cord connecting the stone to the rear wheel comes from an old sewing machine, the extra rear wheel and axle on the sharpening stone come from discarded bicycles, and the knives for sale are secured by recycled inner tubes on a display board whose edges are softened by flattened, worn-out bicycle tires.

Sohail cycles great distances to reach customers scattered around northwestern Mumbai—traveling, on average, twenty-five miles a day, six days a week—but it was clear from its use that his bicycle is not just for transportation. When he pulls up to small snack stalls (most of his customers are small roadside fried food and snack vendors), he swiftly lifts the cycle up from the rear and lowers the kickstand in one motion, bends over and loops the cord to connect the sharpening stone to the small rear wheel, sits just behind the saddle on the rear rack, and gently pedals. As his power is transferred to the slowly spinning stone, he takes out a knife, wipes it down and then gently touches it to stone, creating a shower of bright orange sparks. He continues to pedal while slowly angling the knife to get a consistent edge. Sparks continue to fly, blackening the display board resting on the handlebars. As the metallic shrill of the knife rubbing against the spinning stone rises above the din of traffic, his bicycle is no longer only a mobility device; it has been transformed into a workplace.

Morning Deliveries

I often encountered people whose work, mobility, and relationship to cycling challenged commonsense categories. Consider Iqbal, a man who sells biscuits door to door. I met him one day in Chembur after he had delivered a large package of his product to a liquor shop there. He was rearranging his items for sale in a large metal box perched on the back of his bicycle and supported by two thick metal rods. I introduced myself and the book project and, before diving into a conversation about cycling and its relationship to work, he opened a package and forced me to eat a biscuit. "You've come from far away so at least have one," he said. Iqbal, a broad-shouldered man with a thick mustache, a carefully ironed blue button-down shirt, and gray trousers, looked down on me as I quickly chewed the buttery, flaky biscuit.

As with Dinesh and Mohan, Iqbal's utility-oriented cycling does not quite conform to the image of the "captive" cyclist found in transportation literature. Iqbal sells baked goods to a long list of customers he has cultivated over the past decade. His most popular item is the type of biscuit he shared with me and purchases from a large bakery in central Mumbai. He sells them at a 20 to 30 percent markup, so for each kilogram of biscuits he makes roughly twenty to thirty rupees. The amount of profit he gets depends on the neighborhood. "People in slums pay less, but I can get a higher rate in nicer neighborhoods," he said. He structures his week so each day takes him to a different neighborhood—Vashi one day, Kurla the next, and Jogeshwari the day after. Some of these destinations are more than ten miles from his home.

This work arrangement is not lucrative, but Iqbal said it gives him freedoms his previous job—tailoring in a small workshop—did not. Bicycle delivery offers an alternative to what he described as the claustrophobic, monotonous, and unhealthy work of tailoring. Bicycle delivery also appealed to his sense of independence, evinced in his description of his work as "dhandha." Although literally meaning "business," dhandha in this context means one's own work rather than wage work. For instance, he said, "Even if I come ten or twenty minutes late [it] doesn't matter, it's my business" (Das bees minute late pohoonchenge toh aisa kuch problem hai nahin dhandha toh apna hi hai). Anthropologists Aditi Aggarwal and Tarini Bedi have also observed how the term "dhandha" in working-class Mumbai signifies an ethic of entrepreneurialism and "self-employed labour more broadly," thus challenging social scientists' assumptions about what freedom looks like.[14] According to these authors, "Dhandha also takes place in spaces where workers, even those who are poor and whose lives are precarious, have some autonomy over their time and their work conditions."[15]

Iqbal described the positive aspects of bicycle-based delivery work in terms of how he feels and the effects of cycling on his body. Certainly, navigating traffic on a bicycle also comes with stress and risk of physical injury. He told me he is constantly on guard for swerving motorcycles and autorickshaws, which had been the cause of two crashes—fortunately not serious. "That's why I ride very carefully through the traffic and sometimes get down and walk if I have to. Those guys will just cut you off," he said. But he also emphasized the embodied and sensory benefits of this work: "I got attracted to this trade because I would get body aches [from tailoring] and was worried about gaining too much weight," he said. I asked if he enjoyed cycling, to which he responded, "When you go up an incline and you take these deep breaths, it is so good for your lungs. I really like taking these deep breaths.... When you cycle up a bridge it becomes a bit difficult, but when you go to down a flyover [overpass], and there is the wind all around you, it feels so good. The cycle just flies. Whatever distance it may be, say one or one and a half kilometers, it feels really good."

For Iqbal, a bicycle also provides a specific practical benefit: it enables him to access city spaces that would otherwise be out of reach. He estimates that 30 percent of his clients live in slums. These neighborhoods often have very narrow lanes the width of three people standing shoulder to shoulder, 90-degree turns, and uneven concrete and tile surfaces interrupted by clusters of water pipes. Those lanes are only accessible on foot or on a bicycle; "because those areas have small lanes, a bicycle is perfect there," he said. Whereas people with motorcycles have to park them near the entrance and walk the rest of the way on foot, cycling allows him to navigate those narrow passageways. Many lanes are even too narrow or bumpy to ride on, so he gets off and pushes his bicycle like a handcart: "I can take out the box from behind my bicycle, then push the cycle through the lane, and then bring the box. With a motorcycle, I don't think I could do that," he said. With a focus on what Iqbal does with a bicycle, it became clear that cycling offers something more than affordability. For him, cycling enables him to grow his business.

Iqbal, like many other people, emphasized the theme of accessibility and the pleasures of being on the road. However, this does not mean that financial considerations are not part of the equation. I recognize that talking about cycling because it is affordable can be embarrassing. It is possible that Iqbal, and many other working-class people quoted in this chapter, deliberately avoided talking with me about the financial benefits of cycling, even if that might be an important factor in their use of this mode of transport. For instance, during his research on working-class mobility choices in Ahmedabad, Rutul Joshi observed that "many participants were not comfortable talking about issues related to income or affordability. The poverty situations were often underplayed in the conversations.... 'Not affordable' was often projected [in surveys] as 'not convenient.'"[16] However, as Joshi also noted, people frame mobility as a personal choice even if, from a generalized, socioeconomic perspective, it seems like there is a lack of choice. This is because people may desire to assert a sense of autonomy and dignity in personal decisions. As Joshi adds, "This attitude of 'being on one's devices' was an important part of being a working woman and man."[17]

Indeed, talk of the practicality of cycling—or whether it is a convenience, as Joshi observed—falls into a gray area of meaning between affordability and autonomy. The slipperiness of these two motivations is demonstrated by people who use bicycles to make early-morning door-to-door milk deliveries in working-class areas of Mumbai. For instance, consider Sunil, a man in his early twenties who does milk deliveries starting at 5:30 a.m. and then attends college classes. For him, cycling is a necessity that financially enables access to the city; delivery work represents both constrained choice and opportunities for independence. Teasing out one or the other seems to be missing the point.

Sunil starts his day before sunrise, using the light from his cell phone to illuminate the narrow alley near his home while pushing his bicycle out to the main road. On the day I cycled with him, in front of the alley where Sunil lives, a milk wholesaler sat adjacent to a tower of milk crates. At that time of day, cawing crows dominated a soundscape that would soon be taken over by honking. Autorickshaw drivers waited in a long line for gas. Four young women dressed in flight attendants' uniforms got into a van. Middle-aged women jogged toward the nearby beach, and men in white kurtas headed to a nearby mosque for morning prayer. Sunil, dressed in a black tank top with fluorescent yellow lining, sweatpants, flip-flops, and an army fatigue hat, walked his bicycle to the wholesaler and wordlessly draped polypropylene bags containing three dozen milk packets around the handlebars of his cycle. He crisscrossed the bags' straps over the handlebars and then, while struggling to get on, muttered to me that there's "a balance problem."

He later revealed that the balance problem is not much of an issue because he cycles with this heavy load only briefly. I followed behind him as he cycled a few hundred feet, dismounted, and pushed his bicycle through a small lane wedged between a print shop and a sugarcane juice stall. The lane was wide enough for his bicycle and one person to pass by in the other direction. The surface was firmly packed dirt. The left side was lined with bits of paper, paan packets, and potted plants. The right side was lined with dozens of three-inch-wide water pipes. We turned left and negotiated the narrow spaces between people's homes, trying to avoid bumping into stoops, water barrels, parked bicycles, and clothes hung to dry. Streaks of light appeared outside, but the lane was still dark. I heard crows cawing and the occasional metal clang of our bicycles rolling over water pipes.

Sunil arrived at his first customer's home at 6:00 a.m., lifted a towel covering a blue water barrel, and slipped a half-liter packet of milk underneath. He continued pushing his bicycle down the lane. At each home, he placed milk packets in different places—in a small shopping bag hanging from a hook, under a tarp, and through a metal grille and onto a window ledge—like hiding spots. A woman was setting up a tea stall at the end of the lane. Sunil handed her six milk packets. The neighborhood slowly woke up as he finished this round of deliveries. A man in a perfectly pressed white shirt and groomed mustache and his partner walked behind us, pushing their bicycles. Bags full of idli and cooking utensils, plates, and napkins hung from one side of the handlebar. Metal tiffins of coconut and red chutney hung from the other. He was on his way to his spot on the side of the road, a few hundred feet away, where he runs a breakfast stall. In this lane, at this time of day, it seemed that there was nothing other than bicycles on the move.

People on bicycles rule many Mumbai streets at dawn. For instance, while Sunil makes milk deliveries, a few hundred feet away Amit starts delivering pao, a popular bun-like bread sold throughout the city. His day starts at 5:00 a.m. His first stop is at the wholesale bakery to pick up the slabs of pao for his first round of deliveries. As he parks his bicycle, a bakery worker starts layering the freshly baked bread on the glass counter. Amit locks his bicycle and then slowly inspects each slab. He picks at frayed edges and checks for inconsistencies. Meanwhile, in a small room next to the display area, a three-person team continues baking pao. One man carves a mound of loose, pliant dough into fist-size chunks and tosses them down to another man sitting beside a scale. He forms the dough into loaves, places them in a metal tray, and then hands the tray to a third person managing the oven. Across the narrow lane men fresh off an overnight shift, covered head to toe in flour, sip rich tea in the only other shop open at this time. Five minutes later, satisfied, Amit tucks the bread into yellow polypropylene bags. He drapes the bags around the handlebars of his bicycle one strap at a time, using the bell to keep the straps from slipping, and then adds an extra layer of plastic on top to protect the bread from the rain.

While riding with him just after sunrise one day, he told me that he's built up his list of clients over the years. At first he rides very slowly. The two bags heavy with bread that hang from his handlebars make it difficult to maneuver with much agility. They occasionally bump into his legs as he rides. To avoid rubbing against the bags he bows his knees outward with each pedal stroke. Like Iqbal, he works independently, and his business is also dependent on cultivating reliable customers. "I've been coming here since this area was built twenty-five years ago. Everyone knows I'm the paowala for this area," he said as we cycled side by side through the quiet streets of the early-morning hours. "What happens when a new building comes up?" I asked, pointing to the towers rising behind the one-story homes of the longtime residents. "The security guys figure out who is the paowala in the area and find me. I've been coming here for twenty-five years, so others don't come," he said, then rings his bell. We've arrived at the first stop of the morning. He steps down from the bicycle, counts out three slabs, places them in a plastic container on a street-facing counter of a small corner store, and pedals off to his next destination.

Around the corner from the bakery where Amit starts his day, Prakash operates a small ice business out of his home. The structure he owns consists of two ten-by-ten-foot rooms—a ground floor, which he uses as a warehouse and workspace, and a small bedroom, connected by external stairs to the workspace. This vertical architectural style is common in Mumbai's informal settlements. Researchers Rahul Srivastava and Matias Echanove call this style a "tool-house," an appellation that captures this mix of living and working, as well as the element of adaptation and flexibility.[18]

One morning, with his bicycle parked outside, Prakash lifted the gray shutter of his shop and peeled off layers of burlap and tarp to reveal a recently delivered, two-hundred-pound block of ice. He immediately got to work breaking down the block. He began by chiseling a line with a small pick. *Tik-tik-tik*, he stabbed at the ice from top to bottom to create a shallow but perfectly straight line. He went over the line again and again, each time going slightly deeper, until a large block of ice cracked off. He put that block aside for one of his sugarcane vendor customers. He broke another large piece and shaved it into thin slivers—that was for fish vendors. *Tik-tik-tik*—he cracked off two more large blocks, roughly ten pounds each, which he would deliver to fruit juice vendors. He then wrapped each bunch of ice in burlap, stacked them on the back of his bicycle, and secured them with old inner tubes. While holding the handle bars, he raised the kickstand and, in one swift motion, gave the bicycle a little push, swung his leg over the top bar, and started pedaling.

He did not have to cycle very far—his first customers are fish vendors who live at the end of the lane. They had left their baskets out for him the previous night, so he quickly uncovered the baskets, filled them with shaved ice, and moved on. He made three more stops on his lane—at a sugarcane stall, a juice stall, and a sweet shop. Next, he cycled a few minutes to a wealthier neighborhood nearby and parked in front of a shuttered restaurant. He lifted the rear of the bicycle onto the kickstand, untied the straps on the back of his bicycle, and unveiled what remained of the slab of ice. A shop assistant ran out of the shop and handed him a bucket. Prakash cut the ice in half, put it into the bucket, and stabbed at it with a pick. Little bits of ice and water droplets flew onto the sidewalk.

Like the other people discussed in this chapter, Prakash is a small-scale independent entrepreneur. His profits are slim, and his relationship to cycling is often utilitarian. However, this relationship is not defined entirely by utility alone. In addition to chopping and delivering ice, he manages his business, takes orders from customers, and carefully cultivates a client list. He also owns land in Bihar on which he grows potatoes, onions, and wheat. Curious about his continued use of the bicycle even though it seems he could afford a scooter, I asked him about it. "With a cycle, I'm healthier," he replied. "My body, how I feel, how I'm going. It feels better. Whatever petrol I save, I eat." He patted his belly; "I put it all inside," he said, and laughed.

Bicycle Enterprise

Mohan, the incense manufacturer whom I mentioned at the beginning of this chapter, similarly described the utility of cycling alongside a set of other meanings and associations. He framed his work as a choice he made within the constraints of his limited education and his lack of connections and funds to start a business. As I sat with him one afternoon in his home, which doubled as a workshop, he explained that when he arrived in Mumbai from his village in Gujarat ten years ago, he did not want to take whatever work was available: "I thought if I do a job, my whole life will be spent doing that job. But I don't have any special education, so I couldn't become a doctor, engineer, or lawyer." He sought out something to sell that could withstand the rapid technological changes he's witnessed in his lifetime. "In ten years, no one will be buying radios, clocks, or TVs, just like there are no more STD/PCO [public phone] booths because of mobile phones," he said, but items related to household worship have a staying power: "Scent is at the center of all religions—Muslims must wear perfume before praying, Hindus light incense sticks for the gods, and even Catholics light incense, although a bit less, of course."

Floor-to-ceiling metal shelving lines the walls of his home, holding dozens of bottles of perfume concentrates, each carefully labeled with the name and instructions for dilution. Large plastic jugs containing chemical solutions for incense are scattered on the floor. Dozens of bundles of raw incense sticks, in bright pink, red, and blue cellophane, mingle with household items like pots, glasses, and plates. Intricately framed pictures of gods, dozens of plastic containers holding pens, vials of perfume, other supplies (tape, scissors, cotton swabs), and a scale are arranged on a countertop. A small TV perched up above a cupboard silently plays the twenty-four-hour news.

Mohan sat on a short stool as he explained how he started this business. "After bathing in the morning, what do we do? We touch the feet of god," he said as he dunked bundles of raw incense sticks into a thick blue solution—being extra careful not to stain his beautiful white shirt with blue flower patterns. "We offer flowers and water, and after that, we light incense. I can't manage flowers, and water is available in every household. So, I thought, why not sell incense?"

Three times a week, Mohan buys dozens of kilos of raw incense sticks—which are a light tan, similar to the color of unfinished plywood—brings them back to his home, cleans them of wood shavings by pounding them on the floor, ties them in one-pound bundles, and then dunks them, a bundle at a time, in a bright blue liquid. While sitting on a low stool, he shows me the process. He dunks the bundles in the liquid, lifts them out to drain, then dunks again. He repeats this twenty times per bundle, rotating the sticks slightly between each dunk to make sure they get an even soak. After the final dunk, he places the bundle on a metal tray that has a small hole in the corner to drain the liquid. Each tray can hold thirty bundles. Each bundle contains one hundred sticks. That's three thousand sticks in each batch, which he sometimes does three times a day. After eight hours of drying, the sticks come out looking a deep, reddish brown, glistening with the perfume. He wraps one-pound bundles in bright red cellophane, stuffs them in his leather bag, and sets out to make his sales. "Making incense is easy," he said. "But marketing and selling them, that's a much bigger deal."

Unsurprisingly, his home hit me with a cacophony of odors whenever I entered: the fruity-smokiness of lit incense; the pungent, chemical scent from the raw solutions; the light floral smell of the dozens of perfume bottles; as well as the hint of dish soap his mother was using to wash pots and the caramel-like scent coming from the pot of milky water boiling on the stove. Knowing little about incense and perfumes, I asked for a tutorial. "People know a dozen or so, but *there are thousands of beautiful smells*," he answered, emphasizing the last point with dramatic exaggeration. Slowly, and with great relish, he reeled off a few names: "Gulab, chandan, jasmine, raatrani, black cobra, Charlie, jannat, kasturi, romance, China." That afternoon he was making "Charlie," which he categorized as a "flower scent."

One day, after he soaked the last bundle, he put it aside to dry, washed his hands, packed a black leather bag with fifty pounds of incense, and secured it to his rear bicycle rack with two old inner tubes. We both pushed off toward the neighborhood where he needed to make the first set of deliveries—a low-income neighborhood near the airport. Clusters of two-story structures divided by narrow lanes dominated the area. As the sun set, I followed behind Mohan as he swiftly maneuvered through dense rush-hour traffic. At the first intersection, a bus slowly pushed its way through a throng of cars by honking loudly. The bus briefly blocked traffic, opening space for Mohan to go forward. He quickly jumped in front of the bus and sped down the momentarily empty road. At the next intersection, he maneuvered to the front of a long line of stopped cars, saw a gap in the traffic, and jumped ahead.

A few minutes later he turned off the main road. We cycled down a narrow lane that barely fit the two of us. The lane was lined with two-story structures, each having a ground-floor shop or warehouse with small stairs that led to a residence on top. With each turn, the lane narrowed. We entered a narrow passage, got off our bicycles, and walked them in single file. When people passed us, we stepped to the side and pushed our bicycles and bags flush against the wall. We continued walking until we reached a brightly lit open space paved with slabs of tile and lined on one side with a thick cluster of pipes. Here, Mohan leaned his bicycle against the wall, slung his leather bag over his shoulder, and walked a final few feet to his customers. I stood back, trying to stay out of view while he made his sales of incense wrapped in purple cellophane, small bottles of perfumes, and soaps.

When I first met Mohan in 2019, his business was thriving. He told me he had hundreds of customers and was only limited by the production capacity of his two-person workshop—himself and his sister. With all this success, I asked, why didn't he switch to a motorcycle? As he explained, "I do my business on a bicycle at least eight to ten hours a day. I prefer a cycle more than Activa and Kinetic [motorcycle brands]. My business can't operate from those vehicles." This is because much of Mohan's commute involves navigating neighborhoods that have densely packed, narrow alleyways, where private life spills out into the public and where it would thus be inappropriate to roll through on a loud and relatively large motorcycle, if space even permitted it to pass through. But as we talked further, he mixed practical reasons for using a bicycle with other reasons that are abstract or have to do with feelings and sensations:

With a bicycle, I can cut through traffic and signals, I can park wherever I want, and I don't have to worry about RTO [the government transport authority] or towing guys taking my cycle. The second thing is that I get full exercise for my body. This is better than going to a gym. Each and every body part gets completely rejuvenated each day and I sleep so well at night. The problems people have with knees and joints—when you cycle that doesn't happen. The third reason is that I save money on petrol. And the fourth reason is that it is good for the environment. People who take a [motorized] two-wheeler for five kilometers—they could have cycled! They produce so much pollution!

To Mohan, cycling has multiple, overlapping meanings. He cycles because his work requires it—cycling enables him to skip ahead of traffic, navigate crowded lanes, and unobtrusively ride up to people's homes. But he does not talk about cycling in strictly practical terms. As much as talking about its usefulness, he talks about the embodied aspects and sensations of cycling—the feeling he has while riding and the good night's sleep he has afterward—as well as the positive impact cycling has on the urban environment. This mix of attention to utility and the senses is what gets lost in the "captive" and "choice" cyclist categories that are commonly used in transportation literature. Part of the problem is that these categories encourage interpretations—based on the bicycles people ride, the clothes people wear, and the items they carry—that are often misleading. But Mohan, despite cycling for work, described cycling in terms of neither total compulsion nor total choice; the utilitarian nature of his cycling does not preclude him connecting it to pleasure and self-making.

Challenging Stereotypes about Cycling

Misreading cycling was an important topic for many middle-class professionals who regularly cycle to work or for fun. People often talked about how coworkers, family, and passersby read cyclists' clothes, bicycles, and helmets as signs, or clues, for some underlying circumstance or message—that they are cycling to save money, or to signal environmental virtuousness, or some other supposedly hidden reason. These readings overlook the fact that many people cycle simply because it is practical, fun, or makes them feel good. For instance, Arvind, an IT worker who commutes to work on a bicycle, shared a story one morning after an early Sunday morning group ride. We were taking a break at Carter Road, Khar, a popular spot for its beautiful view of the sea, its fresh air, and its public gathering spaces. A group of us sat on a low concrete wall and were chatting when a young man mentioned cycling to work. Arvind told him that he's cycled thousands of miles doing his regular commute. And during those rides "you hear all kinds of comments. That's how people look at us. That's their perspective. You need a *lot* of patience to cycle to work."

Arvind told us that while stopped at a traffic light while cycling to his office one morning, he overheard a man on a motorcycle talking about him. "Look at what people are doing to save money these days," said the man to a female passenger behind him. And what did she see? An IT worker cycling to his office. He wore a helmet, a T-shirt, and shorts; carried a backpack; and was riding an imported bicycle with a colorful frame, flat handlebars, and multiple gears—objects that signal to others that he is a middle-class professional. However, he was not riding a bicycle for fun but for practical purposes. The man on the motorcycle interpreted cycling to work as a sign of financial distress. He assumed that he was riding a bicycle out of desperation—"to save money." Otherwise, the choice made no sense. As this man's misreading demonstrates, commuting to work on a bicycle defies the seemingly distinct categories of middle-class economic need and captive-versus-choice cycling.

I often heard stories of this disconnect between the intimate meaning of cycling and how cycling is externally perceived—either by family, passersby, colleagues, or a more abstract "society." Among cycling groups, stories circulated about people misreading transportation choices: the jewelry shop owner who inadvertently led his family to believe he was going bankrupt when he started cycling to work, the security guards at high-end office buildings who refused to believe someone arriving on a bicycle actually worked there, the scientist who made sure to arrive at work before her boss because cycling seemed too eccentric, the lawyer who had to use a secret side entrance so people wouldn't see him arrive on a bicycle, and so forth. A newspaper editor once told me that when he started taking the train to work, it set off panic among his junior colleagues. "I used to drive to the office, but it would take one and a half hours; it was horrible," he said as we chatted in his office one afternoon. "So I started taking the train and found it to be so much faster and a much better experience." While pointing to the open area with cubicles where junior writers sit, "a rumor started there," he said. "There was talk, like 'Why is he taking the train? Will my salary be cut? Is there a problem with my job?' That's what people think. They think, if you don't drive a car, then what image are you showing?"

The bicycle's image problem is frequently a topic on neighborhood-specific cycling WhatsApp groups. A daily bicycle commuter once wrote, "Unfortunately a lot of people feel low-class or kid-ish on cycles, especially the older generation. So, to maintain their prestige or whatever they think it is, they won't opt for cycles." The people he refers to are other middle-class professionals who are anxious about maintaining an outward appearance of professional success. They are people like himself who have stable salaries and housing but do not live in the city's wealthiest neighborhoods. A reply comes a few minutes later: "Totally agree. People want a gym in their building but never use it. Their bicycle is in the garage just to rot and they think it's a sign of prosperity." These cyclists understand the importance of perception in maintaining class status; a fancy building lobby, a car, an on-site gym—these are all taken as signs of success, just like, ironically, a bicycle under a thick layer of dust because it has never been used. Prashant Nanaware, a journalist, blogger, and cyclist explained it like this: "Cars are a status symbol. People feel, 'If I am able to afford a cycle or car, then why should I ride a bicycle?'"

This theme of the bicycle's stigma appeared often in conversations with middle-class professionals. "In a sense, the bicycle doesn't fit the image of Mumbai, which is fast-paced, commercial, and rushed," said Rohit as we sat together in a Lower Parel café during his lunch break. He told me he got "hooked" on cycling after joining a group near his home in order to lose weight. "I'm a programmer, so I sit for eight to ten hours a day at a desk. We have irregular hours too. It is really stressful. I noticed I was putting on weight because of work." An "old passion for cycling" was rekindled when he met a local cycling group. He only rides on the weekends. Wistfully, he added, "cycling to work is only a dream" because he lives thirty miles from his office in central Mumbai. As with many people, the most difficult and stressful part of the day for him is the commute on an extremely crowded train. Traveling two hours each way "gets on your nerves," he said. "At the end of the day you just want to get out of the traffic, out of the crowds, and have your own transport." He related the crowded trains, the traffic, and the general sense of entrepreneurial bustle that, to many, characterized Mumbai's soul to the negative image of the bicycle: "Here everyone is in a rush, always going from point A to point B. Cycling doesn't seem to fit that. It is like, if you are cycling it means that you are slow. That you have a lot of time." But despite family and friends saying that the responsible thing to do is to save money for a car, to Rohit "that doesn't make any sense. It doesn't fit me. It doesn't fit my way of doing things." Embracing the bicycle means doing things slightly differently—at odds with what people around him expect.

Engaging the City

What else do people do with bicycles in Mumbai? So far in this chapter I have focused on people who primarily use bicycles for work or commuting. However, recreational cycling is also an important part of the city's cycling landscape. For instance, every weekend, dozens of neighborhood groups organize social rides to attractive spots in Mumbai and around its edges, such as to Nariman Point in the south, Sewri on the eastern seaboard, Gorai village in the far northwest, as well as forts, famous temples, and famous bakeries. The people who participate in these rides are usually middle-class professionals—such as lawyers, IT workers, real estate agents, and human resources professionals. As with the other people I've discussed in this chapter, I cycled with them in order to learn what motivates them to ride, how cycling fits into their lives, and what cycling means to them.

Most writing on recreational cycling in India, as with most social science writing on middle-class practices, approaches the topic with skepticism. Expensive bicycles, athletic clothing, and shiny helmets seem to ask for an analysis that centers class-based experiences. In this writing, the act of recreational cycling itself, especially in deeply unequal cities such as Mumbai, is nothing more than an expression of class privilege. But my initial encounters with middle-class cyclists showed that alongside the symbolism of the activity were embodied experiences that showed other possible meanings. In the early part of my research, my hunch was that the novelty of cycling—and the novel associated sensations and bodily experiences—opened a space for surprising interpretations and multiple, overlapping meanings. For instance, might recreational riding be not only a reflection of class status but also a space for people to creatively rethink their relationship to the city? To explore this further, I knew I had to go beyond reading the symbolism of riders' gear and instead ride with them, to understand what cycling means to them on their own terms.

One of the over two dozen social group rides I joined was to Upvan Lake, in Thane, just over the northeastern municipal limits of Mumbai.[19] The night before the ride, my phone buzzed with messages from people eager to plan the ride, talk about previous rides, or simply enjoy a community of people who have made cycling an important part of their lives. Most people in these groups were in their thirties and forties, middle-class professionals, and much like myself at the time, new to cycling as an adult and to the experience of the city on two wheels. On that occasion I typed "I'm in," which committed myself to getting up at 5:00 a.m. to join the group.

Six hours later I woke up, quietly sipped coffee while reading other riders' messages of encouragement—"Good morning," "Leaving now," "It's going to be a good ride today"—and slipped out of my apartment while my family slept. I held a half-eaten banana in one hand and the handlebar in the other while I cycled to the start point.

As I slowly rolled through residential streets delightfully free of traffic, a young man in a bright orange shirt, shorts, and sandals passed me. I noticed he was brushing his teeth while cycling. He saw me looking at him and said light-heartedly, "I don't have any time to do it at home!" A pao delivery man rang a bell, announcing his arrival to customers. In the distance I heard a hollow metallic sound like two chains hitting each other. A middle-aged man in a white kurta cycled past me. Two large metal canisters dangled from the sides of his rear rack. The canisters banged against the metal as he rode over a speed bump, making that clanging noise again. He rang his bell and disappeared down an alley.

I joined the group under a centrally located bridge, and we slowly made our way north. Along the way, cycling groups from other neighborhoods—Ghatkopar, Powai, Bhandup—joined us. After thirty minutes we formed a convoy of fifty riders. We increased our speed on the edge of the flat, smooth, and uninterrupted Eastern Express Highway. We passed other people riding in the same direction: college students on their way to school and people cycling to the gym, to work, and to local parks. We passed men riding on ghoda cycles and dressed in security guard uniforms, as well as a woman in a deep purple sari riding a step-through framed cycle with plastic bags of marigolds dangling from the handlebars. A man with gray hair and wearing a white button-down shirt and trousers cycled up to me. He rode a black ghoda cycle with double top tubes. A folded newspaper was tucked between the brake cables and handlebar. He asked, "Is this a race?" He rode with me for a few minutes and told me about cycling to his job at a power plant every day. "My family tells me to get a car, but I prefer to cycle. Sometimes I ride as far as ten kilometers to visit friends," he said. We passed other people cycling that morning as well—people delivering cigarettes, bread, biscuits, newspapers, and milk, people with electricians' and plumbing tools tied to the back of their bicycles or walking bicycles laden with construction materials such as plywood boards and plastic tubing.

Forty minutes later, we arrived at a prominent intersection in Thane, where we had planned to meet up with other groups joining us for the last section of the ride to Upvan Lake. I glanced around at the eclectic crowd. There were men and women, some self-described cycling enthusiasts, like the man wearing a T-shirt that depicted a bicycle and showing a caption that read "₹0 /litre" underneath, and many more participants who appeared to be cycling for the first time as adults. I saw new imported road bicycles and a mountain bicycle well equipped with a rack, panniers, and new handlebar grips. I also saw also bicycles with rusty frames and chipped paint that looked like they had been sitting in a stairwell for a decade. I could spot the novices by their nervous chatter and experienced riders by their confident talk of upcoming 200 km endurance rides.

"Good morning," said the ride organizer, whose enthusiastic Facebook and WhatsApp posts had drawn most of the group out of bed that morning. He struggled to get everyone's attention. "Good morning," he said again, as people around him continued chatting. He was wearing a blue-and-white jersey with the Bhandup Riders logo on the back and had a thin mustache and a bright smile. He was twenty years old, which made him at least fifteen years younger than most people on the ride. Over the din of the enthusiastic crowd, he addressed the group: "We have some instructions today: ride straight, don't weave, watch out for scooters and go slow. It is not a race." No one seemed to be listening. His voice trailed off, and he looked over to Govind, the other ride leader, and shrugged his shoulders.

Sensing the need to intervene, Govind, who was fifteen years older than the ride organizer, took over the introductory remarks. He implored everyone to pay attention. "There have been a lot of accidents recently, so please follow the instructions," he said. A few weeks earlier, a woman in her thirties had died on a similar group ride on a rural road in Navi Mumbai. This horrible loss weighed heavily on the experienced riders and gave a sense of urgency to Govind's instructions. The cause of the crash was unclear—no one had witnessed what happened, but many felt the tragedy could have been avoided if someone was riding with her. Although he did not mention her death, in his speech Govind emphasized the need for a "sweeper," a designated rider to stay behind the slowest rider in the group. Then he turned to a man to his left not wearing a helmet and chastised him for not following the ride instructions that had circulated online for the past few days. Finally, he explained our route and pointed out the ride leaders and sweepers. One by one, people mounted their bicycles and the group slowly began weaving its way down the road.

We slowly cycled through quiet streets with one ride organizer in front and one in the back. We cycled past clusters of one- and two-story concrete homes—open to the street and thus allowing domestic life to spill out onto it—flanked by new twenty-story apartment buildings. As we slowly pushed ourselves up a hill, the line of people cycling stretched out for half a mile. Occasionally a car would slow down next to us and a passenger would give us a smile, thumbs-up, or word of encouragement. We also shared the side of the road with middle-aged men and women joggers and walkers who were also slowly making their way up to the lake. As we got closer to the lake, the road got steeper. And then, after a sharp bend, we arrived. The sun was still low on the horizon, and a slight breeze flowed down from the greenery of nearby Sanjay Gandhi National Park and out over the water. In the background were a few newly constructed apartment buildings reminding us that we were still in the city.

We lined our bicycles carefully along the water's edge, gathered around a circular concrete platform, and one by one people entered the semicircle and shared why they started cycling again as an adult. An older-looking man in a white-collared shirt, shorts, and black sneakers kicked off an impromptu session by sharing the story of his medical recovery through cycling. "A year ago I couldn't walk; I had knee surgery," he said, while adjusting his helmet. Its straps were so loose that it had slid to the back of his head and wobbled as he talked. "I could hardly move around. And then I started cycling and slowly got better. Now I am fit. With cycling I got all better—." Before he could finish, the group starting clapping and cheering. People nearest him reached out to give him reassuring pats on the shoulder, as his eyes glistened.

Meanwhile, a man in his thirties, taller and broad-shouldered, adjusted his mountain bicycle to make sure it wouldn't fall and walked to the center. He had just returned from cycling to Goa, the state bordering Maharashtra, three hundred miles away. He did the trip on only a few dollars a day—"I only spent money on water," he said. He described riding on the rough roads that hugged the coast, the relentless climbs and rolling hills, and the countless little ferries that took him across creeks, rivers, and inlets. He told us about chatting and riding alongside an elderly man and his son on their way to a pilgrimage site hundreds of miles away—"and on ghoda cycles," he said, drawing out "ghoda" as he said it, to emphasize the simplicity of these bicycles. "People, new riders, ask me, 'Oh, man, what is the best bicycle brand?' I say, 'What best brand?! Just get a cycle and ride.' It doesn't matter . . . it's not about that."

He emphasized the warmth and generosity of the people he met along the ride. "I arrived in one small town on the coast; there was a wedding in the village, so there were no guest houses, no hotels, no place to stay. A man comes up to me and says, 'Come, I'll get you a place to stay.' I was like, hmmm . . . usually this isn't good. But I went with him. He took me to his house. It was very small, very simple. Then he brought me food—what a huge fish! He didn't ask for money, nothing," he said. "He still calls me to see how I am. . . . My contact list now includes fishermen and farmers. That's why I cycle. It is simply to meet people, to understand people and their psychology."

Shweta, a woman in her forties with a chin-length haircut, moves to the center and commands everyone's attention by sharing the story of how she learned about Bhandup Riders: "Last April I was driving in my car. I was having a horrible day. Then I saw two cyclists riding on the side of the highway and I got so excited!" She paused, beamed, and waved to Amit and Govind, the two people she saw that day. "I gave them a thumbs-up. I smiled. I cheered. Actually, I pulled over to talk with them and to cheer them on. From there, I immediately went to Decathlon and bought a basic bicycle." She told us that that day changed her sense of self, her relationship to the city, and her understanding of what she is physically capable of. Seeing those two cyclists on the side of the road opened up possibilities for engagement with the urban landscape that she had thought were beyond her reach. Cycling, she said, allowed her to retrieve something that had been lost—a sense of being in the world and engaging with her surroundings in a way that her previously sedentary lifestyle did not allow. She told the group that her goal is to spread this joy to others. To demonstrate this, she motioned to three young men with flushed faces, still slightly out of breath, sweat staining their T-shirts. "These guys work with me," she said. "I've brought them here." Because of her, she explained, they have cycled for the first time as adults.

When I met Shweta a week later at the cafeteria at her office, where she worked as an administrative assistant, she elaborated on seeing Amit and Govind cycling for the first time: "I felt something—something I hadn't felt since childhood." She explained that as a child in Mumbai in the early 1980s, she viewed cycling as an activity for which friends would pool a few rupees to rent a bicycle for an hour from a streetside cycle repair stall. When she started cycling again as an adult, "memories started coming back. Feelings started coming back." She explained that professional success as an adult means living in a confined world where you inhabit only interior spaces of the city and meet new people only within a restricted circle. "As an adult, you are rarely in an open environment. You are always in a closed room," she said. "Always in an office. So cycling gives you freedom. And it is only you. Your own time. When you are on a cycle, you are with yourself." This was not some naïve attempt to reclaim a past that never quite existed or some search for an earlier, simpler time. Cycling offered the possibility of experiencing a feeling, a sensation, a way of being in the city that she once had and that gave her a sense of purpose in the present and the future. Reclaiming that sense was a way to reinvent herself in the present. It was a way to claim fun and joy now rather than to constantly defer it.

As I stood by the lake that morning, some questions crossed my mind. What was the significance of these stories? And what story could *I* tell about this gathering, in my own form—the ethnography? The themes were diverse: injury, recovery, feelings of rebirth, yearning for discovery, exposure, and freedom. They did not reflect a single phenomenon but created a new sense of bicycles as tools to experiment with and remake oneself. If I described this as a story of middle-class leisure practices or status, every utterance or practice would sound like a reflection of a preexisting and stable social formation. Instead, in this moment of excitement, enthusiasm, and mutual exchange, I saw people trying to work out how the bicycle makes them feel and why it matters. Just as I was trying to work out what people could do with a bicycle, the participants in this ride were also trying to make sense of what this tool means for themselves and their relationship to the city in which they live.

Despite the participants mostly being middle-class professionals with the comfort and security that come with that position, in this gathering—and on many rides after this—I observed a yearning for a different way of inhabiting the city. There was a sense of yearning for connections with the physicality of the city, with its diverse neighborhoods, and with people outside one's social bubble. There was a sense of yearning for something *other than* what had been promised by the consumerist dream that marked post-1990s middle-class urban life.

Later on, I saw how recreational cycling often led to surprising connection with the diverse socialities of Mumbai's streets. This is not a connection or sense of community based on shared subjectivity but on moments of "convivial alliance."[20] These episodes emerge even from silent interactions—a nod here, a smile there, or simply weaving through traffic together for a mile or two. While at tea stalls following group rides, friends chatted about times they were overtaken by utility cyclists carrying massive loads up an incline. People candidly told me the lessons gleaned from these experiences: that stamina, not expensive bicycles and gear, is necessary to cycle fast and that utility cyclists have significant but under-appreciated riding skills. I experienced similar embodied learning; it was difficult to ignore a middle-aged man, pedaling a heavy, rusted bicycle with two massive sacks of rice strapped to the back, effortlessly passing me as I struggled up an incline on my lightweight commuting cycle. It seemed that cycling alongside strangers making deliveries or traveling to work and momentarily sharing space with people next to cars stuck in traffic or chatting with other people cycling on the side of the road produced a sense of empathy. However subtle or fleeting these moments might be, they chipped away at the cold distance that characterizes so much cross-class contact on the street.

During the group rides and chatting time with participants afterward, people showed multiple and overlapping meanings of cycling. Some said they cycle to free themselves from the confines of the office or car, others do it to lose weight, to rediscover their city, or to meet new people. People described small pleasures—like cycling past expensive cars stuck in traffic, the feeling of accomplishment after a long ride, or the excitement of taking risks and enjoying the public spaces of the city that friends and family counseled them to avoid. For some, cycling became almost an obsession. For others, cycling made them newly sensitive toward the army of milk and bread delivery workers who pedal through most neighborhoods at dawn. And for others, recreational cycling led to cycling for more practical purposes like doing small errands and commuting to work.

Interactions

Recreational cycling is, of course, a practice that is made possible by access to disposable income and free time. However, rather than see class as the determining force for people's actions, I found it more useful to see how class functions as a background for people's creative reinterpretations of their relationship to the city and to the many social worlds it contains. Ride participants were not simply reflecting or reinforcing norms but experimenting with new ways of engaging with the city and its publics.

I saw this embrace of new ways of engaging the city on a ride with Dinesh, the denture maker, entrepreneur, and delivery worker whom I discussed in the beginning of this chapter, along with Firoza Dadan and Piyush Shah, cofounders of the Smart Commute Foundation. Like me, Firoza and Piyush wanted to learn more about Dinesh's work and his relationship to cycling. Firoza had clear reasons to learn about Dinesh's life: understanding people's diverse cycling experiences helps her advocacy work, especially when she needs to convince reluctant bureaucrats to see cycling as a significant part of the city's transportation environment. But Piyush joined us for more personal reasons. Two years earlier, he had started commuting to his marketing job in Worli by bicycle, a fifteen-mile round-trip journey from his home. The switch came about because of frustrations around Mumbai's traffic. "I was sitting in my car in traffic one day [and] I said to myself, 'That's it, I'm going to cycle to work from now on. This is the last time I'm driving to work,'" he later told me. His commuting grew into advocacy work. For a year, he collaborated with Firoza on a campaign to get more people to cycle to work. The campaign had mixed success. Piyush was frustrated by the reluctance of other office workers to start bicycle commuting. He was also frustrated by the corporate world itself. He had recently quit a soul-crushing job and had turned to cycling as part of his search for an alternative to a professionally oriented lifestyle. Dinesh, it seemed, represented such an alternative.

As we cycled together on the way to his workshop, Piyush rode up front and complimented Dinesh on his speed and the skillful way he navigated traffic. Indeed, we were all impressed by the way Dinesh seemed to effortlessly manage the late afternoon traffic. As we neared his workshop, the traffic got more dense. We struggled to keep up with him while avoiding being hit by cars, trucks, and buses. Dinesh deftly maneuvered through traffic that seemed impossible to pass and never seemed to stop. As we dove into an opening in traffic, I noticed that he was not even pedaling hard; he was just very skilled at keeping his momentum and avoiding potential bottlenecks without being reckless.

Twenty minutes later, we followed Dinesh as he turned off a main thoroughfare and into a quiet alley, through a beautifully decorated arch, past a group of older women chatting on stoops, and into a courtyard shaded by a tree with an ancient-looking trunk. We parked our bicycles next to a group of other bicycles clustered under the tree. I looked up and saw a dozen children's bicycles stored on top of a shed. Dinesh guided us to his workshop on the first floor of a chawl. We passed open doors showing spotless rooms. The sounds of domestic life spilled out: television background noise, the clink of dishes being washed, and an elderly man speaking softly to a child.

We arrived at the workshop: a single room with a low ceiling and space for three people to work. Three men in T-shirts greeted us warmly and quickly returned to work molding pink acrylic over small flames. Finished dentures, plaster molds, and acrylic chips were scattered on the workbenches. The tiny space only fit one visitor, so Piyush went inside while Firoza and I waited outside on the balcony. I could hear Piyush chatting with Dinesh inside. He asked how he made the dentures, found customers, negotiated with dentists, made deliveries, and expanded his company with so few employees. This lively conversation continued for a few minutes until Piyush came out to the balcony again. He was beaming and still wearing his black helmet and cycling gloves, as if too excited to take anything off.

"Everyone says, 'Oh, I can't cycle and go to work—there's not enough time in the day!' But look at this guy! He does both. He cycles, he works, he can do it. Why can't the others? There's no excuse," Piyush said, referring to the office workers he had fruitlessly tried to convince to start cycling to work. Firoza and I nodded along as he compared Dinesh's cycling and work routine with that of the middle-class professionals who were the target audience of the Smart Commute Foundation's campaign over the past year. They had great success with getting people to do weekend rides, and the yearly Cycle 2 Work rally attracted thousands of participants, but getting people to incorporate cycling into their everyday routine, as Firoza and Piyush do, had been a challenge. Their friends and colleagues often told them that cycling to work seemed too complicated or, as Dinesh quoted them saying, impossible, because "there's not enough time in the day."

"He's got it all worked out!" Piyush said to me and Firoza as we gathered our belongings to leave. "I asked what he needs to take the business forward—and he carefully worked out what needs to be done. He said he needs more guys to deliver. That way he can spend more time in the workshop. He's really thought it through. This guy—he learned the trade while working for someone else, became an expert, and now opened his own workshop. And here I am, waiting for something to happen," Piyush said, referring to his own search for a more fulfilling career. On the workshop balcony that evening, Piyush explained that Dinesh's mobility practices and entrepreneurialism were a productive challenge to himself and to the complacency of other middle-class professionals. Unlike the patronizing accounts of being "inspired" by heroic acts of the poor that sometimes appear in newspapers, this encounter was marked by closeness rather than distance. What began as a fleeting overlap of embodied experience—of dwelling in traffic together—ended with Piyush reinterpreting the possibility for cross-class encounters in the city.

A moment like this, one of experimentation, productive challenge, cross-class encounter, and multiplicity of meaning, gets overlooked when analysis rests on fixed categories. Piyush's expensive bicycle and helmet reflect his class status but say little about what he does with cycling or how he uses it to experiment or find an alternative to the path for professional and personal success he feels has been laid out for him. Likewise, Dinesh's cheap bicycle and the fact that cycling plays an essential, practical role in his work reflect his class status and constrained choices but say little about what cycling means to him or how it fits his business plans or his dreams for the future. The multiple meanings of cycling that Dinesh and Piyush express, as with the other people discussed in this chapter, do not neatly correspond with the commonsense categories that dominate writing on mobility—that is, the idea that the city is divided into one demographic that does menial labor and has cheap bicycles, no helmets, and a tedious life without choice and another demographic that has helmets and expensive cycles and desires self-improvement and a life full of options. This approach leads us to overlook the complex and shifting motivations of individuals *in addition* to the structures of power in which we are all enmeshed.

What motivates people to ride, how does cycling fit into their lives, and what does cycling mean to them? The vignettes I have provided in this chapter show that the bicycle can be a tool to get from one place to others, to make money, or to remake oneself—sometimes all at once. Some people deliberately *choose* to cycle because it offers a lifestyle that is more enjoyable, healthier, and less constrained. For a particular person, cycling can be seen in terms of affordability *and* health benefits. It can be argued that bicycle-based delivery is difficult and not very profitable *and* is associated with autonomy, as well as "pride and dignity."[21] Some people might use a bicycle for work but are not necessarily "captive" to it. These are some of the more counterintuitive observations I made. The uses of the bicycle show the need to see cycling in terms of overlapping signification. Focusing on what people do with bicycles, what cycling means to people, and the sensory experiences of cycling challenges commonsense binaries and categorizations while also encouraging other, less reductionist ways of interpreting people's relationships to transportation.

3 Embodied Freedoms

🚲   *Everyone dreams of a job with no boss.*

I quickly wrote that note in June 2019 after an afternoon chatting with Mohammad, a bicycle mechanic who does mobile bicycle repair throughout Mumbai. Although only twenty years old, Mohammad was already well known in Mumbai's recreational cycling community. He grew up in a small city near the northeastern edge of Mumbai. While he was in school, his father commuted two hours a day to a neighborhood in the western part of Mumbai, where he sold tomatoes on the street. After dropping out of college because he couldn't afford the fees, Mohammad bounced around jobs until a friendly bicycle mechanic took him on as an apprentice. During the day he worked in the shop, and at night he tore down and rebuilt bicycles to understand how they worked, read manuals on obscure bicycle components, and voraciously consumed YouTube videos about bicycle repair. In three years, he went from fixing flat tires in a small shop that primarily served the repair needs of food delivery workers to being part of the technical crew in national-level bicycle races. Summing up this professional journey, he once told me, "I've repaired cycles worth ₹4,000 and ₹4 lakhs."[1]

By learning how to repair high-end bicycles, Mohammad had stumbled upon a rapidly growing professional niche in India. New, recreationally oriented bicycle shops like Trek and Trail were opening in small towns and cities around the country. Unlike the traditional shops that stuff dozens of plastic- and cardboard-wrapped utility-oriented bicycles in cramped spaces, these new shops are spacious, air-conditioned, and have a uniformed staff who circulate among carefully displayed high-end bicycles. These shops are colorful and polished, well lit, and surrounded by large photographs of people cycling in beautiful landscapes, and they need professional mechanics like Mohammad.

The problem is that those jobs do not fit Mohammad's vision for a free life. "In India, stores are selling good bicycles now, but there aren't enough people to fix them," Mohammad said. As a result, he has received multiple job offers, all of which he has turned down. Despite promising pay that doubled what his father made as a street vendor, they did not offer what, to him, bicycles truly offer, and that is the ability "to make your own image" (aap ki khud ki image bana sakte ho).[2]

As he carefully packed up his tools in a shaded courtyard of IIT Powai (a university, where he had been tuning up a customer's bicycle), he shared a bit more about his life goals and the place of bicycles in them: "Doing this, here, like this, people see me. But if I worked in a shop, I'd be stuck in the back. I wouldn't meet anyone. The owner will just keep me there all day and say, 'Don't go anywhere.'" He explained that those jobs offer the pay, and even the respect, that his father never got selling vegetables on the side of the road, but there would be a boss watching his every move. He would not have control over his schedule, or over his career, Mohammad said, and the freedom he associated with bicycles would be lost.

I often heard people associate bicycles with a sense of freedom. I heard it from people who cycle for fun, for commuting purposes, and for work. Sometimes it was explicit, such as when a forty-year-old administrative assistant who occasionally cycles to work told me that cycling gave her "freedom." She said, "You are with your time. Only you. When you are on a cycle, it is only with yourself." Or when Sarita, who works at a bank and regularly attends early-morning group rides, said cycling is freeing because it is the one time she is not "bound" by the schedules of others. She said that on a bicycle "you can think and no one is intruding in your thoughts." Other times the bicycle-as-freedom theme was more implicit. For instance, Sujay said that the best part of being a dabbawala is not having a boss. He tried working in an office once, but he couldn't take the boss's demands for constant displays of deference: "If someone said something in a tone I didn't like, my temper would become hot. So I quit." Likewise, Iqbal, who sells biscuits door to door on a bicycle, described his work in similar terms: "It's my business, and so there's no one to tell me anything."

There is a long history in India, as well as elsewhere around the world, of associating the bicycle with freedom.[3] This connection has been expressed in literature, film, music, and advertising. Perhaps most importantly, in India the idea that bicycles are freeing has shaped important women's education initiatives promulgated by state governments. Since the 1980s, programs in Bihar, Maharashtra, Tamil Nadu, and elsewhere have given away hundreds of thousands of bicycles to women and girls. The journalist P. Sainath documented an early bicycle program in Tamil Nadu's Pudukkotai District. In his account, women described how bicycles enabled them to no longer be dependent on men in their families to access educational resources and new income opportunities. But he also noticed that recipients of bicycles did not only describe their value— and the freedoms bicycles offered—in terms recognizable by an official developmentalist discourse: "It would be very wrong to emphasise the economic aspect over all else. The sense of self-respect cycling brings is vital. 'Of course it's not economic,' said Fatima, giving me a look that made me feel rather stupid. 'What money do I make from cycling? I lose money. I can't afford a bicycle. But I hire one every evening just to feel that goodness, that independence.'"[4]

What is notable in this account is that even in developmentalist projects that explicitly frame the freeing nature of bicycles in practical terms (as in, a bicycle offers autonomy that expands opportunities that lead to particular outcomes), there is also the possibility for excess.

The desire "to feel that goodness," as Fatima said, goes beyond simple understandings of freedom that reduce it to the practical. The "goodness" and pleasure of cycling emerge from an embodied quality of freedom that often gets ignored. Instances of overlooking the embodied aspect of the bicycle's freedom can be seen elsewhere. For instance, Susan B. Anthony, who, in an interview with Nellie Bly in 1896, famously said that cycling "has done more to emancipate women than anything else in the world"—a quote that is included in bicycle advocacy literature around the world—also emphasized the pleasure and joys of this freedom, in addition to its practical implications. To continue the quote, she said,

"It gives women a feeling of freedom and self-reliance. It makes her feel as if she were independent."[5] By emphasizing embodied experiences of cycling, the feeling of freedom is no longer subordinate to the abstract idea of being free. It also means being open to the excess that sometimes gets lost in the idea of freedom as total autonomy.

The kinds of freedoms I witnessed in Mumbai were similarly expansive, "open-ended," and "heterogeneous" on account of their embodied qualities.[6] For Mohammad and so many other people I spoke with, the bicycle-provided freedom is not a freedom *from* something but a freedom *to do* something; it is a creative, generative, and experimental freedom. People emphasized mundane things like freedom to not have a boss, freedom to stop at a tea stall whenever they want, or freedom to do work they love. It could also mean freedom to take risks and to be vulnerable.[7] Like the sense of freedom Aman Sethi shows in his book *A Free Man*, this kind of freedom can be a complicated and unsettling thing because it could seem counterproductive or irrational. This might be simply the freedom to have fun, or it could just mean freedom to do things that don't make sense to anyone other than yourself.

Certainly, the freedoms we have access to are shaped by our bodies and identities, as the research on gendered experiences of public space in India—notably the writing of Shilpa Phadke, Sameera Khan, and Shilpa Ranade—has shown.[8] Moreover, research on gendered bodies in motion in particular has highlighted the overlap of autonomy and the embodied experiences of mobility. For instance, Julie Gamble describes women's playful appropriation of the street through creative bicycle races in Quito, Ecuador.[9] Writing about women's experiences with affordable scooters in Kathmandu, Nepal, Jan Brunson similarly observes that "scooters offer a way out of the socially policed realm of a young woman's home and neighbourhood... leading to the exploration of a space for creating intimacy with other young men and women."[10] The link between pleasure and women's enhanced autonomy is also an important theme in writings on car driving in India. For instance, Sneha Annavarapu's writing on women's experiences of driving in Hyderabad highlights the way access to cars leads to less dependence on male family members and male-dominated transportation options, along with increased access to the multiple spaces of joy that the city offers.[11]

The embodied freedoms of cycling discussed in this chapter are similarly linked to autonomy even as they often exceed it. Sometimes these freedoms are empowering, as in giving people mobility where there was none before. But as I show here, it also means messy freedoms as well, such as the freedom to take risks, to immerse oneself in the city, to sense landscapes, or simply to feel free. The embodied bicycle freedoms I describe are open-ended freedoms and do not necessarily lead to a particular political end or practical outcome, but they allow us to see the meaning of cycling, and of the streets it takes place on, differently than narratives about mobility we take for granted.

An Unsettling Freedom

As the sun set in a lane lined with small recording studios in Lokhandwala, Mumbai, I introduced myself to Anil, a man in his twenties who was wearing a red polo shirt and a large boxy backpack slung around his shoulders. Anil was standing by a scratched-up blue bicycle while casually checking his phone in the shade. By his stance, red shirt, backpack, and the large smartphone in his hand, I could tell he delivered food by bicycle for an app-based food delivery company and hoped he would have a few minutes free before the next order came in.

I learned that Anil does food deliveries part-time, six to seven hours a day, and spends the rest of his time studying filmmaking. He said he is pursuing a dream that motivated him to quit his civil engineering job in Uttar Pradesh, leave a comfortable life with his parents, and move to Mumbai. The delivery work pays the rent but also comes with a surprising benefit: traveling around the city delivering food gives him ideas for scripts. "I learn new things with every customer I meet. While doing this work I am meeting new people, seeing how they behave, learning their stories—." A new order alert flashes on his phone, interrupting his sentence. I see the alert and tell him not to worry about my questions and that he should take the order. But as if to make a point, Anil puts his phone away and continues to talk. "I can go and come whenever I want. With my degree, I could get an office job for ₹20,000 a month. But there would be so much work pressure. A boss would pressure me. I wouldn't get freedom. Now, I am free—." He pauses, gives me a huge smile, throws his head back, and adds, "I am happy. I am totally free" (Boss log humko pressure rahega. Azaad nahin paoonga. Abhi azad hoon. . . . Abhi khush hoon. Main ekdum free hoon).[12]

App-based bicycle delivery workers would often describe the advantages of the work in terms of the freedoms it offered. For instance, I would often chat with Khalid in a small, informal hangout spot for delivery workers adjacent to a street lined with restaurants. Two stoops in front of shuttered stalls served as a bench for workers to sit on while waiting for orders, while a cluster of bicycles and a large tree shielded them from traffic. One evening with Khalid, I asked how his work compared with previous jobs he had had. He used our conversations as way to illustrate the freedoms of bicycle-based work: "There's quite a difference between the two. Here I am free. I'm talking with you now. If I get an order and don't deliver it, no one's asking, 'Why are you standing here? Why are you talking with him?' In my previous job I got humiliated [by the boss] whether I worked or not. No one scolds me here."

Most writing on gig economy workers such as Anil and Khalid describes how *unfree* they are. They describe how app-based food delivery jobs are exploitative and point out how companies like Zomato have almost no responsibility for the welfare of their employees. Journalists and researchers describe problems such as low pay, lack of compensation for injuries sustained on the job, few possibilities for upward advancement, and the inability to unionize or to contest suspensions or bans from the platform.[13] Social scientists are especially skeptical of this work because it seems so neoliberal: nothing better embodies the idea of the enterprising citizen than an industry consisting entirely of independent contractors. And so, the journalists, activists, and social scientists who write these critiques imply that the gig economy's promise of freedom is false because it is freedom at the expense of security.

The juxtaposition of Anil's and Khalid's words about their freedom and writers' insistence on their unfreedom is striking. It leads to a question: what does it mean to feel free—or at least to say you feel free—when, from a structural perspective, you are not? And, how can we make sense of the embodied freedoms of the bicycle that are not easily explained by larger narratives? Answering this requires grappling with our own assumptions of what freedom means or should look like. As the anthropologist Moisés Lino e Silva puts it, "Can we take other people's freedoms seriously as freedoms without resorting to a normative apparatus?"[14]

I got closer to answering these questions about the embodied freedoms of cycling with the help of Kabir, another man in his twenties who does food delivery in Mumbai. I met Kabir while seeing him leaning against his cycle and checking his phone as I cycled past him one afternoon. I pulled over, introduced myself, explained my book project, and asked if I could chat about his work. But unlike with Anil, this brief conversation turned into a longer relationship. We spent that afternoon cycling together, followed by dozens of meetings, many more rides, and WhatsApp messages over the following four years.

Kabir grew up in a small town near Patna, in Bihar, and as a teenager in the mid-2010s he moved to Mumbai, where he now lives in a single room in Dharavi that he shares with four other young men. He has a wisp of a mustache and wears a long-sleeve shirt, khaki pants, and sandals regardless of the weather. When he was two, he contracted polio, which has resulted in a slight limp when he walks and a slight twist of his right foot as he pedals. Nevertheless, he cycles thirty to forty miles a day, six days a week. On the seventh day he cycles fifteen miles because he works half the day. He rides fast when he has to, but more often, he rides the pace of Mumbai traffic, which is a relaxed 5 to 10 mph. He squeezes through the small space between autorickshaws stalled in traffic jams, maneuvers around cars trying to turn, then pedals into an open stretch of road. With one hand holding on to the handlebar, he answers phone calls from friends

An app-based food delivery worker navigating traffic to make a pickup.

and family with the other, puts a headphone in his ear, and chats loudly with them as he rides down the road smiling and laughing.

I typically cycled with Kabir as he crisscrossed his two-mile-by-one-mile delivery area, which includes three contiguous northwest Mumbai neighborhoods. Because he has been working for the company for three years, he gets the privilege of working within this relatively small area, resulting in more frequent and shorter deliveries. Moreover, because of the high density of restaurants and wealthy people who order from them, the area is relatively lucrative. The first day I joined him, he logged on at 11:30 a.m. and a minute later the first order came in: pickup at a KFC with delivery to an apartment building one mile away. We got on our bicycles and pedaled down a central thoroughfare toward KFC. Inside the restaurant, people at the counter recognized him from his uniform and backpack. He showed them the order number on his phone and they handed over the food. This pickup was swift and efficient. However, the delivery was more of a challenge. The customer's address was confusing. Kabir circled around the block three times and had to call the customer twice to find it.

After the KFC order was delivered, Kabir tapped "Order Complete" on his phone and waited for the next one to come in. A minute later he got an alert. Pickup: Chocolate Heaven. Customer: Rohan. Distance: 1 km. Payment: ₹30. The café was around the corner. We got there early and waited on a bench outside. Five minutes later an employee came out carrying a tray of three large iced chocolate drinks topped with whipped cream, a box of brownies, and a cupcake. Kabir put it all in his backpack and pushed off.

Over the course of that day we worked out a rhythm: we chatted while waiting outside restaurants, while food was being prepared, or while waiting for an order to come in. We also managed to chat while cycling side by side on quiet side streets. I learned his cycling patterns too. For instance, I saw that he rides slowly when going to a pickup because that minimizes waiting outside the restaurant while the food is being prepared. I was careful to avoid being seen with him when he interacted with customers because this would attract attention that he did not want. I did not accompany him while he went inside apartment buildings to deliver food and would wait outside next to his bicycle. Watching over his bicycle while doing drop-offs and helping him locate restaurants and apartment buildings on Google Maps were two of the small ways I could help during these ride-alongs.

At 2:30 p.m.—or three hours, eight deliveries, and fourteen miles into his workday—Kabir parked his bicycle in front of a small dosa stall, told me it was time for a break, and tapped "Off Duty" on his app. After eating, we took a seat on a concrete ledge of a roadside utility box to wait out the postlunch low. Behind us was the high concrete retaining wall of a luxury apartment building with a Starbucks on the ground floor. In front of us a shoe repair worker, just returning from lunch, laid out his tools on a piece of cloth on the ground. Kabir and I sat for a few minutes silently taking in the scene.

He seemed in no hurry to go back on duty, so I asked him what drew him to this work. "Before this work, I was a clerk in a clothing store in a mall," he said. That involved sitting behind a counter, having few breaks, and dealing with a boss who demanded constant deference. Explaining his life plan, he told me, "I will do this for a few years and save up money to open a small stall like the ones on Linking Road," referring to the small roadside clothing shops that, by his estimate, cost the equivalent of about two thousand dollars to open. He told me that it is a joy to be out in the city without a boss to worry about, and he enjoyed being allowed to take a break whenever he wanted.

As we sit by the side of the road, two Zomato delivery workers drive by on a motorcycle. I turn to Kabir and ask about using a motorcycle instead. On a bicycle, he said, you can move around the city "leisurely." Generally speaking, bicycles allow more flexibility, and the authorities treat him like a pedestrian. "With a motorcycle, you are always worried about police or RTO fines, you can't go down the wrong way on one-way streets, you have to wear a helmet, and there's the stress of parking," he said. But with a bicycle, "there isn't much tension. They are comfortable enough. I just need to pedal."

"But this is difficult work," I said in an attempt to empathize, although I immediately regretted it. After a moment of awkward silence he told me that at first the work was physically demanding but that it got better with experience. "For the first three months, it was difficult on my body. On my hands, look—" and he showed me callouses on the balls of his fingers, where they met his palm—"that's where it hurt. But after three months I felt fine. Now my body is strong and I feel good all over."

Talking about hard work made him more quiet than usual. I sensed he interpreted my comments as pitying. But I was thinking of what he had told me a week earlier, when he had to make deliveries through three days of torrential rain. He described the flooded streets, discomfort, and hunger he had experienced. One day that week "it rained the entire day. Even with a raincoat, everything got wet. It was cold but I continued working. I also got so hungry in the afternoon because I couldn't find time to eat—the deliveries kept on coming. There was no time to stop. I did a record number of deliveries that day," he had said, looking up at me and smiling. I had been thinking about that conversation when I mentioned the difficulties of his work. But I had forgotten what he really said. Yes, the work was very challenging, but he described it as a challenge that he overcame. He was hungry because "deliveries kept coming," and so he chose not to stop. He also felt compelled to do more deliveries because he got paid more that day because of the rain. By focusing on the physical demands of the work, I reduced something he was proud of—the "record number of deliveries"—into an abstract labor problem. He was trying to describe his subjective experience, but what I heard was a story of structural inequalities.

We stayed together silently for a few more minutes, then he took out his phone and tapped the "On Duty" button. Thirty seconds later he jumped up and told me a delivery order had come. It was a pickup at Sindhful for a customer named Mohit. Distance: 1.5 km. Payment: ₹30. He accepted the order, and we got back on the road.

I left him three hours, eight orders, and another ten miles later. While we said good-bye, another order came in. Kabir declined it. "You aren't going to take it?" I asked. "It's too far. I don't need to take those."

That evening I messaged him on WhatsApp to thank him for letting me spend the day with him. He wrote back at 9:02 p.m.:
"Thanks.
I stopped working
I'm going home
21 orders"

I couldn't help but think Kabir was urging me to see his work not just in economic terms. Doing twenty-one orders—and cycling thirty miles along the way—is an accomplishment. And there is pleasure in that, even if ephemeral. It is certainly hard work and comes with little pay, but it is work done on his own terms, without a boss pushing him or monitoring his breaks. It seemed the app too was part of the pleasure of the job. "It's all in the app," Kabir said one afternoon a few months later. We were riding together in an autorickshaw because he had just gotten a flat tire, and we were on our way to the only open shop in the neighborhood to get it fixed. While we were stopped in traffic, he pulled out his phone and showed me his company's app. His work information was presented in a visually appealing graphic. The amount of money earned that day and that week, the number of hours worked, and the number of orders he completed were displayed in colorful concentric circles. He told me he appreciated that the app was clear and lacked vague elements. But most of all, it seemed the app's appeal was that, unlike with a boss, he could turn it on and off. "I just need to pedal," he said. The job's appeal was not just in the money he could make, which was not a lot—some deliveries paid as little as fifteen rupees—but in the freedom of doing work on his own terms and feeling in control of his own day.

Kabir's experiences resonated with other bicycle freedom stories I encountered, even as I met other delivery workers who did not describe their work in terms of freedom. For instance, Varun, a thirty-year-old man who delivers for Domino's Pizza and whom I met at a bicycle repair stall, saw his work in terms of lack of opportunity. As we both waited for our flat tires to get repaired, he described food delivery on a bicycle as a struggle that was in part shaped by the poor image of cycling. "In India, people want to look good by showing the latest things, like new cars or motorcycles. A bicycle—that doesn't look good," he said. He uses a bicycle because he cannot afford any other mode of transportation, just as he can't afford a lifestyle that involves hanging out and eating pizza with friends, he said. Because of how I introduced myself and my research (I usually say a version of, "I am writing a book about cycling in India"), someone like Varun who dreams of ditching their bicycle for a motorcycle might not feel they have something to contribute to this project.

Thus, Kabir's story does not simply show that a bicycle, or the work he does, is freeing; like any other object, bicycles do not have an inherent quality. In this case, the bicycle's meaning is an effect of a convergence of particularities of mobility and work. Kabir associates cycling with freedom from having a boss and lack of stress because police do not fine people on bicycles. Moreover, the app also mediates his work, daily rhythm, movement through the city, and sense of self. But in neither case—the bicycle nor the app—should the technology be equated with a narrative of total liberation; a bicycle enables a range and flexibility of movement that other transportation modes don't allow, while also exposing him to the dangers of traffic, just as the app enables autonomy from a boss and gives him freedom over his own time without offering job security or a livable wage.

The writers who emphasize the unfreedom of app-based delivery work—and I would have put myself in that camp until I rode with Kabir— do so because they are telling a larger narrative about the changing nature of work, policy, or economics in the city. This is a narrative that documents the lack of fair pay and benefits for workers in the contemporary city, compared to an earlier time, before the liberalization era, that is imagined to have been more equitable or worker-friendly. Such a narrative is a critique of the present in order to envision a better world for the future. But it does not take seriously subjective experiences such as Kabir's, which are shaped by desires for autonomy and freedom *now*. The desire for messy freedoms in the contemporary, and certainly imperfect, world will not always fit progressive narratives. This insistence on futurity has led to the "stubborn refusal of the left to consider pleasure."[15] As Stuart Hall has written, "The project of the left is directed at the future, at the socialism that is still to come, and that is at odds with the direct experience of pleasure here and now."[16]

Enterprising Freedoms

Mohammad, the bicycle mechanic profiled at the beginning of this chapter, associated bicycles not just with work but also with the potential for fun. This partly explains his parents' response when he told them he would pursue a career in bicycle repair: "My parents scolded me. They said, 'Why do you want to do puncture repair?' They felt this way because I am from Uttar Pradesh, and people there underestimate cycle-repairing work. They think it is a menial job. My parents weren't convinced that there is any future in it." As he explained, bicycle repair in India conjures the image of a man wearing a greasy T-shirt and squatting on the ground, tools scattered around his feet, hammering away at a rusty utilitarian bicycle. Even the commonly used term "puncture-wala" has a belittling tone to it;

the assumption is that minimal skill and craftsmanship are really required to fix a hole in an inner tube.

Mohammad got into bicycle repair after being forced to drop out of college because his family could no longer afford the fees. He told me he couldn't do what his father did—work as a street vendor in Mumbai's relatively wealthy western neighborhoods. "I couldn't do that job. He would come home every night completely drained. There was no enjoyment in it," Mohammad said. He tried doing data entry but quit after a month. A stint as an air-conditioning repair trainee ended after two days. Data entry was mind-numbing, and air-conditioning technology rarely changed, so he felt there was no potential for future growth. And, he added, "there was no fun in it."

For Mohammad, fun and professional advancement go hand in hand. He said that in those jobs, like other options he listed—furniture making, tile work, and gardening—"there is no future opportunity" (koi scope nahin hain). They involve going on "duty for eight hours a day and exiting the workplace when their shift is completed. But we should do work that gives satisfaction and happiness. When we make our job our passion, then we will do great work." He uses the English term "duty" (a word that is commonly used by Hindi speakers) to refer to work that comes with security but does not inspire passion. The daily routine of going on and off duty is like turning a water spigot on and off; when it is off, it is off. When you are not on duty, you don't think about it or pursue it further, whereas work that you are passionate about feels like a hobby. It combines fun, pleasure, and the possibility for growth; with such work, you are never fully removed from your work life.

Mohammad found this satisfying work with the help of a friendly older mechanic who took him on as an apprentice. The mechanic taught Mohammad the basics of repairing the affordable and utilitarian bicycles used by people in their working-class neighborhood. At night, Mohammad practiced skills learned during the day by breaking down and reassembling his own bicycle in a makeshift workshop he built in his home. He read whatever technical manuals he could find and watched hundreds of instructional videos—"YouTube was a good friend to me," he once said. Within a year, he got a job with a bicycle company that specialized in high-end, recreationally oriented bicycles. His experience with working on complicated and delicate bicycle components got him an invitation to be a mechanic for professional cyclists competing in the Indian National Championships. He went on to join the technical crews at cycling events such as the Tour of the Aravallis, the Deccan Cliffhanger, and a solo ten-day ride traversing the country, from Srinagar in the north to Kanyakumari in the south. This work gave him experience with a wide range of bicycles and components like disc brakes that most mechanics in the city's ubiquitous small roadside stalls do not know how to fix.

Companies such as Trek and Trail were opening recreationally oriented bicycle shops in small towns and cities around the country and desperately needed new people to staff them. And so Mohammad became a bicycle repair instructor. He traveled around western India, visiting small cities such as Dhule, Nashik, Solapur, Dharwad, and Belgaum whenever a new shop opened. He led workshops for mechanics, teaching them how to diagnose and fix problems, as well as about different types of bicycles and components, their different uses, functions, and maintenance needs, as well as how to deal with customers. He taught students bicycle repair, as well as demonstrating what passionate professionalism looks like.

Returning home after doing these training sessions, Mohammad started to notice a change in his family's and neighbors' attitudes toward bicycle-related work. "My parents saw me traveling and felt, 'This is a good field to be in.' People living near me who weren't interested before—who thought it was just puncture repair when I joined the company—they said, 'Okay, okay. Teach me how to do cycle repairing!'" Sensing an opportunity for young people in his neighborhood, Mohammad opened an informal workshop near his home where he taught unemployed teenagers for free. In 2018, the first of his students got a decent-paying job at a bicycle shop. Three others got jobs the following year.

Mohammad's fun approach to his work helped him as a teacher. His students often had little classroom experience, and the experiences they did have were alienating. So he invented a new, more approachable way to teach bicycle repair. He swapped out technical words with his own way of describing cycle parts and how they interact with each other. "I saw that if I use words like 'limit screw,'" he said, "people won't remember all this." As he worked on a bicycle one day, he demonstrated his pedagogical style. Pinching the barrel adjuster—a tiny cap that adjusts a gear cable's tension—he said, "This is the havaldar." Like a traffic cop, "he maintains how much it [the gear cable] moves." Pointing to the L and H screws, two small screws behind the derailleur, which shifts the chain from gear to gear, he said, "This is the BSF [border security force]. This does the BSF's work—doesn't let the chain go too far inside or outside." Smiling, he added, "Like the BSF, it doesn't let anyone in or out of India and Pakistan." His explanation of how to adjust a brake caliper, which holds the two brake pads that pinch the wheel rim, was also creative: "You know what happens in school, one kid works and the other doesn't?" he asked as he adjusted a two-pronged brake caliper that was off balance. Gripping one side, he explained, "So, I pulled the ear of the student that wasn't working in class." While adjusting the other side, he added with a smile, "Now, I took some help of the other student, the one who was working. And now they are working properly together."

One afternoon I accompanied Mohammad on a client visit in Goregaon. For the past two years he had worked for a company offering home-based bicycle repair and deep cleaning. This can be a labor-intensive process that often takes up to three hours per bicycle. Doing all the work at clients' homes also has challenges. Sometimes it requires him to travel for hours across the city only to arrive at a tiny flat whose owner offers a square meter of unventilated stairwell landing for him to work. Everything on the bicycle is stripped bare, and every piece, down to the smallest bolt, is given a thorough cleaning. This is done by dipping it either in diesel—the jugaad, or improvised, way of doing it, he said—or using a more expensive product called MucOff (which, he noted, is "how it is supposed to be done"), and then scrubbing the parts with an old toothbrush until they are shiny. After that, he checks the whole bicycle to see if all parts are working together properly, which is a laborious process of constant adjustments and tweaks, until everything interacts smoothly.

I reached the client's home before Mohammad did, so I waited for him on the street. The house was perched on a leafy hill facing the sea. A light breeze flowed through the thicket of tall apartment buildings that lined the road. A few minutes later, Mohammad rode up the hill on his small white motorcycle. He held his phone in one hand and the handlebar in the other. A checkered scarf was wrapped around his neck. His clothing—a tight-fitting gray polo shirt and black cargo pants—suggested calm efficiency. A large black backpack containing tools was nestled between his legs. His brother sat behind him, carrying a long, thin canvas bag containing the bicycle stand.

We entered the compound together, and I told the client that I am writing a book about cycling cultures in India and that Mohammad's story would feature in it. While we chatted Mohammad set up the bicycle stand in an open space next to the garage and spread out some tools on a table tennis surface. His brother spread old newspaper on the concrete floor and carefully laid out the rest of the tools, spare parts, lubricants, and rags. The client handed him a mountain bicycle with a thick layer of rust; it looked like it had not been ridden in years. Mohammad took one look at it and said, "Where did you leave this?" The client responded, "I rode with it through the monsoon and left it here when it stopped working right," pointing to the wall behind us; it was shaded by a plastic roof but still exposed to the elements. "People who have nice cycles, they never leave them outside," Mohammad admonished the client. "Really? Where do they keep them?" the client asked, chuckling at the thought of keeping a bicycle inside his house. "Inside their home, always." As the client looked on skeptically, Mohammad explained: "When you keep it outside, people see it and think, 'Wow, what a great cycle,' and then do this"—he grabs the gear shifters and pretends to click them. "Then when you go cycling it won't be in good condition."

Mohammad hoisted the bicycle onto the stand and got to work. He pulled off the brake cables; chiseled through a thick layer of rust in order to open the bottom bracket, cassette, and free wheel; opened the brake set; then took apart the front derailleur, rear derailleur, and inner cables. With each piece, he described the effect of the rain, mud, and rust on them and commented on the parts that seemed to be damaged from something that struck them, what needed the most cleaning, which parts needed replacing, and what the client should do to keep the bicycle in better repair. An hour later, the client brought out a tray of tea and biscuits. Seeing that Mohammad was about to go back to work, he insisted that everyone take a break and drink.

Many ethnographically informed accounts of craft focus on tactile knowledge.[17] These writings show how people develop an intimacy with objects and substances after years of working with them. The craftsmaker learns by handling, manipulating, and coaxing objects and, in doing so, comes to understand how they behave. Bicycle repair consists of constant adjustment and fine-tuning of multiple parts. It is a process of trial and error until that seemingly magical moment when everything functions together perfectly. Experience enables mechanics to understand how each bicycle component interacts with the others to create something larger than the individual parts. Mohammad emphasized this point when he explained how brake calipers work by way of his parable of the naughty student whose ears need to be pulled. With the client's rusted mountain cycle hoisted on the stand, he also showed me how he makes adjustments by feeling the tension of cables: he opens and adjusts derailleurs by positioning his thumb just so, sensing tension with his hand then pulling slightly. Mohammad also assesses how parts work together by listening. A scraping sound suggests a derailleur is not in the right position, a slight click means the crank is loose, a high-pitched squeak means the brake pads need to be replaced, and so on.

But the more we talked, the more obvious it was to me that the appeal of this craft came not just from this intimacy with bicycles and their constituent parts but also with the life he was able to make with it. This is partly because of the novelty of the bicycle repair field. "New equipment comes daily, new gears and new shift systems. There is no end to the learning," he said. Indeed, he seemed to have an insatiable desire to learn about new bicycle components. One time he had me track down a technical manual that was only available in Germany; he wanted this particular manual because it included a section on installing and repairing electronically controlled gearshifts. But most of all, he insisted that what matters is that the work is fun. After the client took away the dirty teacups, Mohammad stopped what he was doing on the bicycle stand and explained why "there's great joy [mazaa] in this work":

> When I go to customers' places, they give me lots of respect. Like here, he offered me tea, coffee, and juice—whatever I needed. So I feel happy working here. My father was a hawker. The work he did, walking around all day carrying a basket of biscuits—he walked ten to twelve kilometers all over Bandra every day. That was all hard physical labor. The income was low, and there was no fun in it. This work is hard too—all work is a struggle. But people don't respect hawkers. More than the money, if you get respect, that's what matters.

Freedom and Embodiment

For whom does the bicycle offer embodied freedom, on what basis, and what does this freedom mean? For Kabir and others making deliveries, as well as mechanics and other workers like Mohammad, the meaning of freedom is shaped by their work: bicycle-related work offers autonomy and opportunities that were otherwise not available to them. However, to others, such as recreational riders and middle-class bicycle commuters, the meaning of the bicycle's freedoms is, in the first instance, often shaped by bodily experiences. And of course, your ability and identity all shape the freedoms available to you.

Several middle-class cyclists in Mumbai told me that the joy of cycling comes from feeling or sensing the city differently. On a bicycle, they said, they notice the varying road texture and gradients, the city's microinfrastructure, subtle changes in elevation, and even varying wind patterns and microclimates; they are attracted to the sensory experiences of cycling and the sense of openness to the outdoor world of the city it offers. Delivery workers also talked about embodied experiences and the pleasures of being "sensorily open to the environment."[18] However, recreational riders most explicitly centered embodied experiences in their accounts of cycling.

The focus on embodiment among middle-class cyclists is partly due to comparisons with driving. For people with more transportation options—and for whom driving is the primary frame of reference—one of the first things they notice is that "the body interacts with the city in a unique way" while on a bicycle.[19] On a bicycle for the first time, people often comment that they feel exposed because there is no longer metal, plastic, or glass separating them from the surrounding environment. For instance, the lack of a barrier separating the rider from the outside world is the first thing Disha Srivastava noticed when she started cycling as an adult. During lunch one afternoon, she told me, "Before cycling, I was always in a car. But the car is a protected shield around me. If anything happens, it will happen to the car first. While I'm on the cycle, [if] anything hits, it will hit me first. The cycle will not take the damage; I will take the damage. But once it was done—then there was bliss. I crossed that blockage. I could see that I can ride. I felt that the roads knew me, and I knew the roads."[20]

I first met Disha on one of the popular group rides she organized. The ride started near Powai, in northern Mumbai. As we rode side by side up a rain-slicked overpass in Kemps Corner, eighteen miles to the south of our starting point, she said that she cycled because of its openness to the city. To her, cycling was characterized by exposure in all senses of the term. It meant exposure to the elements (such as the rain, heat, humidity, and dust), exposure to the physical environment (such as the concrete, gravel, and asphalt roads, which she sensed in her fingertips as she cycled over them, and, on two occasions, in deep gashes in her skin, when she crashed into those surfaces), and also exposure to life worlds outside her work, family, and friend bubbles. To her, cycling "is quite literally a way of exposing oneself to 'the social,'" as one writer notes, as well as to the physical environment of the city.[21]

As we shared a meal together a week later, I asked Disha to describe her first experiences of cycling as an adult. In between fielding calls from colleagues and her sons, whom she was helping study for their upcoming exams—she explained that those early rides were a struggle to free herself from seeing the city in terms of the car: "I realized that I was living in a different world in a car. The AC set to a comfortable temperature, music blaring so I don't hear honking. No pollution. No dust, mud, or sweat—what nonsense!" To her, driving was comfortable and safe but also disconnecting. But a bicycle, by exposing the rider to the outer world, enabled a new intimacy with the city and its infrastructures.

The idea that cycling meant a rejection of the middle-class professional world was often what troubled Govind, a ride organizer I met during a group cycling event. Govind, a man in his forties, started cycling to work because it was faster than driving, despite his being not especially athletic and having little history of doing physical activities. One afternoon in his one-bedroom, ground-floor apartment turned office, he shared his family's interpretation of his choice to switch transportation modes. When his father heard he had sold his motorcycle to pay for a bicycle, he pulled him aside and asked, "Is everything going okay, financially?" Govind's eyes watered as he shared this story. "Why do people ask a question like this?" he asked me, rhetorically, and continued: "This is how people look at the bicycle!" We sat together for a while on a weathered couch in his office while children playing cricket screamed with delight outside the open door. A ceiling fan whirred noisily above us. Govind nearly shouted to make himself heard, or perhaps because he was frustrated that people in his social circle see the bicycle only as a symbol of professional failure.

Govind had a reputation for idiosyncratic professional decisions. In 2000, he quit a job at a call center that provided technical support to American customers. "I quit it in the middle of a call!" he told me at a bar one evening, slapping the tiny table so enthusiastically that it nearly overturned our plate of fried fish. After he quit this job, his parents did not talk to him for two days—"Just 'eat' was all they said. They thought I was completely crazy." To his family, cycling continued a pattern of refusing to act as one should. For now, his family accepts this idiosyncrasy as long as he does not cycle near his family's village. "There are great trails near my ancestral village," he told me, "but if people there see me dressed in a cycling kit [outfit], they'll wonder, who is this crazy guy cycling in his underwear?"

For Govind, the bicycle was not a symbol but a tool that enabled him to interact with the city differently and to encourage others to be more open to the city as well. Bicycles, and the desire to cycle, are all around us, he said. In nearly every apartment complex, bicycles gather dust on balconies, in stairwells, and in basement garages. His goal was to reignite the long-dormant desire—a "hidden passion"—that those dusty bicycles represent. As Sarita, whom I cycled with on group rides, put it, "As you grow up, there are very limited areas where you get to meet other people, not the same strata, social background, whatever. . . . The fact that you are out in the open, with the wind hitting your face, discovering new places, and not getting in the car—there is a joy of discovery and reliving childhood memories." It is a yearning to experience the city differently, perhaps as one did as a child, when you embraced its physicality—the heat, humidity, rain, dust, and dirt—and when you considered the street not as a space to merely pass through on your commute to somewhere else but as a destination in itself, a space of pleasure as well.

Certainly the embodied freedoms that cycling enables are shaped by gender. It is for this reason that Disha called cycling in Mumbai "an adventure sport" with the "adventure" including things like navigating in-laws who tell her to stay at home, aunts who think she is neglecting her children, and uncles who think she is "crazy" for cycling. "For women, just getting out of the house is an adventure. And then, cycling on Mumbai's streets is an adventure in itself! With this terrain and the potholes, you don't need to go off-roading," she laughed, before turning more serious. "And then there are those guys at the traffic signal with popping eyes, who say,

'Ooohh, you are cycling,' and look you up and down, in every possible direction. You have to just continue on, but it is disgusting. I just think to myself, 'Cool, now go tell your girlfriends, maybe they'll cycle too.'"

Disha has taken an active role in organizing group rides and encouraging more women to cycle by reactivating a long-dormant bicycle group in her neighborhood. Every two weeks she leads groups of two dozen mostly middle-aged men and women with little cycling experience on slow rides to popular destinations around the city such as Bandra Bandstand, Worli Sea Face, and Nariman Point. Organizing these rides is a challenge because she has to juggle work and the demands of her family. She schedules the rides early, usually starting at 5:30 a.m. and ending by 8:00 a.m., thus enabling her to return home to make breakfast and get her children ready for school. But still, she knows that not everyone has the ability to do this. She identifies the problem of low female ridership as a problem with the domestic sphere, rather than a problem of the road. Street-related problems are certainly there—Disha described numerous incidents of men on motorcycles following behind her slowly, or leering men who drive by and go "oooh, wooow" in creepy, exaggerated voices—but she emphasized that the primary impediment to women cycling comes from the home, from the gendered division of labor: "Getting mothers to cycle is a revolution. It changes the dynamics in the family. The husband, kids, etc., realize that with the mother gone for a few hours—even an hour—everything doesn't fall apart." She hopes that through her group rides, women can enact alternative gendered expectations.

Disha focuses on cycling in particular because "going out" on a bicycle involves occupying public spaces and having particular sensory experiences in those spaces, which is the opposite of exercising in a gym. "Looking in the mirror at myself only all the time: what is so great about that?"—she said while we were eating lunch one afternoon. The gym is sterile, controlled, and cut off from the outer world. It encourages an inward-looking view that, like the office and the air-conditioned car, becomes an extension of the domestic space. By contrast, cycling forces riders into the outer world, where they are free to embrace the city's pleasures and discomforts or perhaps to embrace the pleasure *in* the city's discomforts. As if speaking to an imaginary middle-class and timid person, she bangs on the table and exclaims, "Go out! Face the humidity. Face the sun. Face the heat. Face the dirt. Face the pollution." Her voice rises with each challenge. She slaps the table again, arches her back, and opens her eyes wide. "Let your lungs get dirty. See the city. It's so beautiful when you go out. Just go out. It feels so liberating. I feel so free. I can feel the air around me. Rushing down the flyover, going down. The way the wind hits you—it's amazing." For her, cycling offers a freedom to dwell in and have fun in public spaces on her own terms, separate from expectations of friends, family, and colleagues.

Sensing Freedom

The question of which bodies can have fun in public, or how the bodies we have shape the freedoms available to us, was a central theme of my conversations with Divyanshu Ganatra. When he was nineteen, Divyanshu became blind because of glaucoma. One of the first things he noticed was that he found himself increasingly isolated. At first, elevators, steps, and transport, all designed for sighted people, became mobility impediments. He loved the outdoors, but he was told that activities like hiking and cycling were no longer possible. Then his friends started excluding him from their plans. He noticed that not only was his mobility restricted but his social world was rapidly shrinking as well.

Divyanshu described these experiences to me one afternoon at the office of Adventures Beyond Barriers Foundation (ABBF), an organization he started in 2014 and runs out of his two-bedroom apartment in Pune. He started the organization when he noticed that the impediment to a fulfilling life was not his vision loss per se but how others responded to it. ABBF provides opportunities for people with disabilities to participate in adventure sports like trekking, rafting, and long-distance cycling. Their underlying philosophy is that disability is produced by the lack of a support structure, or what disability scholars and activists call the social model of disability, in which "it's the *interaction* between the conditions of the body and the shapes of the world that makes disability into a lived experience, and therefore a matter not only for individuals but also for societies."[22]

Divyanshu makes disability a "matter" that is "for societies" to address by deliberately including people without disabilities in his events, such as in his annual ten-day, two-hundred-mile bicycle ride from Manali to Leh, in the Himalayas.[23] On this ride, people who have limited vision or blindness, have had amputations, or are nondisabled complete this physically demanding, high-altitude route in pairs on tandem bicycles. Divyanshu hopes that, by participating in events like this, sighted people learn that disability is produced by lack of a support structure and of the availability of appropriate technologies: "Our handicap is that we don't have tandems," Divyanshu explains. "When you remove that handicap, we experience freedom. Give blind people tandems, then you are removing the handicap that blind people can't cycle."[24]

By emphasizing play, fun, and the joys of being in the outdoors, Divyanshu offers a deliberate alternative to the traditional approach to visual impairment in India, which typically involves teaching technical trades in institutional settings.[25] Whereas that approach is joyless, isolating, and pitying, ABBF's events are playful and emphasize connection, collaboration, and understanding. "The biggest challenge in this country is not my disability but social and attitudinal barriers. But when you get people with disability out in the open, doing things the world has told them they can't do, and you get them to play with able-bodied people—the mainstream community—that shatters stereotypes. It builds empathy," Divyanshu says. While doing something fun together, "you see each other as equals. You are blind but you use your phone, you might be a software engineer, et cetera. If it is just me, they will write me off as an exception. But if they see others leading a full life, going outdoors, playing together, then there's huge potential for change."

That afternoon, the ABBF office buzzed with activity because the next day, a group of eight people—four visually impaired and four sighted— were about to embark on an ultra-cycling race called the Deccan Cliff-

Sighted and blind tandem bicycle riders competing in the Deccan Cliffhanger
ultra-cycling endurance race, 2017.

hanger. ABBF riders would be the only disabled participants in the event.
They would complete the relay-style event in pairs, taking turns cycling for
thirty minutes or an hour at a time for thirty-two hours (any longer would
lead to a "DNF" or Did Not Finish status). The race route starts outside of
Pune, takes riders up the Sahyadri mountain range, along the windy, cool,
and flat hilltops past Mahabaleshwar, down into the hot, open highways of
southern Maharashtra, then up through another section of the southern
Sahyadris in Karnataka, winding through a wildlife sanctuary, and then
into the tree-lined, red earth-stained Goa roads, and finally ending at a
small beach-facing village called Bogmolo.

As I chatted with Divyanshu, the event's staff, friends, and supporters
came and went, finalizing the logistics: when and where to do the transitions, the target speeds for each section, and how to manage sleep and nu-
trition. Meanwhile, the support crew of six—a doctor, a mechanic (a "cycle
doctor," as everyone called him), two drivers, a physical therapist, and an
event coordinator—were given a clear idea of their roles and the route.

Amid this activity, Divyanshu was an oasis of calm. He sat at a small
dining table covered in papers, ABBF literature, laptops, and computer

cables, calmly answering everyone's questions and solving problems. As if on guard against the solemnness that could creep into this setting, he lightened the mood with a constant stream of jokes. "Social change doesn't have to be this 'we are sad now we are doing this' thing," he told me one day in a monotone voice, mocking people who take themselves too seriously. "No! You can learn so much through fun! Through play. Through being outdoors and through building friendships."

Tandem cycling is uniquely suited to encouraging sensory interactions, as the anthropologist Gili Hammer observes. In an ethnography of non-sighted-with-sighted tandem cyclists, Hammer writes that tandem cycling is characterized by "'intersensory' performance, emphasizing visual, sonic, tactile, and olfactory experiences, as well as kinesthetic sensations of movement in space."[26] Indeed, Divyanshu organizes these events because they are fun *and* because they produce empathy, teaching others what people with visual impairments can do and what freedoms a bicycle offers. For instance, sighted riders say they learn to sense things—landscapes, roads, the movement of their own bodies—differently and more intensely while participating in ABBF-sponsored tandem rides. Raju, a sighted man in his forties, told me that cycling with blind and visually impaired people got him to see landscapes more completely. He told me that on rides with visually impaired people he observes new things—the brightness of the moon, small bumps on roads, the snap of a twig, and how scenery changes are associated with different smells. He became attuned to these after many hours of riding a tandem cycle, often at night, while deprived of sleep. He said that in these moments, his visually impaired partner "pushes" him to notice the landscape, the road, and each other's bodies.

The "intersensory experience" of tandem cycling is a particular kind of sensory experience because it involves collaboration mediated by the objects that make up the bicycle: the chain, crank, frame, seat post, and so forth. Tandem cycling is not like two people riding side by side on separate bicycles, walking together, or even dancing, although it comes closest to the last. A single chain connects the front and back pedal/crank system. That means the rider in front (called the "captain") and the rider in back (called the "stoker") are effectively connected; when one pedals, the other will feel it via the chain. Tandem pairs aspire to pedal in sync and with similar force, which requires constant adjustment and compromise.[27] And communicating these adjustments often happens through the force applied to the chain.

Tandem cycling is thus a "collaboration."[28] To stay safe, to avoid falling over, to ride efficiently, and to maintain morale, the partners have to constantly sense each other. Divyanshu tells me that after days of cycling together, stoker and captain develop a "language" that gets communicated through pedaling:

> We've built a language—how much to push, when to slow, how to center your weight, when the captain is tired, or if a bump is coming up. I can't see the road. If there is a bump coming up, I have to rapidly respond. They warn me [verbally] that a bump is coming. Or I can tell a bump is coming in the way they brake or their pedaling changes. The minute they see the bump I can sense it. I can feel it. The minute he sees a bump he makes adjustments. It's a beautiful tango. It's like a dance that is happening.

The "intersensory" aspect of tandem cycling is not just a question of noticing and then communicating but a question of sensing things together. It is an embodied experience of cycling that changes how both riders perceive the world.

Sensing things together does not mean sensing things the same way. Prasad, a visually impaired man and regular participant in ABBF cycling events, told me that one of the great joys of tandem cycling is the feeling of autonomy it offers, which is not something his sighted partner associates with tandem cycling. When Prasad was a teenager, he enjoyed cycling and participating in short- and long-distance running races at school events. However, once he lost his vision, he had to stop doing these activities. "I thought I would never cycle again," he told me while we chatted at the ABBF office one evening. "For fifteen, twenty years, no running or cycling.

Then I saw this tandem event. I felt I could do something that has been robbed."

The first time I saw Prasad he was cycling up Pasarni ghat, a few miles from Panchgani, Maharashtra.[29] His sighted partner was Raju. The two of them were pedaling with hard, consistent strokes up a steep, narrow, winding road that overlooked a lush green valley. At the time, they were five hours into the Deccan Cliffhanger. Because the race requires at least one tandem pair to be on the road at any given time, there are no opportunities to check in to a hotel, take a shower, or have a leisurely meal. Riders just get brief sleep breaks in support vehicles. It also means there is a lot of cycling at night. At first (the race starts at around 5:30 a.m.) they cycle for hours amid buses and trucks in the periurban areas of Pune; later that evening they ride the smooth and flat highways of southern Maharashtra; and after midnight, they move through the narrow, sometimes rough and forest-lined roads that wind up and over Chorla ghat and into Goa. The soundscape changes dramatically over the course of the thirty to thirty-two hours it typically takes to complete the ride. Car and bus horns and the whoosh of traffic dominate the soundscape on roads outside Pune. On the Sahyadri hills and plateaus, wind blows in off the open landscape and bells around goats' necks replace traffic sounds. Near Satara, riders hear trucks screaming down the open highway and the slow chug of tractors carrying sugarcane. And going up Chorla ghat, they hear a cacophony of insects, the rumble of bicycle tires on the asphalt, and the support vehicle's idling engine.

Prasad told me that it is moments like going up Chorla ghat at night that he enjoys the most: "I have a bit of vision. I can perceive some light. During the day I can see my tandem partner a bit, so it doesn't feel like I'm cycling alone. But when I'm cycling at night I just see total darkness in front of me. The best thing I can feel is that I am cycling alone. Like you are in total control. I feel like I am back on the cycle alone." At night, he feels like he is not being guided but doing the guiding.

Tandem cycling brings two kinds of freedom. The first is freedom in the literal sense, as in having the option to move when and how you want (as Prasad said, cycling was one of things that was "robbed" from him when he lost most of his vision). The tandem bicycle brings the joys of cycling—of feeling the wind in his face, the burn in his legs, the camaraderie with other riders, and the sensation of rolling through changing landscapes. In this way, the tandem bicycle is a mobility assistive device, enabling increased opportunities for movement.[30] The second kind of freedom—what Prasad seems to emphasize more—is the *sensation* of autonomy that occurs. As he explained, "When I say 'freedom,' it is not about freedom to go this place or that place. It is a freedom at a mental level, in your mind. It means you are able to do things that you were not able to do in the past."

Freedom to Take Risks

The more I explored what people do with bicycles, the more I saw that their freedoms are not limited to literal mobility or choice. The bicycle offers people the freedom of movement. It enables people to access new places, opportunities, and resources. However, it also enables freedoms without practical outcomes. These are ineffable freedoms—that might simply involve experimenting with ways of being in the world.

I was cycling home alone one morning when I first met Meera Velankar, someone whose cycling represents embodied freedoms that are not always understandable to others. We were stopped at a traffic light on the edge of the Eastern Express Highway when we met. As we waited for the light to change, I learned that she had just completed a sixty-mile training ride that took her far outside Mumbai. She had momentarily lost contact with her training partner, so she asked to borrow my phone to contact her. She told me that despite her husband's pleas, she doesn't carry a phone on long rides like this. "I tell him, 'If I am alive, I will find a way to call you. If I am not, someone else will call!'" I would learn that for Meera, cycling offers the freedom to inhabit spaces outside the home on her own terms, including the "chosen risks" this dwelling in public space entails.[31]

With her friend safely located, Meera and I cycled together to a nearby mall to continue our conversation at a café there. It was late morning and the asphalt radiated heat. Sweat poured down my forehead as I zigzagged through patches of shade provided by trees, while Meera seemed to ride effortlessly. I was sure she slowed down for my sake. A stream of men on motorcycles veered around us. Trucks barreled down behind us making unsettling clanking noises as they drove over ridges in the road. We turned off the highway and onto a two-lane road. Meera and I squeezed past cars, trucks, and autorickshaws that were at a standstill, blaring their horns in a cacophonous chorus of frustration.

Twenty minutes later, I was walking with Meera through the cool, quiet, and air-conditioned mall. Her cleats clicked on the polished tiled floor. Her hair was cropped at her chin, and she was wearing a small nose stud, a pink jersey, Lycra shorts, and bright pink fingerless gloves streaked with black grease. Passersby—young couples holding hands, families on a Sunday morning outing—furtively glanced at her as she walked by. "When people see clothes like this, all of them are thinking I am absolutely mad. When they see me and others, they either think, 'They are into sports, they are very free, so they are sexually available'—or they think I am totally mad," she said to me as we walked by more people staring at her. A twinkle in her eye as she spoke suggested that she did not mind the impression of madness, or at least of breaking expectations, and that she enjoyed challenging what is considered proper, acceptable, or comprehensible.

Meera started cycling seriously in 2011 after briefly living in the United States as a microbiology postdoctoral fellow. At the time, she was frustrated by not finding a job that matched her qualifications, and, she said, she was looking to lose weight after the birth of her second child. "I am a scientist, so I approach things systematically," she said. Her rides gradually got longer and longer. She connected with others who did long-distance cycling. Then she learned about events called brevets organized by the local chapter of Audax India and about its associated style of cycling called randonneuring. On a brevet, the goal is to ride a specific

Meera Velankar taking a break
during a long-distance bicycle
ride. Photo by Utkarsh Verma.
Used with permission.

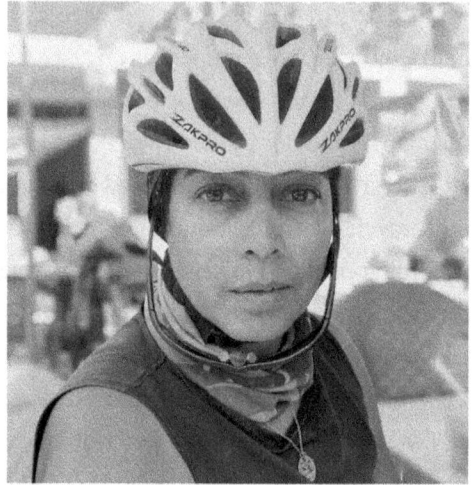

distance within a set time limit. They are not races but more like tests of participants' "capacity to endure."[32] Meera completed a 200 km brevet organized by the Mumbai Audax group, then the 400 km, and finally the 600 km brevet. Accomplishing the three major distance milestones in under twelve, twenty-seven, and forty hours, respectively, all in one year made her India's fourth "Super Randonneuse." She then moved on to cycling extremely long distances on a tandem bicycle, such as a 6,000 km ride from the northern to the southern tip of the country. In 2021, she also cycled from Kolkata to Mumbai and then on a loop that included Bengaluru, Kolkata, New Delhi, and Mumbai, becoming one of the few people to accomplish this.

Meera calls these long bicycle rides "raw," referring to both the freedoms of being out on the highway, far from home and its comforts, and "the hazards that are ever present at [the] edges [of this freedom]."[33] These rides allow her to get out of her social bubble in Bengaluru and see different landscapes and people in "different frames," as she put it, as in different contexts and situations. Cyclists must endure intense heat, sleeplessness, discomfort, and boredom, as well as real and imagined threats on the road. "After three hundred kilometers, the situation turns drastic," Meera told me. "Since you've been awake for most of the time, your body is sore and everything is in pain. Everything hurts and you have bruises all around. Especially where you sit. It is messed up. Mentally too. Sometimes you hallucinate. One time I saw sunflowers dancing on the road. You get confused. I think, 'If I stop now, I won't know what direction I came from and where I should be going.'"

On these long rides, Meera has to navigate the complexities of gender dynamics and the mix of responses people on rural highways have to the sight of a woman alone, dressed in Lycra, and riding a sleek-looking road bicycle. She encounters men on motorcycles who are aggressive and angry, men who reach out and try to touch her, as well as others who "appreciate I am breaking barriers. The random truck driver who gives me a thumbs-up. The random vegetable vendor asking about my journey." She encounters people who are hostile to the idea of a woman riding a bicycle on the highway, then, a moment later, people who "think that I have some special powers—so sometimes the attention is good. They stare, wave, and respect your strength. But when it comes to touching, it is totally crazy."

Once a group of men frantically waved at Meera yelling, "Don't go, don't go!" as she cycled toward them. She thought they were just hostile to the idea of a woman on a bicycle, so she ignored them. They kept shouting and waving at her to stop, telling her, "There are rampaging elephants ahead!" She later learned that one of those elephants had charged a man on a bicycle on that road minutes earlier, tearing his leg and breaking his bicycle in two. Another time, while cycling at night, she passed by a village shrouded in darkness. An old man stopped her and said, "Take my torch. Come home and have some food, tea, and water." Then there are other, more terrifying moments, when men's questions don't stop. They ask what she is doing, where she is from, whether she is married and has children. "They don't understand what I'm doing alone on a bicycle," she said. In those moments, she says, "I tell them I am neither a man nor a woman. That ends the conversation."

As I listened to Meera tell these cycling stories—in a café, on the side of a busy road, while riding together in an autorickshaw, at bicycle shops, or, one time, while at her daughter's swim practice—I wondered, why do this? Why commit to days and weeks of continuous cycling, with so little sleep that you see "flowers dancing on the highway"? Why choose the pain, discomfort, and dangers? That is often the question that extreme endurance-oriented activities elicit. The goal of these activities is to push boundaries and test limits; they are no longer comprehensible in terms of exercise or physical fitness. They are more about experimenting with what you can do on a bicycle and, in doing so, engaging the world on your own terms.

Meera finds autonomy while cycling immense distances on India's highways. "As an adult, you are mother and wife. You need to behave in this and that manner. But on the highway, when you are cycling, you are just yourself. There is no one. No one asks anything of you. I won't say it is freedom—I can wear whatever I want in my house or whatever—it is *beyond* freedom. It is meditative. It allows me to reflect. On the past, the good and the bad. They flash by like a kaleidoscope." When Meera shared this with me, I was struck by her use of and discomfort with the word *freedom* (she is a fluent English speaker and the conversation took place in English, so she knew the word's associations). On one hand, "freedom" conveyed what long-distance cycling meant to her: being able to do a single physical activity for long stretches of time, roll through the country's diverse landscapes, encounter its diverse social worlds in their unsanitized form, and be "alone," momentarily outside familial obligations. But on the other hand, "freedom" did not capture her experience—"it is beyond freedom," she said, as if uncomfortable with the word. And so she hesitated for a moment and clarified, "I won't say it is freedom—I can wear whatever I want in my house," later adding that she has a loving and supportive husband, and so being on the highway has nothing to do with escaping a bad domestic situation. To her, long-distance cycling in, ironically, a conservative part of the country where she experiences many *more* restrictions on clothing choices than at home, offers the freedom to reinvent categories such as woman, mother, wife, and professional; this embodied freedom of cycling is not the antithesis of oppression. It is an idea of freedom to experiment with ways of being in the world, to sense landscapes differently and encounter public life on one's own terms.

There is an inherent tension in writing about—and therefore fixing—meaning that is always in flux. But I hope to have shown that embodied bicycle freedoms change over time and context. Indeed, most of the meanings of freedoms that I write about in this chapter were worked out over the course of multiple conversations. And of course, what I write is my interpretation of Meera's interpretation of the role of cycling in her life—similar to what Clifford Geertz called "constructions of other people's constructions of what they . . . are up to."[34] But this multilayered interpretation is how people often approach cycling. Recall Prasad, who also clarified what he meant by the freedom of cycling. He distanced himself from its clichéd associations when he said, "When I say 'freedom,' it is not about freedom to go this place or that place. It is a freedom at a mental level, in your mind." He was referring to kinds of movement and sensations of autonomy that his limited eyesight prevented him from experiencing. For him, the tandem bicycle was a tool to regain a subjective way of inhabiting the world and not simply about going to "this place or that place."

Focusing on the intimate and embodied ways people relate to the bicycle opens new ways of understanding its meaning and place in the city outside narratives of urban or sociological change. When a bicycle is seen in purely symbolic terms (such as how it reflects class status) or only through the lens of policy (such as how official discourses treat cycling), its varied meanings and potentials get flattened. But looking at what people do with bicycles—and how they experience landscapes with them—highlights immanent possibility and reveals the potential bicycle futures that already exist, which is the focus of the chapters that follow.

4 Navigating Traffic

🚲 "There is no direct hostility towards cyclists here. We haven't gotten there yet!" joked Mirza Saaib Bég, a lawyer who, at that time, cycled to work daily in Mumbai. He said that playfully as we compared traffic interactions in India, the United States, and England, where he had once lived, at a northern Mumbai café one morning. He had just completed a ride and had on a green jersey, threadbare black shorts, and gray cycling shoes that showed the signs of thousands of miles of use. While we shared a sandwich, I told him about hostile drivers I had encountered while cycling in Massachusetts. He responded by invoking, with deliberate irony, a surprising developmentalist teleology: Mumbai does not have the antibicycle hostility I experience in the United States because the city is still far from achieving car hegemony—or what social scientists call automobility.

Mirza was well suited to study traffic environments from the perspective of a bicycle. He commuted twenty-four miles daily by bicycle from his home in Powai to his office in Bandra Kurla Complex, where he worked as a lawyer for a government agency. He had begun his two-wheel commute after law school in order to save money and avoid the hassle of Mumbai's severely overcrowded trains. "I cycle to work every day despite working for a bureaucracy. People should know that! People think all government workers are lazy," he said with a gleam in his eye when we first met. After months of bicycle commuting, cycling occupied a large, and steadily growing, part of his life to the point where he once confided to me, "Now all my thoughts revolve around cycling." In addition to bicycle commuting, he participated in recreationally oriented group rides, completed endurance events of up to four hundred miles organized by Audax India, and took two-thousand-mile rides around India, which he did as fundraisers for an orphanage in Kashmir and for low-income law students.

After cycling tens of thousands of miles through a variety of road conditions, traffic environments, and cultural contexts, Mirza insisted that cycling in India is relatively comfortable because of the unspoken rules of traffic. During our conversation about cycling in America and England, he added, "Cyclists aren't considered a nuisance here. Drivers in India won't come right behind you and start honking. If you hold the line, go straight, and don't make any sudden turns, then it's all good."[1] As long as you bicycle "straight," he said, other street users will maneuver around you; they won't see you as occupying road space that is theirs but as one among the many people, activities, and objects that they encounter in a diverse street environment.

Mirza's point was not that cycling conditions in Mumbai are perfect, or even ideal, but that there is something accidentally forgiving about the city's traffic environment. Certainly, he recognized that not everyone finds Mumbai's traffic environment welcoming for cycling. Gender, age, and ability are also important factors in people's sense of comfort on the street, and such factors shape how welcoming the city's traffic environment feels. But what I took away from my conversations with Mirza was a way of seeing and interpreting traffic and the bicycle's place in it: meaning evaluating cycling conditions based on the norms, assumptions, and ordinary practices of traffic interactions. In other words, Mirza's embodied experiences of cycling led him to a similar point made by the anthropologist Adonia Lugo: "that it [is] the people, not the traffic infrastructure, who [decide] the order of the street."[2] I argue that this perspective offers a glimmer of hope regarding the place of cycling in urban India: if we do not singularly focus on policy or infrastructure provision (or the question of how much street space is allocated for people on bicycles), we might identify immanent possibilities for the sustainable city.

Of course, transportation planners, architects, and journalists see urban Indian traffic, as well as the bicycle rider's place in it, quite differently. They consistently say that cycling conditions in India are poor because there is no space for people on bicycles and few policies that take cyclists into account. A newspaper article on cycling in Mumbai includes a typical assessment of the city's cycling conditions: "Paresh Rawal, a transport planner based in Mumbai, said, 'It is not safe to cycle in the city because there is no supporting infrastructure.'"[3] The authors of a working paper on nonmotorized transportation in India similarly write, "Cyclists are forced to either remain on the sides with tattered edges making cycling unsafe or they have to ride on the road space meant for motorised traffic . . . [which slows] down the entire traffic."[4] Another overview of cycling in India notes that "the major shortcoming of almost all development proposals in Indian cities is that bicycle tracks have not been planned as an integral part of the road networks."[5] And, "until recently, Indian cities had almost no separate cycling infrastructure at all, forcing cyclists to ride on overcrowded, deteriorating roads together with a wide variety of motorized traffic. . . . The mixing of so many different modes of transport, with large variations in size and speed, causes severe problems of traffic safety."[6] The assumption that cycling conditions should be evaluated nearly entirely based on what has been planned for in the past echoes the design-centric approach of mainstream sustainable transportation writing in Europe and North America, which begins from the assumption that design and physical infrastructure are the primary factors affecting people's cycling experience.[7]

While design and policy are certainly important, those are not the only factors that shape bicycle safety and comfort. As Mirza points out, norms regarding the use of the street edge, the composition of traffic, and implicit mobility codes also shape the experience of cycling. And so, rather than focus on what is planned for people on bicycles, I have explored what I believe to be the more important, and often neglected, question: how do people on bicycles navigate the traffic and street environments that already exist? I have explored this question because people's cycling practices represent an embodied understanding of the city. Specifically, these practices reflect an understanding of the implicit ideas, practices, and norms that create a street environment conducive to cycling and might be used to shape new ideas for promoting sustainable transportation.

Holding the Line

Early one morning I was cycling with Rashid on Linking Road, Bandra, as he delivered bread to small shops and restaurants. Rashid is a short man in his thirties with a thin black goatee and a wide smile punctuated by the gleam of a gold-capped tooth. He seems to have a white earphone permanently in one ear, with the cords stuffed in the front pocket of his button-down shirt along with a small pad, a pen, and a cell phone.

I was riding with Rashid on streets glistening from the previous night's rain. A plastic tarp covered the bread Rashid carried on the back of his bicycle. After cycling for a mile, we reached a line of motorcycles, cars, autorickshaws, and trucks backed up behind a traffic light. Slowly, Rashid weaved his way to the front of the line. I inched forward as well but got stuck behind a small delivery truck. An autorickshaw was to my right and cars were in front. I was blocked in. Meanwhile, Rashid broke free of the stopped traffic, moved to his right, and rested his foot on a median made of concrete blocks covered with faded yellow paint. The median acted like a footrest, giving him enough leverage to stay balanced while still seated on the saddle and offering a brief moment of relief. This small feature of the median saved him from the awkward maneuver of getting a bicycle rolling that is laden with bread. The light changed, and he rang his bell and rolled forward with a slight push off the median. A gap in traffic opened, and I pedaled fast to catch up. Glancing down at the ledge where he placed his foot, I saw a spot amid the dirty gray blocks, polished smooth by the hundreds of other people who took advantage of this accidental bicycle-friendly infrastructure.

At the start of each delivery, Rashid drapes two large polypropylene bags of pao from the handlebars of his bicycle. Four more bags draped in a layer of blue plastic are tied to the rear rack. Rashid can carry six large bags at a time, each bag containing six slabs of bread; each slab contains six pao, so he has to periodically return to the bakery to load up again, for a total ride of about three miles for each delivery circuit. Rashid's bicycle—a roadster-style black Atlas, the classic Indian-made utility bicycle—is well maintained, other than a squeaky chain, which makes a scraping noise with each pedal stroke. His seat is extra wide, with thick padding and support provided by three thick springs. It is set at the lowest possible spot, which makes his legs bow slightly as he pedals. The benefit of having the seat so low is that it makes stopping and starting easier. I envy the graceful way he gets on the bicycle when it isn't loaded with bread. While standing and holding the handlebars, he lifts the kickstand, lowers the bicycle slightly, and in a swift motion walks the bicycle a few stops, gains momentum, swings a leg over the top bar, and starts pedaling.

With this implicit bicycle infrastructure of the median footrest in mind, I caught up with Rashid and asked him to share strategies for riding comfortably and safely in the city. We cycled side by side in silence for a few hundred meters. I knew that asking someone how they bicycle doesn't really make sense. It's like asking someone how they walk, eat, talk, or perform any other embodied act. You just do it. The traffic got denser as I waited for a response. We were no longer able to ride side by side, so I slipped behind him. Sensing the pressure of traffic behind us, we crossed a seam where the concrete roadway meets the asphalt road edge. Rashid calls this seam the "lining" and often warned me that it is one of the biggest dangers people on bicycles face. Getting a tire trapped in that lining and hitting a newly formed pothole after a heavy rainfall are some of the biggest causes of crashes, he said.

With the traffic bearing down on us, Rashid moved farther to the left, weaving around a utility hole cover with sharp metal ridges, broken asphalt around its edge, a metal grate, and puddles. He pointed down at one puddle saying, "You don't always know what is underneath those." A moment later the traffic thinned out again, and we resumed cycling side by side on the smoothly paved concrete section of the road. He then answered my earlier question about riding strategies. "Maintain your route. Stay within your limit. If you waver outside the line, then you will have problems," he said. He explained that a key strategy for staying safe while cycling is to maintain a straight line. The English words he sprinkled in (he spoke Hindi the rest of the time)—"line," "limit," and "route"—collectively convey this sense of consistency. His point was that you should ride as if you are tracing an imaginary line, a line that stretches back from where you've been and extends forward to where you are potentially going; in other words, consistent riding enables others to anticipate your movements.

His words reminded me of the many times the idea of "maintaining your line" came up in earlier conversations with people who bicycle in Mumbai. A security guard who cycled to work for twenty-five years told me, "Always ride on your line. Don't deviate or cut another's line, or swerve, like when you drink. That's how you prevent accidents." Iqbal, the door-to-door biscuit vendor; Faisal, the bicycle shop owner; Firoza, the bicycle advocate; and Mirza, the lawyer, all told me something similar: the key to staying safe is to maintain a straight line and let traffic flow around you. The view seemed to cross differences in class and types of cycling. "I hold the line," Mirza once told me while we chatted about cycling strategies at his home one evening. "The problem with some cyclists is that they go side to side and aren't holding the line. But if I am holding my line, going straight, then drivers can go around me."

All these comments reflect an intuitive knowledge of Mumbai's traffic and mobility context. They reflect an understanding of the logic of mobility in the city, which includes how people in different vehicles interact with each other and how people read each other's movements, communicate nonverbally, and anticipate actions. These interactions reflect "embodied codes which guide actions," and traffic environments in every city have them.[8] Rashid subtly encouraged me to focus on the implicit norms, behaviors, and unspoken rules of traffic—behaviors that are at "once cognitive, sensual, affective and instinctive."[9] They are visible in the "manouevres, forms of etiquette and gestures of annoyance, for instance, [that] are [considered] 'proper' in particular contexts."[10] These norms shape our expectations for how street space is used and how other drivers, cyclists, and pedestrians will interact as we travel near them. They include expectations of how the street edge can be used (do you expect the side of the road to be free of people selling things, or do you expect it to be occupied by street vendors?), attitudes toward traffic flow disruptions (is a person chatting next to a friend in the road considered an annoyance or an obstacle to be avoided?), what honking means (an aggressive act or a helpful "I'm coming up behind you"?), what is considered acceptable distance between vehicles (is two inches too close to the nearest vehicle when stopped at a light?), expectations about behavior in traffic (when a traffic signal turns green, is it rude to turn left in front of oncoming cars?), and expectations about the traffic itself (are people and vehicles moving at mixed speeds considered normal?). Answers to these questions offer something like a grammar of traffic.[11] This is because they reflect an implicit set of codes, or structure, that guide movement without dictating it. This grammar is a product of accumulated behaviors, as well as the historical accretions of varying forms of street construction and mobility practices that shape mobility contexts. As Allison Truitt writes, "Urban traffic [is] shaped by local systems of meaning and subject to historically constituted constraints."[12]

The Social Landscape of Cycling

A few minutes before sunrise one day, I am silently cycling up an incline of a wide arterial road in central Mumbai. The darkness is pierced by a line of blinking red lights of other people on bicycles, the dim yellow glow of streetlights, and the glare of passing vehicles. Trucks carrying farm products roar past, kicking up dirt and dust as they head toward markets in the center of the city. Smoke from a slow-burning fire at the nearby garbage dump drifts by. The women and men in front of me have scarves wrapped around their faces to protect themselves from the pollution. As we push up the ramp, their body language shows the challenging conditions. A man wearing a bright red shirt stretched over a slight paunch gets off his saddle, grinding his way to the top. Another cyclist slows to a walking pace. No one talks. Lively conversations about neighborhood events, children's schools, frustrating bosses at work, and funny incidents that happened in previous rides will come later over tea and idli, after the ride is over.

On that day, the group was larger and more eclectic than usual. There were eight men and three women ranging in age from their late twenties to fifties. They worked in real estate consulting, IT, used car sales, and NGOs; some were unemployed and some focused on taking care of their families. Their riding abilities varied considerably. A man in his thirties said he was following his doctor's orders to get some exercise and that this was his second ride. A woman of roughly the same age had been riding with the group for six months. A man in his fifties boasted that he'd just completed a forty-eight-hour, 400 km endurance ride despite being a regular smoker.

Before we reached the top of the grade, the group tacitly agreed to slow down to the pace of the slowest rider. I noticed that two of the more experienced riders stayed in view throughout the ascent, while two others moved to the back, bringing up the rear and keeping the group tight as we navigated this treacherous stretch of road. Over a year and half of organized rides, the group had worked out an established practice for navigating roads like this one: ride in a single file, don't zigzag, and stick to the safe part of the road. I remember thinking how different the feeling of riding in a group was compared to my solo trip on this road weeks earlier. The stress of the trucks, air pollution, fatigue, and darkness was compounded by having to decide on which part of the road I should ride. Should I go left and avoid the trucks? But that's where the asphalt chunks, loose paver blocks, gravel, dirt, and garbage were. My head hurt from the constant vibrations caused by this detritus. With each jolt, I imagined bolts coming loose, wheels flying off, my body hurtling to the pavement. So I was tempted to ride on the smoothly paved surface. But that's where the trucks were flying by. I ended up looking for safety and comfort in the constantly shifting intermediate zone between the central travel lanes and the road edge.

The sun rises as we enter the geographic center of the city and pass Sion, Mahim, and Dadar, the neighborhoods that lead us south to our final destination, Nariman Point. As we head south, groups from neighborhoods around the city merge with ours—messages had circulated on WhatsApp earlier that week for multiple bicycle groups to join in one large ride. The line of bicycles grows longer. By the time we reach Dadar, there are forty riders, stretched out over a few hundred meters, taking up the left side of the road. I notice most people are very accommodating. Despite the size of the group, they are careful not to occupy the road. At one intersection a bus driver, not expecting such a long line of people on bicycles, gets stuck. The group quickly opens a gap for him and he navigates through.

On rides like this, I saw how group ride participants "use their bodies to create temporary zones where they transformed the street."[13] Amit, a group ride leader, told me one afternoon that the goal is to create a "virtual track" on the side of the road; what the city lacks in physical bicycle infrastructure, it makes up in this simulated version. A well-run group ride, Amit said, creates a cocoon that keeps the less experienced riders somewhat sheltered from traffic. Cycling in this virtual track is like a protective blanket rather than a bubble—you are certainly in and amid traffic and its dangers, but there is nominal protection from immediate bodily harm. On that group ride, for instance, the string of red blinking lights that we created as we rode up the overpass was hard to miss. Trucks and buses made an arc around us. Men on scooters slowed down to ask what we were up to or to simply smile and give a thumbs-up. After many rides together like this, members of the group refined how they collectively used the road and interacted with other traffic. We learned to ride predictably but confidently, acknowledging the expectations of other road users, implicitly working with, and finding a place in, the flow of traffic around us.

Group rides play an important role in helping new riders get comfortable cycling in the city. But what enables those rides in the first place? What enables and normalizes this scene of dozens of riders cycling in relative comfort on the side of a road that was not designed for them?

Firoza Dadan, the city's best-known bicycle advocate, helped me answer these questions. By 2015, when I first met her, Firoza's "Cycle 2 Work" rallies had garnered widespread attention from the media because they attracted thousands of participants. The rides were fun, unique for Mumbai, and resonated with middle-class professionals who yearned for an engagement with the urban landscape that did not involve cars, offices, malls, or air-conditioned gyms. Her work has grown to planning group rides for college students and children living in low-income neighborhoods. She has also collaborated with companies to encourage bicycle communities among employees and is regularly consulted by the municipality on bicycle-related issues. However, the part of her work I witnessed most often was her one-on-one outreach with the people she calls the "real cyclists" of Mumbai—the people who ride simple, Indian-made, single-speed roadster bicycles, colloquially called ghoda cycles, as a practical means of getting around the city.

Nearly every ride with Firoza included numerous pit stops during which we talked with people about their experiences cycling in Mumbai. Sometimes these interactions took place at traffic lights, but more often they would happen as we all cycled together. As we talked one morning at a tea stall where we had stopped for a snack, passersby approached and furtively glanced at Firoza's orange folding bicycle. A young man fiddled with its brakes and gears, while another tweaked the seat. She used this as an opportunity to strike up conversations with them about things like bicycles and their designs, such as the differences among hybrid, mountain, and road bicycles. Some of the men walked away, eyebrows raised, puzzled; others smiled, sharing childhood cycling stories and expressing nostalgia for that rush of excitement when flying down the road on two wheels. Firoza used the bicycle to start conversations, to learn about and engage with the diverse mobile socialities of the city.

"I am thankful to the delivery guys," Firoza told me one morning while we cycled past an army of food delivery workers in the narrow streets of the Bandra market. "Because of them, motorists know that there are cyclists on the road. That's why motorists are alert for cyclists. That's why they share the road. [We] cyclists who wear fancy helmets and have expensive gear, we are indebted to them. They've created an invisible cycle track on the side of the road." Firoza was careful to distinguish the experiences of riders such as herself—and myself—from the vast majority of people who bicycle in Mumbai: the delivery workers who do not have the privileges of middle- and upper-class status or the privileges of gender, race, and nationality that I have as a white man and US citizen cycling in Mumbai.

Her point was not to universalize people's cycling experiences but to acknowledge the connections across difference.

We occupy an "invisible cycle track" on the road made possible by the generations of working-class people who have cycled before us, explained Firoza—the tens of thousands of people who deliver food from restaurants, caterers, and small general stores; the people who deliver newspapers, laundry, construction materials, and flowers; and the large swaths of the service economy who commute by bicycle, such as security guards, electricians, plumbers, cooks, and child caretakers. In their journeys through the city, they collectively normalize cycling. They create the eclectic traffic conditions that shape drivers' expectations for how roads and roadsides are used. Firoza suggests that they even create a figurative space for cycling in the collective imagination of the city. The "invisible cycle track" that cyclists create, Firoza said, might not be recognized as bicycle infrastructure but opens a space for cycling nonetheless.

The people who have created the biggest symbolic space for cycling in Mumbai are the famous dabbawalas, or lunch delivery workers. There are five thousand dabbawalas in the city, and most of them use a combination of bicycles and trains to make their deliveries. As mentioned in the introduction, Firoza's fundraising pitches at corporate offices (which she visits hoping to both appeal for funds and boost support for bicycle commuting) often includes a reminder that dabbawalas are Mumbai's original commuters. "They were the first people to cycle to work. They've been here for a hundred years. They are why we exist," she said at one meeting with representatives at a telecommunications company. The audience members listening to these pitches—middle-aged men and women—usually nod along and smile. Dabbawalas are an accepted part of the landscape, and so it is a clever way to win over people who are skeptical of the idea that anyone can cycle to work. But doing so is more than a tactic; Firoza makes an important observation about the work dabbawalas have done in facilitating a mobility landscape that accepts cycling.

One morning Firoza and I cycle with Sujay, a dabbawala, during his early-morning rounds in a quiet residential area of Jogeshwari, in western

Mumbai. Sujay has worked as a dabbawala for fifteen years. He is a tall, lean man in his thirties who lives with his family in a small one-room home in Andheri. I cycled with him as he did the morning pickups—dabbas stacked on each other and wrapped in cloth or tucked in a bag. He attaches the bags to hooks hanging off the rear rack of his bicycle, looping the rest around the handlebar. Despite these bulky items, he is still nimble. He speeds through intersections often faster than motorized traffic, goes up bridges with ease, and squeezes through narrow gaps he locates in the traffic.

After doing the morning pickups, he left the main thoroughfares and turned on to a narrow lane. Suddenly he made a sharp right and turned into a space barely the width of two people cycling side by side, wedged between a small corner store and the high concrete wall of an apartment building. The path widened; we were now in an open space surrounded by residences, like an informal courtyard, with small paths leading to nearby streets. Elderly women sat on the stoops, watching us go by. As we cycled, the surface changed from concrete to tile, to gravel and dirt, and back to concrete. Other dabbawalas, coming from separate directions, joined us. A hundred meters later, we reached a road paved with asphalt, merged with motor vehicle traffic, and continued on toward the station, where the dabbas are transferred to a train. I saw that through their daily practices, these cyclists piece together this series of conjoined spaces to create what was, in effect, a quiet bicycle lane completely separate from the honking cacophony of motorized traffic a hundred meters away.

In her novel *Kartography*, Kamila Shamsie describes an ephemeral alley created by women in Karachi, Pakistan, during the month of Muharram. During this time women weave their way through a series of connected domestic spaces to reach a neighborhood shrine, so they can travel while still staying in purdah. Like this alley, the space Sujay cycles through is an "alley without [a] name."[14] It is not an officially recognized path. It too is ephemeral; the addition of a small extension to a shop, a concrete barrier, or a new gate could potentially close it off. But like the alley created by women in Karachi during Muharram, the route created by dabbawalas

Dabbawalas cycling on a path that is inaccessible to motorized vehicles.

might even tell you more about the city than what "you'll find on a street map."[15]

After picking up his final lunch box that morning—from a newly built luxury apartment complex that towers over the low-rise construction that dominates the area—Sujay cycled a few minutes to the nearby train station. Along the way, more dabbawalas converged with us to form a group of six. At the station, he locked his bicycle to the metal fence near where two dozen other dabbawalas were arranging that morning's pickups. Over the next thirty minutes they sorted the dabbas according to their final destination—most often, offices in Bandra Kurla Complex and south Mumbai. They loaded the bags onto a train with a luggage compartment that, during these delivery times, is reserved for the dabbawalas' exclusive use. Sujay rode the train to a neighborhood in south Mumbai, where the dabbas were again re-sorted to accommodate arrivals from other parts of the city and then loaded onto another bicycle, which he kept locked near that station, and delivered to nearby offices.

This is not lucrative work—for instance, Sujay can only afford a single

room in a crowded Andheri neighborhood with his wife and two children. However, being part of the dabbawala community, which garners
wide respect for its historical lineage and the vital service they provide,
comes with its privileges. The most valuable one is space. A long, centrally
located stretch of roadside adjacent to nearly all train stations is reserved
for their use, either to sort dabbas, sit and chat, eat lunch, or park their bicycles. Near Andheri Station, for example, there is a bicycle parking stand
that holds up to forty bicycles. So in a way, dabbawalas have the exclusive
right to one of city's rare dedicated-bicycle amenities. Raghunath Medge,
president of the Mumbai Dabbawala Association, explained that this is
an unofficial yet widely acknowledged entitlement that comes from the
dabbawalas' long historical presence in Mumbai, as well as for providing
a service used by all strata of society: "We've been doing this system for
125 years. So we don't have any space problems outside train stations. We
have all types of customers—police, RTO officers, businessmen."

Dabbawalas using the street outside a train station to park their bicycles
and sort lunch deliveries.

While riding with Sujay, I could also sense that his membership in this occupational community shapes *how* he cycles as well. Sujay exudes a professional confidence as he cycles down busy streets, navigates complex intersections, passes through the high gates of apartment buildings, and breezes past guards. He does the work fast and efficiently. He occupies the residential spaces he navigates with a sense of ownership and belonging. For instance, while standing in front of the manicured greenery of a luxury apartment building waiting for a pickup as other service providers timidly come and go, Sujay casually leans against his bicycle and checks his phone or chats with a friend. The nature of the dabbawalas' work and their iconic status, history, and importance to the city's functioning open up a space for his bicycle-presence in the city.

But not all participants in the social landscape of cycling are as iconic as dabbawalas. The other tens of thousands of people who cycle primarily because it is convenient or affordable rely on—and create—a less visible bicycle infrastructure. For them, it is informal relationships with people along the roadside—such as with security guards, shopkeepers, and residents of nearby apartment buildings willing to keep an eye on their bicycles—that enable their movement through the city.

Mohan, a small-scale entrepreneur whose incense business I described in chapter 2, showed me some striking instances of the everyday social practices that support cycling in Mumbai. After spending time at his home, where he and his sister make incense and perfumes by hand, we traveled together through Andheri East. He was taking me along on his weekly route, where he sells incense door to door. Toward the end of the ride he turned from a main thoroughfare onto a rocky, semipaved lane. As dusk fell, the lane became occupied by kids playing and adults walking home from work. There were few streetlights, so the area was lit only by the apartments adjacent to the road. Despite the bumps and vibrations, the cycling was pleasant and I expected Mohan to do his usual routine: cycle to a dense residential area, park his bicycle on the road, lock the wheel to itself, swing his heavy leather bag containing bundles of incense and perfume over his shoulder, and then go off on foot for his door-to-door sales calls. But on this evening, as we got close to a large structure built to house previously evicted slum residents, with dozens of one-room apartments lit up, women hanging out on front balconies, and young kids playing on the street in the dark, he did something different. "We'll leave them inside there," he said, pointing to a nearby building with a security guard sitting in front. As we walked to the compound, I asked why he doesn't just lock his bicycle on the road. "Because some of those kids will let air out of the tires just for fun," he replied. We arrived at the gate and, as if expecting us, the guards created a space for Mohan to keep his bicycle. He left it there, unlocked, slung his bag over his shoulder, and climbed up the apartment stairs to make his sales.

As I rode more with Mohan that evening and on subsequent days, I saw the larger social landscapes that sustain cycling in Mumbai. He took me to other places in the city that facilitate his incense business: an ashram around an old shrine whose caretaker allows him to store his bicycle and incense-making materials, a lane closed to motor vehicles that provides a convenient shortcut between two major roads, support beams near train stations that function as improvised bicycle racks for people making deliveries in the area, and more security guards in front of apartment buildings with whom he has an informal agreement to watch over his bicycle as he works nearby.

Mohan's appearance also seems to reflect how he occupies public space. He carefully chooses clothes that project a business-like quality. For instance, when Mohan goes out to make deliveries, he changes into a shirt with bright patterns and stiff collars, freshly ironed pants, and polished shoes. Setting off from his home, he speeds through the city with an earphone in one ear, talking loudly with friends, family, suppliers, and customers. He occupies the center lanes and uses whatever tricks he can to get ahead of traffic. One afternoon I saw him navigate a complex intersection with ease. As he entered the intersection, traffic slowed nearly to a standstill, but he sped up, quickly maneuvered to his left, moved behind motorbike drivers inching into the lane, turned right, and returned to the center of the road, having cut in front of a line of stalled cars. He then used a bus as a shield by weaving around it to the left to take advantage of its ability to clear a path through the cars in front of it. Whether rushing to customers or to pick up raw materials or when we cycled together to his hoped-for new manufacturing space, he seemed to ride as if physical and social mobility are linked.

Navigating the Road Edge

One afternoon I was cycling back home after spending time with Dinesh, the man who makes and delivers dentures around the city's northwest neighborhoods (discussed in chapter 2). I had a small GoPro camera mounted to my helmet to record his trips between his denture workshop and the dentists who were his customers. I cycled behind and alongside him as he criss-crossed neighborhoods in western Mumbai, often going faster than traffic on notoriously clogged SV Road. Exhausted from trying to keep up with him and to maneuver safely amid the traffic while keeping mental notes of fieldwork interactions, after leaving his workshop at the end of the day I forgot to turn off my camera. And so, as I passed neighborhoods that buzzed with activity, my camera captured street scenes, such as the one shown on the following page.

A streetscape I rolled through that late afternoon contained autorickshaws, groups of children walking home from school, and men and women, three and four people deep, walking and hanging out around shops. The road buzzed with activity. On one side, people stood near a vegetable stall chatting with friends. On the other side, a small flower stall the size of a coffee table was placed against a concrete wall. A woman in a bright pink sari sat by the table, twisting garlands. Meanwhile, elderly men and women stood on the street praying in front of a temple, and a young man sat on a parked motorcycle, smoking, while other adults held children's hands as they crossed the street.

Navigating this intersection on a bicycle required slow pedaling and

Heterogenous traffic on a Khar, Mumbai, street whose edge is used for a variety of purposes.

quick decision-making. It required twists, sharp turns, and sudden stops. The moment after I passed the street section shown here, I braked when the two men on a red motorcycle cut me off. A few pedal strokes later, I slowed down for a group of schoolchildren on the right to cross the street, then maneuvered around an autorickshaw picking up a passenger. I was grateful to be riding a single-speed commuter bicycle. Its upright frame made starting and stopping easy. This proved essential a few seconds later as I twisted my handlebar to the left when another person on a bicycle came close to me on my right. I then had to jerk my bicycle to the left to stay upright. The kids laughed at my awkward maneuver. I was going walking speed or less, with barely enough momentum to keep me upright. A small white car passed through the intersection, and a space opened up in its wake. I sped up to make the gap.

Automobility—the idea that cities have been "reconfigure[d]" according to the needs of the car—structures most conversations around cycling and street design that encourage sustainable transportation.[16] But street scenes like this one in Khar do not reflect automobility. Like many streets in Mumbai, this one is characterized by fluid infrastructure, flexible road edges, and heterogenous traffic.[17] By contrast, cities characterized by automobility have static road infrastructure with clearly marked boundaries, monofunctional streets, and homogenous traffic. As Peter Norton has shown, in North America automobility refers to the complete transformation of the law, culture, and physical environment of cities to normalize and prioritize driving.[18] In that environment, automobility does not simply refer to a city with a lot of cars but to a context where driving is a default for how public space is organized, imagined, and governed; as Pascal Menoret puts it, "Automobility is not only a system of objects (cars, roads, parking lots, garages, etc.) and systems (regulations, markets, services, etc.), but it is also a structure of feeling, imagining, and thinking."[19] Automobility requires particular street characteristics that are uncommon in Mumbai: streets that are highly regulated, that consist of sharp spatial delineations (such as between curb and roadway), and that are used for a single purpose throughout the day. I bring up automobility because both proponents of sustainable transportation *and* its critics assume that all cities are characterized by it; the idea of automobility sets the discourse in which the problem is articulated and delineates potential solutions.

If Mumbai is not characterized by automobility (i.e., car-centrism as a total cultural, political, and economic system), then what alternative spatial arrangement does it have? How does the city offer alternatives not just to automobility but to thinking about cycling as a practice that is inevitably oppositional to driving?

Whereas automobility's critics assume streets have a homogenous and clearly defined edge, the sides of most Mumbai streets are often characterized by mixed use, interactions, flexibility, and slow movement. There are exceptions, such as the streets in the historic districts of south Mumbai, which have high curbs that sharply define sidewalk and road space, and

A blurred street edge and heterogenous traffic in Mumbai.

some central north-south thoroughfares, as well as the few restricted access expressways open only to cars. However, in "contrast with the highly regulated, single-purpose, 'purified' spaces of Western highways," many Mumbai street edges are a gray zone.[20] In Mumbai, that zone is used for many activities: to park vehicles and wash them, to walk, to sell things, and to sit, eat, sleep, push handcarts, and hang out with friends.[21] A significant percentage of public space is also occupied by parked cars. Privately owned vehicles in particular occupy an amount of space vastly disproportionate to the number of people who benefit from using those vehicles. But the diversity of activities and objects found on Mumbai street edges—the store displays, trees, and food, as well as people playing, cooking, talking, and walking, *as well as* the parked vehicles—means that parked cars are not the only feature of the road that shapes the experience of cycling in Mumbai.

"The left side of the road, that's our space, that's where I try to be," Firoza once told me. While riding alone to meetings, or with people as part of doing this fieldwork, I would also often navigate this mixed-use road edge. This gray zone lies between shop frontages and the fast-moving traffic adjacent to a center concrete divider. Instead of a curb, there may be a gradually disappearing roadway that turns to dirt. Instead of a street edge lined with parked cars, there may be a street edge lined with small shops, crates of bread, and small groups of people chatting, where the threat of being "doored" is replaced by the threat of being slapped on the arm by someone, in the throes of an animated conversation, accidentally gesticulating (as I once experienced). The architects Rupali Gupte and Prasad Shetty provide a vivid account of this diversely used street edge, which they call a "transactional space":

> In the electronic cluster of Mumbai, called Lamington Road, shops are very small and are along street sidewalks. During the daytime, the tiny shops extend themselves slightly by placing empty display cartons on the sidewalk. . . . The free walls between the doors of two shops are rented to other shops, which dig themselves one foot within the wall and extend themselves one foot outside. . . . When they shut, they remain folded as a thin relief on the wall. But when they unfold and open, they spill their guts out to reveal the oneiric spaces within. Beyond this play of shop doors, empty cartons, and one-foot shops is another series of shops, which occupy the edge of the sidewalk along the carriageway. . . . At some places there are also shops on the carriageway beyond the sidewalk shops. They alternate with parked cars. At certain times of the day, even the surfaces of the parked cars become temporary shops.[22]

In contrast to the normative street conjured by progressive planners (monofunctional streets lined with parked cars that force people to bicycle in the dangerous "door zone"), cycling in Mumbai means navigating eclectically used, flexible, and dynamic street edges such as those Gupte and Shetty describe.[23] On these street edges, distinctions between public and private, commercial and residential, roadway and sidewalk are not clearly established. This is not necessarily a bad thing. For instance, this "blurred" roadside "accommodates" low start-up cost commercial activities like roadside bicycle repair stalls.[24] These stalls, sometimes occupying only a few square feet of space, function similarly to the "one-foot shops" Gupte and Shetty describe. Stall owners often dangle a yellow-painted inner tube from a pole or tree to indicate they fix flat tires—or punctures, as they are locally called. Parts and old bicycles may be stored behind a fence, off the road, while the repair person sits on a small tarp, with tools spread around them, easily accessible to passersby. Although never officially recognized as such, these repair shops are also an infrastructure that supports cycling.

Moreover, many Mumbai streets lack lane markings or design consistency, which further facilitates the fluidity and flexibility of the street edge. White stripes, center lines, curbs, and sidewalks—all design features traditionally meant to indicate how space is supposed to be used and by whom—exist in some places but are more often absent. As Tarini Bedi observes in her ethnography of taxi driving in Mumbai, "In most places these markings are scraped over or faded." She argues that this shows "that linear thinking and driving along protected, laned, and demarcated road spaces are neither universal desires nor practices."[25] The lack of lane markings signals the importance of seeing infrastructure—even in concrete and asphalt—as flexible. For instance, the life cycle of a Mumbai street does not consist of planning, paving, and then maintenance (such as regular "striping," or repainting white and yellow lines). More often, the street life cycle looks like a pattern of paving, appropriation by multiple users—drivers parking their cars, hawkers selling, shopkeepers extending their displays, infrastructure workers digging up the roadway (often for the laying of telecommunications cables)—then repaving, reappropriation, and so forth.

What matters is not so much why lane markings are absent but how this absence shapes the experience of cycling. As I saw in Khar that day, the street edge was determined not by design elements such as markings but by shop owners, hawkers, people walking, and people parking their scooters. This is also a street edge that is often bumpy, slippery, and potentially full of obstacles. It is a place where road refuse gets pushed, garbage is dumped, and muddy water flows. On the stretch of street in Khar discussed above, the street edge had mud, crumpled packaging, banana peels, and, during the monsoon, small piles of palm fronds, leaves, and branches knocked down from the wind. But there can be more pleasant objects on the roadside as well. Crates of sandwich bread, straw brooms, umbrellas, and children's clothes hang on poles to tempt customers; cooked food, flowers, and toys also shape the experience of moving through this space.

The blurred edge is a further sign of streets that have not been completely re-ordered to facilitate driving. Certainly, this fluidity can enable aggressive drivers to take over space. But it can have the opposite effect as well. In mixed residential and commercial areas, various roadside activities have the effect transportation planners would call "traffic calming" by "friction."[26] Most of the time this does not mean literal rubbing or physical interaction but a closeness of encounter among road users and vehicles that slows movement. Progressive urban planning professionals who advocate and design for reducing vehicle speeds in dense urban areas emphasize the positive effects of this friction. This "healthy interaction" among a mix of road users "induces safer behavior" because it forces drivers to slow down and pay attention to what is happening on the road.[27] Streets that put "drivers in closer contact with pedestrians and cyclists ... [force drivers] to proceed, turn, and change lanes more slowly and predictably."[28] By contrast, the friction-free quality of high-capacity, multilane, uninterrupted roads designed to move car traffic quickly is especially dangerous to people on bicycles and pedestrians.

However, not all transportation planning professionals have a positive view of friction. In fact, across the literature focusing on Indian cities, there is an unresolved tension regarding traffic mode mixing and safety. Some transportation planning publications argue that friction and mode mixing *decrease* safety for people on bicycles, whereas others argue that friction and mode mixing reduce motor vehicle speed and therefore *increase* safety for people on bicycles.[29] This tension is also present in newspaper coverage of cycling in India. For instance, an article on cycling fatalities in Chandigarh blames the frictionless travel enabled by the city's well-planned streets for the relatively high number of cyclist fatalities. A road safety expert is quoted as saying, "Chandigarh has less traffic and good road infrastructure, which is why people speed. We need dedicated cycle lanes."[30] This contradiction can be resolved through greater attention to the specific kinds of street environments the authors are considering, since mixed-mode streets in dense neighborhoods pose less danger to people on bicycles than mixed-mode, highway-like streets (such as found on Mumbai's periphery) with fast-moving motor vehicle traffic.[31]

Moreover, the friction of Mumbai's streets does not benefit everyone at all times. Edges with broken concrete, uneven surfaces, mounds of rubble, and open utility holes also produce friction that makes walking difficult and dangerous. Also, driving in Mumbai *is* stressful, especially for the professional drivers who bear the brunt of navigating the city's complex road environment. However, walking remains the most common form of transportation in Mumbai despite being difficult, dangerous (in terms of the threat from cars), and not accessible. This high pedestrian activity contributes to the heterogenous street edge use in the city. The significant number of people walking in or alongside streets, especially since most streets do not have sidewalks, has a significant impact on the experience of cycling. It means that cycling in Mumbai often involves navigating around people *walking* rather than only around people driving. This is especially the case near the city's many commuter train stations, where pedestrian traffic is so high that even riding a bicycle can feel like an unfair monopoly of space.

In Mumbai's high-pedestrian zones, a person on a bicycle can feel like an invader of *pedestrian* space rather than car space. I discovered this by chance when I made the decision to bicycle near Kurla Station, a major transportation hub, in the early evening, a time of day when, every few minutes, tens of thousands of people leave the trains coming in from the commercial areas of south Mumbai and start their walk home to nearby working-class neighborhoods. At first, I enjoyed slowly cycling on the car-free roads adjacent to the station, cycling past the bustling shops selling snacks, drinks, clothing, and gadgets along the many lanes emanating from the station. But soon the crowd got more dense, and I slowed to a walking pace. Then, no longer able to stay upright, I dismounted and pushed my

Cycling in Mumbai often means navigating street space primarily used by pedestrians.

bicycle. I tried making my way toward Bandra Kurla Complex, but the crush of bodies became so dense I could no longer even push my bicycle, so I had to lift it above my head and walk the last few hundred feet to the highway. Streets so full of pedestrians that even pushing a bicycle is physically impossible are rare in Mumbai, but this extreme case highlights the paradox of Mumbai's streets: although they are not designed for walking or cycling, some streets are pedestrianized organically.

Certainly, Mumbai's streets include a lot of cars; car traffic is incredibly dense, drivers can be aggressive and assert a sense of ownership over the public space, and, judging by recent development projects, officials give disproportionate attention to the needs of the tiny percentage of the population that travels via car. But an urban landscape with many cars and even a political sphere focused on drivers does not equate to a city characterized by automobility. This is where my account of the experience of moving in Mumbai diverges from other writing on transportation politics in India. For instance, Govind Gopakumar argues that a "pervasive force transforming streets in the pursuit of world-class city status has been the rise of private automobile use in urban India."[32] Focusing on megaprojects, official documents, government discourse, and policies, he argues that driving and car ownership fundamentally shape the urban experience in India.

While the car in Mumbai may be culturally and politically dominant, it is not hegemonic.[33] In Mumbai, there has not been a total reorganization of city life around the needs of the car, such as what took place in US cities in the mid-twentieth century. The street edge remains eclectically used and without spatial clarity. Driving is neither the organizing principle of public space and urban sociality nor the default mode of thinking when it comes to mobility. The incomplete re-arrangement of culture, space, law and politics does not necessarily make the city's streets safer or more comfortable to walk or bicycle on. But it does highlight the need for close attention to specific mobility contexts, even when officials might speak the language of automobility. And certainly, tensions around street planning in Indian cities involve more than just bicycles. Proponents of public transit, and in particular, bus rapid transit systems (i.e., bus lanes) in cities such as Ahmedabad, New Delhi, and Bengaluru also confront car-centric thinking from the authorities.[34] And car-centrism is clearly a factor in officials' failure to consider the needs of people who cycle in India. However, my point is that the official discourses should not dictate how cycling experiences are understood and represented. As I argue throughout this book, the official world of architects and government officials is often less important in shaping the experience of cycling in Mumbai than the everyday practices of people who use the street.

Adjustment

After Rashid finished his second round of bread deliveries, we cycled together back to the bakery. The roads dried as the clouds parted; the sun came up and traffic became more intense. Earlier that morning, we managed to ride on the smoothly paved concrete section near the center of the street. Occasionally, people on motorcycles would honk behind us while coming up on our right. The honk—more like a series of beeps—was the drivers' way of announcing their presence. In this traffic context, honking is rarely considered an aggressive act. Drivers honk to communicate their presence behind us and that they were about to be at our side.[35] In fact, rather than telling us to move, honking is often a message to stay put—or as Rashid put it, to maintain our line.

A mile later, we turned to the right into a narrow lane that led toward the bakery, one of a dozen or so in the city's northwest neighborhoods that specialize in pao, a key element of numerous iconic Mumbai snack foods. Like so many others, Rashid's bakery has a small, street-facing counter catering primarily to people arriving on foot. In the back, there is a small, partially covered courtyard with a large water tank, a small alcove where Rashid and ten other delivery men and bakery workers sleep, and a space to park a dozen bicycles. Having started when neighborhoods like Bandra, Vile Parle, and Andheri were villages, these bakeries are often located amid narrow lanes of dense market areas. Cycling in this streetscape no longer involves maneuvering among motorized vehicles but weaving around women laden with large bags of groceries, street vendors pushing four-wheeled carts piled high with radishes, and young men pushing massive sacks of flour on two-wheeled handcarts. So, as we enter the market area, we slow down to maneuver around this eclectic traffic. We no longer hold our line as we did on the arterial road but accommodate the other users of the street.

Rashid's riding style encouraged me to see the street as a flexible, shared space rather than one of competing territorial claims. This suggested the first implicit rule of Mumbai's grammar of traffic: once you occupy a space, people will maneuver around you. In other words, I saw that, in a further departure from the automobility norm, Mumbai traffic is characterized by adjustment rather than territoriality. I deliberately use the term "adjustment" to describe Mumbai's traffic because the English word "adjust" is commonly used among Hindi speakers, especially in the phrase "adjust kar lo," which tells others to move over a bit and accommodate.[36]

Firoza articulated this idea of adjustment explicitly while we were cycling together one afternoon. She told me that when she cycles, she tries to keep a straight line, which, ironically, is complementary with adjustment because she expects people will flow around her. "Stay to the left and never zigzag," she said. Addressing hypothetical car and scooter drivers, she said, "If you want to move, then move. If you want to move around me, then make your way around me."

Assuming that traffic will flow around you as you cycle—that traffic will adjust to your presence—reflects a mobility context that operates differently from what is expected in a landscape defined by automobility. Streets organized according to the needs of driving are characterized by a principle of territoriality. In these contexts, the experience of mobility is shaped by occupying road space that has been allocated to you by design, law, or custom. Curbs, white lines dividing lanes, yellow lines dividing traffic flow, and bollards separating bicycle lanes from roadways are all manifestations of the territoriality principle. In US cities, for instance, territoriality can work both ways; it is a mobility principle reflected in drivers' sense of ownership over the road *and* implicit in cycling advocates' attempts to reclaim space in the form of bicycle lanes. For instance, an American author arguing for the importance of bicycle lanes puts it this way: "People traveling by foot often feel under siege from both speeding cars and unpredictable bicycles. Like many street-level conflicts, this one is about *territory*. Who owns the streets?"[37]

A clear example of Mumbai mobility *not* being about territory is the space spontaneously created for cyclists and scooter drivers during periods of dense traffic. On many of the city's major thoroughfares, people riding scooters and bicycles or pushing handcarts self-"segregate" on the "curb-side" of the road.[38] This has the effect of creating a "lane" for people on bicycles and scooters in the absence of physical dividers or markings on the road meant for this purpose. This lane is fluid and constantly changing; it expands and contracts depending on the number of vehicles, the width of the road, the number of pedestrians, or the presence of obstacles. This phenomenon is especially visible at traffic lights. Cars, buses, and trucks become tightly packed together on the right, leaving open space for a spontaneous two-wheeled vehicle lane on the left. People on motorcycles and bicycles will also slowly move around each other to occupy whatever space is free. In these instances, movement is enabled by momentarily occupying whatever space is possible. The important point is that the "lane" for people on two wheels is the effect of road users adjusting to changing road conditions rather than claiming prior allocations of space.[39]

Another example of the adjustment principle replacing the principle of territoriality is the unspoken rule of traffic that you can take up as much space as possible and simply move over when you have to.[40] This is not the same as the "might is right" principle, which critics of urban Indian traffic often blame for a lack of roadway discipline. For instance, a common practice among drivers is to occupy the center of a road, even if there are lane markings. Drivers are expected to move to the left to let faster vehicles pass on the right, then move back to the center when the road is clear. Of course, there are exceptions, such as highly regulated restricted-access motorways where following lanes and maintaining consistent speeds are the norm. But mobility is far more commonly guided by this logic of ad-

During rush hour traffic, a "lane" for bicycles and scooters is often spontaneously created on the left side of the road.

justment, in which drivers temporarily occupy as much space as possible and then readjust when other vehicles approach.

To casual observers, these traffic behaviors could look like chaos: traffic movement is not always guided by lane markings, road space allocation changes according to traffic conditions, and there is often little physical separation between people and vehicles going different speeds. As Sneha Annavarapu documents in her ethnography of driving in Hyderabad, Indian road safety reformers interpret drivers' refusal to abide by lane markings as a sign of a poor driving culture.[41] Safety advocates see the practices I describe—such as driving on white lines or grouping vehicles according to speed—as an absence of "lane discipline." For them, anything less than complete denunciation of existing practices is considered the romanticization of a dangerous road environment.

Rather than evaluate whether these driving practices are good, it is more useful to understand the logic of mobility they reflect. As Annavarapu argues, these mobility practices reflect an "embodied expertise" in traffic interactions.[42] For example, driving *on*, rather than adjacent to, a lane marker can be a response to heterogenous road conditions, as Geetam Tiwari suggests.[43] This is because occupying the center of the road and then moving to the left to let faster vehicles pass enables drivers employing a variety of vehicle types, traveling styles, and speeds to use the same tight road space. In this way, drivers' relationship to the road is more similar to pedestrians' mobility expectations than the expectations of a driver in a homogenous, car-centric street environment. Like people walking, drivers on Mumbai's roads rarely expect straight, monotonous, uninterrupted movement. They do not expect incessant "linearity."[44] Rather, they anticipate a driving experience that involves navigating around others going various speeds and directions.

These ideas were crystallized in conversations I had with Divya Tate. As the director of long-distance endurance rides in India for over a decade, Divya has close-read traffic, especially how drivers relate to cyclists. She is also an experienced crew member and official in cars following cyclists participating in the transcontinental Race Across America, and she offers a valuable comparative perspective on mobility contexts and cyclists' place in them.

The first of our many meetings was at an empty café near her home in Pune. With tanned skin and well-worn denim shorts that suggested a life lived outdoors as much as possible, Divya exuded a sense of practical enthusiasm. Like so many other experienced cyclists in India, she had little patience for planners' and architects' idealized street design scenarios. She was more interested in how people can cycle within the conditions that already exist than in transportation planners' talk of how streets should be. With characteristic candor she said, "The traffic here *is* chaotic. But everyone is constantly aware that there is chaos!" She chuckled at her observation and then elaborated: "Constantly, you know—in some way, we are preparing for chaos. But in the US, everything is supposed to be this way or that way. For the most part everybody obeys the rules, so when you have a slight aberration, nobody is prepared for it! When it comes to the use of space, basically, culturally in India we are much more accommodating than elsewhere."[45]

Divya emphasizes the mobility environment created by actual driving, cycling, and walking practices, rather than how traffic *should* interact. As Annavarapu puts it, "The heterogeneity of the traffic . . . created not just a space of physical and physiological variation but also [a space of] mental and interpretive [variation]. Being in traffic, in a way, was being used to being in a space of heightened difference."[46] The driver habitus prevalent in India, which Divya calls "accommodating," does not reflect the norms of automobility, which are instead characterized by an ideal of incessant movement "without obstruction, effort, or engagement."[47] Importantly, Divya suggests that this failure to abide by the norms of automobility may in fact benefit people on bicycles—people who otherwise represent an "obstruction" in the car-centric vision of the city.

One of the most vocal advocates of this non-normative approach to Mumbai traffic is Faisal Thakur, the experienced cyclist, bicycle mechanic, and owner of a small bicycle shop discussed in chapter 1. His clientele comprises wealthy people who live nearby, including celebrities who go on casual weekend recreational rides that he organizes. His bicycle shop is set up like a small meeting space, which makes it easy for me to stop by, chat with him, or sit at his desk while he fixes bicycles or deals with customers. One afternoon he took a break from adjusting a derailleur and explained the message he tells new participants on his group rides: "Autorickshaw, bus, and truck drivers—they will come close, but they won't hit you. They don't want to waste their time! They have very good judgment. They might come close to you. They might come within two inches—you'll think 'I almost had an accident'! But they won't touch you." Of course, sometimes drivers of autorickshaws, taxis, and trucks do crash into people on bicycles in Mumbai, sometimes with fatal results. However, most serious crashes involving cars and trucks happen on highways on the outer edge of the city, which is not the traffic environment Faisal had in mind.

In this message, Faisal sought to teach his wealthy customers the logic of how vehicles interact on Mumbai's streets or at least get them to recognize that there *is* a logic to Mumbai traffic, rather than just chaos. He explained that prior to owning a bicycle, most of his customers, and the participants of the rides he organizes, had only traveled through the city by car, often with a chauffeur at the wheel. Many had also traveled to Europe and seen dedicated bicycle infrastructure there. He tells them to get rid of visions of these other cities with broad avenues and dedicated bicycle lanes. Instead, he tells his clientele, people should recognize the skills of those who navigate Mumbai traffic daily—the autorickshaw, bus, and truck drivers—whom his customers, before their cycling days, likely ignored. The new cyclists "need to know that those autoguys know how to drive, they aren't going to bump into you, they know how much space there is between you and their autorickshaw."[48]

Like his message to new cyclists to find a place amid the eclectic traffic rather than carve out a separate space, Faisal's small shop is nestled amid a laundry stall, a tea shop, and a small open space often occupied by kids playing soccer. This bustling environment is what attracted him to this area in the first place, he says, and he tried to design the space so it was integrated into the neighborhood. For instance, the shop consists of one small room open to the road. A mix of bicycles and bicycle stands, parts, and seats are usually strewn outside. People come and go, few of whom are actual customers. People often stop by after a ride to use the bathroom, chat, or eat idli from the next-door shop, and Faisal, who is never short on conversation, welcomes these visitors. On one such occasion, he told a middle-aged woman, who said she had started cycling weeks ago, his views on how to stay safe. "Hold your line, that's the most important thing to do. Don't do 'J-riding,' going in and out," he said, while making hand motions mimicking someone going unpredictably left and right. Like Rashid and many others, he advised riding as if there were an imaginary line on the road: "When you are riding straight, you are telling the motorist this is the amount of space you are going to take. Riding straight allows people to make a judgment. That way they will know that this is where you will be going."

During a mini lecture he gave to a new customer one afternoon, Faisal described the serious consequences for not reading Mumbai's traffic. The customer, an athletic-looking young man who worked at the Thai consulate, had brought in a glossy red carbon-framed bicycle for a derailleur adjustment. Faisal sized him up quickly as a newbie. The customer's unblemished, expensive bicycle and spotless white bicycle shoes gave him away. "Bicycles like this," he said, stroking the handlebar of the customer's bicycle, "are designed for speed—and that can get you in trouble."

Sensing the man was in need of instruction on how to negotiate Mumbai traffic, Faisal shared a story of a recent horrific crash. While the customer pedaled slowly on a stationary roller, set up to enable Faisal to see how the gears shifted, Faisal explained his version of events. A few weeks earlier, a young man was cycling very fast on the side of the highway that connects Mumbai and Ahmedabad. A truck driver, assuming the cyclist was going slowly, turned left. The young man was going so fast that they collided. On a long, flat highway outside the city, athletic cyclists can go more than 30 mph, he said. But a truck heavily loaded with goods goes barely faster than that. Faisal explained that the truck driver thought he could make the turn safely because he assumed someone on a bicycle would be moving slowly. "Always remember that truck drivers do not realize how fast you can go on a bicycle," he said.

Faisal maintains that while Mumbai's traffic is accommodating, cyclists have to *accommodate to* the traffic as well; they have to observe how autorickshaw and bus drivers navigate the roads and understand the traffic environment, and they have to constantly adjust to how they move, communicate, and negotiate complex interactions. In moments like this, I saw that, whereas transportation planning professionals focus on what the city needs, how driving should change, and what the streets lack, people who have made cycling a central part of their lives focus on how traffic actually operates in the present. This approach to cycling in Mumbai is without judgment, refusing to fixate on what an ideal traffic pattern should look like. It focuses on how traffic moves, how drivers behave, and what the streets feel like from the perspective of someone cycling, without an implicit comparison to normative bicycle-friendly cities elsewhere.

I argue that focusing on how people actually cycle in Mumbai, rather than what is planned for ideal cycling in Mumbai, opens a space for understanding mobility outside the paradigm of automobility—a paradigm that, ironically, is shared by both proponents *and* critics of car-centric planning. The automobility paradigm assumes that traffic is homogenous and that road users seek territoriality over space. But Mumbai cyclists show that mobility contexts can be guided by other principles. In place of homogeneity, mobility in Mumbai is characterized by heterogeneity, and, in place of territoriality, underlying the city's mobility context is a principle of adjustment. These features are not unique to Mumbai, nor do they inherently make Mumbai's streets more safe or enjoyable. Streets and mobility in *all* cities are shaped by localized practices, expectations of behavior, and shared cultural codes, but these local specificities are often overlooked by transportation planners and advocates alike.

What Mirza, Rashid, Divya, and many others who bicycle in Mumbai, including myself, often observe, is that the "mundane choreographies of the road" in Mumbai can be surprisingly accommodating to people on bicycles.[49] This does not mean cycling in Mumbai is completely safe or free from stress, nor does it mean that everyone benefits equally from this accommodating traffic. Crashes, including fatal crashes, happen far too often; like all cities, Mumbai has its share of reckless, careless, and drunk driving. Mirza himself experienced this early one morning when an autorickshaw driver, who was likely drunk, crashed into him head-on while driving on the wrong side of the road. This crash severed 70 percent of a ligament in his knee and prevented him from cycling for six months. But despite this crash, Mirza insists that people on bicycles benefit from the particular qualities of Mumbai's mobility context. This mobility context is shaped by the extent to which the city's physical form, politics, culture, and laws have been reorganized to normalize driving, but also by bicycle communities and collective cycling practices that, as transportation equity researchers have shown, can be as important as any hard infrastructure.

In this way, Mumbai's "virtual tracks" and "invisible bicycle lanes" created by tens of thousands people who cycle each day offer an alternative vision for urban planning. The virtual track constitutes an "infrastructure" that is made through intuitive and, at times, collective practices and is thus a fitting metaphor for the city's emergent bicycle cultures, in part because it allows for cycling now rather than waiting for the infrastructure to come. It also means refusing the "not yet," or postcolonial delay, of urban sustainability in India.[50]

5   Are Bicycle Lanes the Future?

欺 The first major dedicated bicycle infrastructure project in Mumbai opened in 2012. It consisted of eight miles of bicycle lanes painted bright green and separated from the roadway with plastic curbing. The lanes were located in the Bandra Kurla Complex (BKC).[1] This area of the central Mumbai business district was developed in the 1970s by the Mumbai Metropolitan Regional Development Authority (MMRDA). BKC is an exclusive commercial zone that contains corporate office complexes, financial institutions, and five-star hotels. The buildings are set back from the street, have high fences, and are fronted with wide sidewalks that are watched over by security guards and cameras. This planned and heavily surveilled street edge makes it unique in Mumbai. The street edge is delineated with curbs, uniform in appearance, and characterized by static use throughout the day—all features that enabled the MMRDA to create long stretches of uninterrupted bicycle lanes without having to contend with the many competing claims to the street edge that exist elsewhere in the city.

The BKC bicycle lanes are now widely considered a failure. This is because the lanes had numerous design flaws: they had sharp curves, the plastic curbing separating them from the street made them challenging to enter, and there was no connection to nearby residential neighborhoods or to the busy commuter train station that serves the area. The lack of connectivity indicated that authorities responsible for the bicycle lanes envisioned them as a place to exercise rather than as part of the city's transportation infrastructure. But separation from the city was not just a mistake; it was fundamental to the project's vision. The street characteristics that made bicycle lanes possible—uninterrupted, surveilled, and homogenous streets—also made it impractical for people to cycle on them. Within months of the project's completion, the green paint faded, the surface cracked to reveal bumpy paver blocks, large potholes emerged, and trenches dug up by telecommunications companies were never refilled. Plagued by lack of use, these maintenance problems, and parking enforcement issues, the project was abandoned almost from the start. By 2014, the MMRDA had officially declared the neglected bicycle lanes a failure and started the process of removing the remaining curbing. Today, a few sections of plastic curbing bolted to the street and fragmented stretches of green street surface lying beneath parked cars are the only reminders that these bicycle lanes once existed.[2]

The remnants of failed dedicated bicycle infrastructure projects like the one in BKC exist in most major Indian cities.[3] Since the late 2000s, dedicated bicycle infrastructure projects have been built and abandoned in such cities as Pune, Ludhiana, Chennai, Bhopal, Bhubaneswar, Lucknow, Bengaluru, Ahmedabad, and Mumbai, among others. And like the project in BKC, these bicycle lanes were conceived of as "islands."[4] Treated as separate from the rest of the city infrastructure, they were not maintained, lacked enforcement, and were rarely used by people who cycle. Media coverage of these projects demonstrates this pattern. Consider these headlines from around the country: "City's Much-Vaunted Cycle Tracks Become Parking Lots," "Mulund Cycle Track or 'Adda' of Romance and Crime?," "Pune Cycle Tracks, Not for Cyclists for Sure," "Chennai's First Cycling Track Taken Over," and "Cyclists on Rise Even as Bicycle Lanes Shrink."[5]

These newspaper articles document numerous problems: poor design, an inaccessible location, lack of maintenance, and the absence of enforcement against the use of the space by people walking, parking, or hawking. Of course, use of bicycle lanes in ways other than how they were intended is not necessarily bad. In cities where there are no sidewalks and few public spaces, the fact that bicycle lanes are taken over by people walking or socializing outside is understandable. But the use of spaces designated as bicycle lanes for many other activities shows that these projects have not achieved their objective—to create an exclusive space for cycling. Certainly, past failures do not mean that no bicycle lane project will ever succeed in Indian cities. However, the past failures—and the continued focus on bicycle lanes as the way to increase cycling—provide an important warning about the prioritization of street design and physical infrastructure over other ways to promote sustainable transportation.

What explains the persistence of infrastructure-oriented ideas such as bicycle lanes as the solution, despite their repeated failures in India, and what political effects does it have? Numerous researchers have shown that the effect of infrastructure often goes beyond the circulation of people, things, and substances. They have shown that infrastructure delivers intangible ideas, or "promises."[6] These might be such notions as modernity, imperial power, developmental progress, or "socialist achievement."[7] Such infrastructural promises can also come with tangible benefits like water, electricity, and garbage disposal provided to citizens.[8] As Rashmi Sadana writes, infrastructure is always "more than the function it serves." Infrastructures "put matter, substances, and people in motion," while also being "a statement of social and technological change."[9] This partly explains why politicians represent themselves on billboards alongside images of large-scale infrastructure projects. For example, prior to Prime Minister Narendra Modi's visit to Mumbai in spring 2016, bridges and overpasses in the city were plastered with banners showing Modi's face alongside those of state and local officials, next to an image of the new Mumbai metro and the white triangular lines of the Bandra-Worli Sea Link. Bridges and roads do not just move cars; they also consolidate and legitimize power.[10]

Bicycle infrastructure projects do not (yet) appear on billboards advertising politicians' achievements, as images of completed bridges, trains, and dams already do, but they have similar charisma. And in part, this charisma has to do with the promise of modernity they bring and their seemingly apolitical, technical aura. For example, efforts like the 2018 Comprehensive Bicycle Master Plan for Pune were framed as apolitical, technical interventions. This plan included significant contributions from a northern European–based design firm whose ambit explicitly *excluded* looking at the politics of implementing street design proposals, or the implications of those proposals on preexisting, often informal claims to the street edge. As a Pune-based transportation activist explained, the consultants' work was framed as providing technical expertise—often, expertise on things like bicycle network planning gleaned from successful projects in northern European cities. They described how this depoliticization was facilitated by the prominent role of design firms: "In a meeting with the commissioner and [the firms], I tried bringing up the politics and the commissioner told me to stop, didn't want to talk about it. Same with the consultant; they don't think about the political system—it's how things work, how things get done. So they come up with a plan of what should be done but don't think about how it will get done." In Mumbai as well, bicycle infrastructure projects are often imagined and planned as figuratively—and sometimes literally—apart from the city. This involves imagining bicycle lanes as separate from the complicated politics of the street, as well as the everyday workings of municipal governance around things like maintenance, repair, and enforcement. In other words, the bicycle lane's charisma enables it to be imagined separately from, as the transportation activist said, "how it will get done."

Transportation planners and advocates around the world make an important argument about the tangible benefits of street design. They say that decades of urban planning have restructured cities to prioritize the needs of people driving, thereby pushing all other transportation users to the margins and creating unhealthy and dangerous streets for everyone but drivers. Creating bicycle lanes (along with other design elements like bus priority lanes and wider sidewalks) reclaims a small part of the street in order to make a more efficient, economical, and environmentally friendly mode of transport a safe option for people of all ages and abilities. For these planners and advocates, bicycle lanes represent a challenge to a car-dominated political, economic, and cultural system.[11] As such, bicycle lanes replace the "windshield view" of the world that sees the city through the needs, desires, and perspectives of someone driving with a "view from the saddle" that reflects the needs, desires, and perspectives of someone cycling.[12]

The advantages of dedicated bicycle infrastructure—for reducing the risk of crashes, improving access to cycling, making public spaces more welcoming for people of all abilities, and improving neighborhoods more generally—have been well documented. But other questions have been asked less often. For instance, does the logic of bicycle lanes make sense in all cities and on all streets, regardless of political, government, and cultural contexts? Does creating a space for people cycling necessarily mean taking space away from people driving? Do bicycle lanes necessarily challenge elite, car-oriented development or do they also, in certain cases, further marginalize and enrich people in power seeking kickbacks and other illicit funds from contractors? What are the politics of the street edge in which bicycle lanes become enmeshed? Does creating an exclusive space for people cycling inherently challenge dominant power structures?

These questions are not just relevant to India. In the US context, academics, activists, and journalists have highlighted the connections among street redesign, power, and urban exclusion. They have documented instances in which bicycle lane projects are connected to real estate interests, gentrification, and efforts to increase police surveillance. Bicycle and pedestrian safety efforts in which policing is central have ignored the reality that street safety for Black and brown cyclists requires safety from police violence and from the racist legacies of US transportation planning.[13] Moreover, US-based transportation equity writings demonstrate the need to carefully trace the connection between street design and power because dedicated "bicycle infrastructure can be easily swept into larger projects working to cater to the upwardly mobile, creative, white demographic."[14] Moreover, numerous researchers and activists have highlighted how bicycle lane projects in the United States are sometimes connected with a new, place-based urban economy of spatial improvement that leads to eviction—such as when bicycle lanes are promoted because they make "places 'special'" rather than improve streets' safety or increase ridership.[15] Thus, what might look like a challenge to dominant power structures (i.e., designing infrastructure to accommodate non-car users) might in fact reinforce those structures, and while intended to be inclusive in a general sense, dedicated bicycle infrastructure has the potential to be exclusionary. As the geographer John Stehlin puts it, "The simplified opposition between car and bike masks a more complicated politics of space and place."[16]

The "simplified opposition between car and bike" that Stehlin observes in US transportation planning also poses problems in Mumbai. The street edges are used by many people to park cars but also to sell vegetables, push handcarts, or sit and hang out with friends. Mumbai's traffic consists of a huge variety of two-, three-, and four-wheeled vehicles; street markings are often absent; street surfaces are not rigorously maintained; and the distinction between roadway and sidewalk is not always clear. Creating an exclusive use of the street for people on bicycles thus entails significant changes to a complex system. It often requires hardening a street edge, increasing surveillance, and evicting people who are not cycling—all of which are counterproductive to the goal of creating safe, equitable, and sustainable cities.

My goal is not to critique particular bicycle lane designs but to critically examine the centrality of the bicycle lane idea in sustainable transportation planning discussions in India. In other words, I examine the effect of seeing bicycle lanes as the *default solution* to problems of bicycle safety and comfort in India. Despite their challenge to car dominance in many contexts, dedicated bicycle lane projects in other contexts also have the potential to exclude marginalized populations and mesh with elite interests. Looking at the connection between bicycle lanes and power in India suggests that many of these projects represent a statist vision and utilize a discourse of urban disorder and a logic of infrastructure that are not so different from the car-centric infrastructure approaches they are supposed to displace.

The Charisma of Bicycle Lanes

"When I say, 'Why not try cycling,' people say, 'Okay, but there are no cycle tracks!'" said Prashant Nanaware one afternoon as we chatted on the side of the road in Dadar. Prashant is a journalist and a founding member of Cycle Katta (katta means "hangout space" in Marathi), a group that hosts informal cycling-related discussions. He also created a YouTube channel called Food Cycle that highlights the city's cycling and Maharashtrian culinary cultures and organized week-long touring trips around India through a local chapter of the YMCA.

Prashant's perspective on bicycle lane projects comes from his experience in working to increase cycling through community building. In conversations with friends, colleagues, and acquaintances about cycling, Prashant observes that the *idea* of bicycle lanes can serve as an obstacle to cycling. He notes that images of beautifully designed streets with uninterrupted bicycle lanes dominate people's imagination of what a cycling-friendly landscape should look like and thus prevent people from looking creatively at the possibility of cycling in Mumbai, whose streetscapes look quite different. Indeed, stereotypes about the impossibility of cycling in Mumbai, as compared to cities in Europe, is a "mind-set" that prevents people from cycling, says Prashant. "Now, people wait ten minutes for a shared autorickshaw to go two kilometers. Or they take a scooter two kilometers to the station, park it there, walk a few minutes to work. But they won't take a bicycle." The image of the perfect cycling city as somewhere other than Mumbai prevents people from cycling the short distances that might make their commutes easier.

Prashant shared his views on street design as we stood on the side of the street admiring an antique ghoda cycle parked in front of a general store. We had just finished a meal at a Maharashtrian restaurant known for delicious snacks like sabudana vada, as part of his research for a column he would later write. The bicycle had a coat of black paint that made it glisten, a double top tube, and a vintage dynamo headlamp. It was beautiful and majestic in a way, with its classic lines and sweeping handlebars, but to him, it also represented the problem with the bicycle lane discourse: the city has a rich, decades-old bicycle culture, and yet many middle-class people suggest that cycling is impossible in the city without a complete transformation of its streets, traffic patterns, and public spaces. In other words, those who say "there are no cycle tracks" are looking past Mumbai's already existing bicycle cultures toward cities like Copenhagen. But Prashant's writings, videos, and work with Cycle Katta promote cycling by building from the cultures and communities that already exist, rather than aspiring for streetscapes found elsewhere. Dedicated infrastructure might be a goal for the future, but in the present, "the bicycle track is not the solution," he said. "With more people on the street, then the government can provide some facilities. Before [bicycle tracks], we can start with small things, like cycle stands outside of train stations and bus stops." First and foremost, Prashant said, "there need to be cyclists on the street. We need to show people that we, cyclists, are part of the commuting community."

Another Cycle Katta founder, Ashish Agashe, similarly emphasized the need for more attention to the symbolic and cultural aspects of the city's existing mobility environment, or what he calls its "soft aspects." An example of a soft aspect is the language officials use to describe cycling. For example, in the spring of 2022 a sign was put up on a municipally owned park in Vashi, Navi Mumbai, that said "Dogs and Bicycles Not Allowed" (Kutari ani cycle yahana parvangi nahi). On a widely read and circulated Facebook post, Ashish pointed out how this sign echoed the racist signs the colonial British used to put up outside clubs: "Dogs and Indians Not Allowed." A reporter noticed Ashish's post and brought it to the attention of the Navi Mumbai municipal commissioner, who ultimately got the sign removed.

"It would have been fine if the sign said 'No Cycling Allowed,'" explained Ashish. "But dogs as an entity are looked down [on] with contempt in India. Bunching them together showed the disrespect towards cycling. I wondered, is this the colonialism of the motorized? If this is how the policy apparatus view bicycles, you could only imagine how people cycling on the street are treated."

Ashish contrasts the "soft" aspects of the city's mobility environment, like language, signage, and communication, with "hard" aspects, like bicycle lanes. To him, signs like "Dogs and Bicycles Not Allowed" present the kind of subtle messaging that people with an infrastructure-centered view of mobility will ignore. Other examples of officials' "contempt" for cycling, as he puts it, include bans on people cycling on new controlled-access highways and the future Coastal Road. Moreover, even the small bicycle lanes that do get built reflect an implicit disregard for people who cycle, suggests Ashish. That is because these projects are never part of a network—that would mean taking cycling seriously as a transportation mode—and instead have all been "created in bits and pieces . . . [as] 'island projects,'" Ashish says. "They are vanity projects that serve crony, corrupt networks. They don't serve the interests of cycling." Moreover, the offensive language on the sign was indicative of a larger problem: that infrastructure distracts people from looking at other ways to promote cycling. As Ashish explained, "Silly spends on islands they call 'cycle tracks' aren't enough to drive a shift in mobility choices for people; it also includes softer, cultural aspects where one does not look down . . . with contempt towards cyclists."[17]

Like Prashant and Ashish, Firoza Dadan emphasizes that the problem is not bicycle lanes per se but the persistent centering of all bicycle discussions on the idea of an exclusive, segregated space for cycling. Indeed, Firoza's ten years of outreach and advocacy make her especially attuned to the unintended effects of the bicycle lane idea. Reflecting on her early years of advocacy one morning, she told me, "When we started, we mostly talked with elite cyclists. At that time, the conversation was always, 'We need cycle tracks.' And then we got that track in BKC. And what happened? It wasn't used. Then people complained. What about that six and a half crore spent on it? But people didn't realize—we didn't focus on ridership, things like public bicycle share or rentals. The conversation just died right there. People didn't understand why it was such a failed project."

Firoza shared this with me in 2021, ten years after the BKC project and ten years after the start of her advocacy work, which she described as initially oriented toward the cycling interests of the elite. She pointed out that a sole emphasis on bicycle lanes can divert attention from other issues, like building ridership. She explained that her thinking about bicycle infrastructure significantly changed after working with children and families living in poor neighborhoods. As she recounted, "Then I went to the slum. And I met those kids. I saw a few on some old, rusted bicycles. I saw their enthusiasm for cycling—and kids living in societies [apartment buildings] didn't have that! That was a turning point for me." Since 2018, she has focused on organizing rides with, and arranging for free bicycles to be given to, underprivileged children. While still sensitive to people's understandable concerns regarding traffic safety, she saw that in Mumbai, the idea of bicycle lanes was an impediment to increasing ridership. It is an infrastructural idea that led to a sense of deferral (among the elite and middle-class professionals whom she was previously trying in vain to convince to cycle to work) and a refusal to engage with the streets, bicycle cultures, and mobility contexts that already exist.

People who cycle in Mumbai such as Prashant, Ashish, and Firoza showed me that bicycle lanes are not just technical interventions on a streetscape. Rather, in dominating the conversation, bicycle lanes can be a distraction from the many ways of approaching the question of increasing bicycle ridership. In this way, the idea of bicycle lanes might well impede grassroots efforts to increase ridership and preclude conversations on the way bicycle safety might be improved beyond the capital-intensive and state-centric "project" approach, as Ashish put it. Firoza summed it up well: "The typical thing people say to me is, 'Give us a cycle track. If we have a track then we will cycle to work.' But tracks aren't everything!"

Bicycle Lanes and State Power

In 2017, a bicycle lane was briefly installed on Carter Road, Khar. The lane was created using multiple materials—partly with yellow plastic curbing, partly with orange plastic bollards, and partly with white paint on the street surface. No Parking and Cycle Track signs were installed to educate people about the new intended use of the space. Although the lane was only a few hundred meters long (this was all the traffic department allowed), the local corporator responsible for the project hoped that the success of this pilot project would lead to more bicycle lanes in the future. Indeed, Carter Road was a promising place for a bicycle lane. The street offers beautiful views of the sea, a wide walkway along the water, benches and low walls to sit on, and many nearby restaurants and cafés. The street is also a popular destination for group bicycle rides. Many rides I participated in included a stop at Carter Road, where a dozen of us would drink tea and share grilled vegetable sandwiches from nearby kiosks. This was already a popular cycling destination, and so it seemed the bicycle lane could work there.

Yet, despite the potential for success, the bicycle lane was a failure from its inception. The space was immediately occupied by people parking cars and motorcycles. The plastic bollards were broken or ripped out and were never replaced, and the Carter Road bicycle lane project was immediately neglected and forgotten. As the author of one of the numerous newspaper articles on its failure wrote, "The track has been constructed two months back but is encroached by motorcycles, cars and hawkers thus making it dysfunctional for cyclists."[18] Media reports rightfully highlighted the failure of authorities to properly design and maintain the lane. However, as with the failed BKC bicycle lane mentioned at the beginning of this chapter, there is another lesson to be learned: the imagining of the bicycle lanes as "islands," as Ashish Agashe put it, separate from the city's politics and street life, was a major factor in its failure.

The gap between the ideal of the bicycle lane and the realities of its implementation in Mumbai was what Faisal Thakur emphasized when I discussed the Carter Road bicycle lane project with him. Faisal, introduced in chapter 1, is a cyclist, mechanic, and bicycle shop owner who grew up near the Carter Road project and cycled on that roadway and adjacent streets for decades. At the time we spoke, he owned a small bicycle shop a few hundred feet from Carter Road and had witnessed the project's evolution.

While he adjusted spokes on a bicycle wheel balanced on his legs one afternoon, Faisal offered his interpretation of the Carter Road bicycle lane failure. First, he explained that the officials created the project to manufacture a bicycle-friendly image rather than actually to improve conditions for cyclists. The small lane demonstrated that they were doing something to improve bicycle safety, but little attention was given to design details. Second, the police refused to get involved in parking enforcement: "They said [to the BMC], 'You will have to handle it yourself,' so people immediately parked their cars there." He paused to adjust a spoke he was working on, then added half-jokingly, "Maybe if they had put in metal bollards, they wouldn't park there because that would have damaged their cars!" Indeed, the plastic bollards they did use got crushed by drivers within a few days: "Everything was crushed. They broke the cones, bollards, everything. Gone. Finished. Total waste of money. It was a mess. Runners were tripping over the flattened bollards and cyclists were pushed *farther* into the street. So after a month, they stopped the test. Why even do it if you don't want to do the right thing?" He then paused to examine a saddle next to him, and our conversation got sidetracked. A moment later, he added that half-baked cycle lane projects like this hurt the cause of bicycle advocacy more than they help: "If cycle tracks aren't done right, then it creates the impression that they don't work at all."

There are multiple technical reasons for the Carter Road cycle lane failure: the lane was very short, it was only meant for recreational purposes, it was not part of a network, there was no coordination with the police or traffic enforcement, and no provision for maintenance was planned. But focusing only on technical failures misses the point, as if a better sign, more maintenance, or a longer lane would have made it successful. As Faisal emphasized, the project's life and death were connected to the everyday practices of local government. Moreover, the project showed that seeing bicycle lanes as the default solution ended up hurting cycling cultures. The performative, poorly planned project made street conditions worse and actually impeded the growth of cycling in the city. Ending his account of the project one day with a characteristic flourish, Faisal said that "it is like saying you are going to give us rice, half cooking it, then saying, 'Okay, we are wasting gas,' then switching it off, and saying, 'Eat it'! That is going to give us stomach pains. Please, don't invite us to your rice party!"

A year after the Carter Road failure, the state threw a much bigger "rice party" with half-cooked rice, as Faisal put it. In September 2017, the chief minister of Maharashtra announced the $40 million "Green Wheels along Blue Lines" project—promising a twenty-four-mile network that would be India's largest dedicated bicycle infrastructure project. According to the plan, a physical path would run alongside the Tansa pipeline, a vital infrastructure that carries water from a reservoir, Tansa Lake, located northeast of the city, to the city center. The proposed project included wide bicycle lanes and walking paths separate from motorized traffic, extensive landscaping, public art, and outdoor furniture. Colorful architectural renderings showed a bright purple, two-way bicycle lane flanked by a wall for art exhibitions, rows of mature trees, benches, and flower beds on one side and a walking and running path, another row of trees, and the pipeline on the other side. In the renderings, the pipeline and walls are eight to ten feet tall—high enough to form a complete separation from the surrounding city on both sides. Without any hint of the adjacent structures, or even the city skyline, this bicycle path was imagined as a utopic space—visually, physically, and symbolically separate from the rest of the city.[19]

Newspaper headlines described the Green Wheels along Blue Lines project as a major contribution toward sustainable transportation in Mumbai; however, the content of the project indicated that the BMC was motivated by a different concern. At the time of the Green Wheels project announcement, tens of thousands of homes, commercial establishments, and informal warehouses abutted the Tansa pipeline. These structures, officially designated as "slums," combined to form dense neighborhoods consisting of one-room, one- or two-floor structures used as homes, as well as for commerce and manufacturing. Within these settlements there were also open areas that served as spaces for socializing, provided shortcuts to a school, and provided parking for trucks and buses.

A few days after Green Wheels was announced, it became clear that this project was focused on demolishing these structures—deemed encroachments—and ensuring that the evicted people did not return to build new homes. In fact, the origin of the Green Wheels project was a

2011 Bombay High Court order that the BMC must demolish the slums abutting the pipeline. The court argued that allowing people to live so close to such an important piece of water infrastructure was a security threat. In subsequent years, no demolitions happened. However, by 2017 significant political pressure had been brought to bear on the BMC to act on the court order. By that time, the increased popularity of cycling had also gotten the attention of the authorities. Ajoy Mehta, the municipal commissioner of the BMC (who is the equivalent of a mayor in most cities), had even attended one of the large Cycle 2 Work events organized by Firoza Dadan. Cyclists represented a constituency that had not previously existed in Mumbai, so incorporating cycling into an anti-encroachment project seemed to be an easy win.

But even for the powerful and well-funded BMC, demolishing slums in Mumbai is complicated and expensive. The primary reason is that the many overlapping uses and spatial claims make demolitions a complicated task, since not everyone who has a stake in access to the space necessarily owns property, lives, or works there. Second, it requires new housing and compensation payments for eligible residents, compensating the large police force required at the time of the demolition, renting equipment for and paying laborers to do the demolitions and clear the rubble, and paying the extensive security to ensure that evicted people do not return.[20] And so, while the BMC and the Maharashtra chief minister's suggestion that the $40 million equivalent for the Green Wheels project would be spent on building world-class dedicated bicycle infrastructure, a vast majority (the precise amount is not known) of that would in fact be used for the slum removal and spatial surveillance that the municipality had been trying to accomplish for years.

Moreover, despite the project being ostensibly for cycling, cyclists following the project were not enthusiastic. "It looks not so much as a traffic solution as a public space creation solution—a recreational park," Divya Tate told me in a conversation shortly after the chief minister's announcement. Others critiqued the idea of a leisure-oriented cycle track removed from the life of the city. Hansel (mentioned in chapter 1), a man with decades of experience cycling in Mumbai, said, "Who the hell wants to cycle in the middle of nowhere? When you cycle, you want to see people, walk around, go [to] the market, buy stuff. Who wants to go to some remote place and cycle?"

The failed BKC project, similarly premised on the notion of a bicycle track separate not just from traffic but from the hustle and bustle of the city, shaped how people saw the Green Wheels project. Divya and others questioned the leisure-oriented cycling implicit in the design, its disconnection from the city's transportation networks, and the lack of important design details in the press announcement. "What about the paver blocks? What about the potholes? What about the drainage grates? What about bicycle parking? What about pedestrians? Signals? How will they be managed? Green paint doesn't qualify as a cycle track," Firoza said when I asked her about the project. Like many other people familiar with cycling in Mumbai, she saw the big promises as a distraction from other, more effective ways to make cycling safer and improve public spaces. People commenting on cycling WhatsApp groups and on social media echoed this concern. They focused on the history of failed bicycle infrastructure in other cities, the lack of facilities for pedestrians, and the overall poor quality of the city's street surfaces.

Sensing this frustration, Cycle Katta organized a public forum on the project. They invited architects and city officials involved in the project along with people active in the Mumbai cycling community. According to Prashant Nanaware, the Cycle Katta organizer, the BMC officials openly told the audience that their primary motivation for the project was to keep the area free of encroachers—the people whose homes and livelihoods would be destroyed by the demolitions. They went so far as saying it was cyclists' "responsibility" to watch over the space and keep it clear. A project architect said the BMC hoped cyclists would "provide voluntary vigilance" to keep the area free from encroachment. The pushback from the audience (which mostly consisted of people who cycle regularly in Mumbai for practical and recreational purposes) was swift. They asked why the BMC was focusing on this big project when street surfaces throughout the city

are so poor. They asked about the details missing in the press announce-
ments, such as the types of surface that would be used, the presence of
bicycle parking, the precise entry and exit points, and whether the area
would be lit at night. Finally, Faisal asked if anyone who cycles in Mumbai
was included in the planning for the project, reflecting the audience's view
that the lack of detail showed a disconnect between the project planners
and the people who cycle in Mumbai.

A few weeks after the Cycle Katta meeting, Faisal summed up the encounter between cyclists and the Green Wheels project coordinators
with characteristic clarity. We were once again chatting at his shop as
he worked on a bicycle. "The BMC's main intention is to clear the space.
They think, it will only stay clear if cycling is happening there. If cycling is
there, they think the hutments won't come back," he said, clearly unhappy
with the idea of cyclists being used to police Mumbai's open spaces. He
also found the cost, combined with lack of attention to design detail,
troubling: "[It's] 300 crore! [Half] of the money will go towards moving the hutments. And they are saying, 'We are going to test whether to
put interlocking tiles or to make it tar.' What do you mean 'test'?! Why
don't you know the right material for cycling? This whole thing, it is not
really for cyclists. At the meeting I was feeling very uncomfortable. I was
thinking, 'Where is the cyclist giving you advice?' We are the ones who
can give feedback." The positive reception the BMC hoped for did not
happen because cycling advocates saw how removed the plan was from
their everyday experiences of cycling in Mumbai. The project organizers
did not seem to value or even acknowledge the experience and expertise
of the city's cycling communities.

The Green Wheels along Blue Lines project never got built. Of the two
dozen miles of open space that was supposed to be created along the pipeline, only a three-hundred-foot section in Mulund was ever cleared. And
of the tens of thousands of homes to be demolished, only a few evictions
happened. As of June 2022, the project had been put on hold because the
BMC was unable to evict the settlements adjacent to the pipeline. The
only physical evidence of the project is the small section in Mulund that

had been cleared and paved. One newspaper article headlined "Mulund Cycle Track or 'Adda' of Romance and Crime" (in Hindi, adda is a meeting space) describes this space negatively, in terms of the supposedly immoral activities that take place there.[21] Indeed, as with so many other failed dedicated bicycle infrastructure projects in India, it is inaccurate to say they are not used; they are certainly used, just not in the way originally intended.

But what happens when a comprehensive dedicated bicycle infrastructure does get built? To answer this question, I made a short visit to Bhopal, Madhya Pradesh, in 2017 to visit a recently inaugurated, eight-mile-long separated bicycle lane—the longest and widest in India. The lane was built as part of a "Smart City" project that included a rapid transit bus and public bicycle share system. The bicycle lane runs adjacent to Hoshangabad Road, a major thoroughfare outside the city center. It is wide enough to be bidirectional and is well marked, painted in bright red, and designed to ensure maximum separation from motorized vehicles. A two-foot-high concrete divider separates the path from the car, bus, and truck traffic on Hoshangabad Road. Bollards placed at the entrance prevent people on motorcycles from using the space, and public bicycle share stations offer bicycles for rent for a small fee at multiple points along the path. Because of the carefully thought-out design and the accompanying public cycle share, the project was lauded as one of the best dedicated bicycle infrastructure projects in the country, heralding a new era of nonmotorized transportation infrastructure.

One of the people responsible for the project was Kartikay Sharma, a man in his thirties who worked in finance before moving back to Bhopal, his home city, to focus on improving civic issues there. "It was nice working on multi-million-dollar deals," he told me while we drove to the bicycle lane on Hoshangabad Road, "but at the end of the day it wasn't satisfying." Kartikay, who described himself as the project's "curator," had pitched the idea to the government during its early stages, helped facilitate discussions involving planning professionals and government officials, and was instrumental in raising the combination of public and private funds necessary for the project.

As we pulled up to a section of the bicycle path, located along a part of the street well outside the dense city center, Kartikay waved his hand in front of us. "You wouldn't believe what all this was like before. There were shanties, rubble, and cars parked everywhere. . . . Then they built this," he said, pausing to allow me to take in the scene. In front of us, the bright red ribbon of asphalt and the four-lane arterial street running alongside it stretched into the distance. To our right was a newly installed public bicycle share station with five well-maintained bicycles ready to go. It was painted in white and green, matching the logo of Standard Charter, the bank that partially funded the project. Speaking over the constant rumble of the Hoshangabad Road traffic, Kartikay said, "Three years ago if I said we'd have a public bicycle share here you would think I am crazy," he said. It was hard to imagine the "shanties, rubble, and cars" that Kartikay said had preceded the path. Other than a few one- and two-story buildings that could be seen set back from the street, the area seemed bare. It lacked the foot traffic and activity found elsewhere in Bhopal.

This bicycle path was well designed and physically separated from motorized vehicles; in a way it was an ideal space to ride a bicycle safely and comfortably. However, it was not used by people cycling. In fact, while I was there, it seemed people on bicycles were *avoiding* the path. With the exception of one person, everyone I saw riding a bicycle chose to ride amid the car, bus, and truck traffic on Hoshangabad Road or on the adjacent, quieter, but bumpier service street. Amit Bhatt, a researcher at WRI and an organizer of Raahgiri, an open streets event in Gurgaon, offered some potential explanations for why people who cycle might avoid the Hoshangabad Road bicycle path, based on his observations of similar behaviors in New Delhi. He observed that for some working-class people in Gurgaon, situated near New Delhi, "there is a real reluctance to use the lanes." He asked some of the people avoiding newly installed bicycle lanes why they were riding on the street, in response to which he learned that some cyclists assumed the tracks were only for the rich and feared that police would chase them away if they tried cycling on them, while others said that they felt no need to cycle in a space segregated from other vehicles because they were comfortable in the current conditions. Bhatt said that "some don't comprehend that something is being done specifically for cyclists. Others feel that they have their regular path and don't feel the need to deviate from it."

Thus, despite its good design, length, and significant funding, the Bhopal bicycle infrastructure project did not fulfill its goal of promoting nonmotorized transportation. During my visit shortly after the Hoshangabad bicycle lane opened, I did see the space come to life in the evening with elderly couples using the path for brisk walks, young men using it to jog, and, in a small section shaded by large trees, children playing in an open space while their parents could watch from nearby benches. The space was not used by people cycling, although at the time it *was* being used. However, within a year, the red paint had chipped away, the surface had crumbled, and large potholes had appeared. The path was not maintained, and large sections of the project were effectively abandoned by the municipality. By 2021, the surfaces in many areas had grown so rough that people no longer walked on them, and cycling on them became impossible. The Green Wheels and the Hoshangabad Road projects show how dedicated bicycle infrastructure is never just a technical intervention in a streetscape but is always embedded in the everyday practices and governance of cities. This embeddedness produces unexpected outcomes. At times, bicycle lanes can provide much-needed public space, and in other moments they reinforce already existing social hierarchies around public space.

The Afterlife of Bicycle Infrastructure in India

Just as the Hoshangabad Road bicycle lane crumbled, bicycle infrastructure projects in Mumbai, Bengaluru, and Pune also lie in forgotten fragments. I often encountered remnants of these projects by accident. For instance, while walking on a quiet side street in Bengaluru with Meera Velankar, I saw the faint image of a bicycle on the sidewalk. It was wedged between three black bollards blocking motorcycles and a parked car and partially hidden beneath dirt, dust, and dried leaves. Ten feet farther, I saw another faded white image of a bicycle. I realized we were walking on the remnants of a bicycle lane. I asked Meera what she knew about these faded images. She directed a dismissive hand gesture toward the bicycle lane and said, "It's just a corruption thing," and she immediately changed the subject back to the bicycle shop we were on our way to visit. Her body language made it clear that the project could not be taken seriously as an attempt to improve cycling conditions.

Indeed, many people who cycle understand dedicated bicycle infrastructure as a tool for corrupt officials to make money rather than as a bicycle safety amenity. "Officials say, 'Cycling tracks, fantaaastic!'" a middle-aged man joked, while riding next to me one morning, mocking a greedy politician. His friend cycling next to us had just brought up the failed BKC lanes. Neither considered the lanes a serious attempt to improve cycling conditions in the city.

Ashish Agashe similarly emphasized that municipal officials see bicycle infrastructure as a money-making opportunity. He explained that for each bicycle lane project, the amount actually spent is far less than the publicized cost. "Suppose they paint a bicycle track that costs ₹10,000," he said. "The expense shown on paper will be inflated. The difference between what's shown on paper and the amount spent will go to the local councilors, people in the BMC, MMRDA, etc." The greater the cost, the more money corrupt officials can make. This has led to additional design features that do not improve bicycle safety or comfort but are there just to increase the cost. For instance, Ashish described a bicycle lane project in Thane, a city adjacent to Mumbai, that had a three-inch concrete edge added at the last minute. This design feature was too low to protect people on bicycles from cars and also prevented people on bicycles from exiting the track. The addition inflated the expenditure, as well as the potential profits for the state functionaries connected to the bicycle lane construction. Moreover, Ashish claimed that because bicycle lanes are relatively small projects, they have less budgetary oversight, making them especially appealing to local-level ward officers who have relatively few opportunities to make money on infrastructure construction.

In Bengaluru, Meera similarly saw previously failed bicycle lane projects, such as in Jayanagar, as something benefiting officials who illicitly profit from such construction rather than as having anything to do with bicycle safety. After the project was completed in 2012, there was inadequate enforcement of the rules reserving the lanes for cyclists, and immediately people began parking cars and scooters in the lanes, making it impossible to ride bicycles there. Meera emphasized that it is important to see the political economy of bicycle lanes and how they are enmeshed in the corrupt networks Ashish described. Meera did not have a principled stance against bicycle lanes. Instead, her point was to look at how the creation and implementation of bicycle lane projects are connected to the way local politics works.

Indeed, since 2020 there have been additional attempts at creating physically separated bicycle lanes in Bengaluru. A notable example is the ten-mile, plastic bollard–protected bicycle lane on Bengaluru's Outer Ring Road. This project was partly inspired by the growth in commuter cycling in the city during the peak of the COVID-19 pandemic. This lane had some initial success despite complaints of poor signage and lack of enforcement (which led to people on motorcycles using the lane in the wrong direction). However, in September 2022 the plastic bollards were removed and the bicycle lane ceased to exist.[22]

Pune's streetscape is similarly littered with the remains of bicycle infrastructure projects. This is a city with a deep cycling tradition; older residents recall bicycle traffic jams at intersections, but it experienced a sharp decline in cycling in the 1980s. In order to reverse this trend, the Pune Municipal Corporation (PMC) initiated one of the first bicycle infrastructure projects in India and has since initiated five more. The first project, in 2006, was a series of bicycle lanes that lined the newly built Pune Bus Rapid Transit (BRT) system, or bus lanes. Since then, the PMC has started projects such as the nonmotorized cell, an entity within the city government devoted to promoting cycling, a bicycle lane on the Pune-Saswad Road, and the Comprehensive Bicycle Plan in 2016, which included the creation of a connected network of physically separated cycle lanes and bicycle parking.[23] However, the bicycle lanes created along the BRT in 2006 were disconnected, poorly planned, and lacking much-needed improvements for pedestrians. According to a Pune transport activist, "Most of those streets [along which the BRT was built] didn't have good pedestrian pathways, so the cycling tracks became de facto pedestrian pathways and were unusable [for cyclists]."[24] In 2014, a group of journalists tried cycling on the city's cycle paths and reported the following: "obstructions every 15 metres," "buses and auto-rickshaws parked on the cycle track," "encroach[ments] by street vendors," "obstructions like electric poles, bus stops and telephone panels," and "missing portions and the sections are not connected to one another." The obstructions were so severe that most paths existed in name only. The journalists wrote, "On paper, Model Colony [in Pune] enjoys a cycle track, but in reality it's a multi-utility parking space [and dumping ground] for the PMC and local residents." The only exception was the path near SNDT College Street, which was "the only well-maintained cycle track with even and wide space for a comfy ride."[25]

Progressive Street Design
and the Politics of the Street Edge

I was on my way to meet Divya Tate when I first encountered the remains of Pune's bicycle lanes. For the past decade, Divya has been organizing hundreds of long-distance cycle rides and dozens of races around the country. She also helped set up endurance cycling–focused groups in ninety cities and towns. But more than a ride organizer, Divya has played an important role in generating enthusiasm for cycling and in building India's new bicycle community. Her experience of collaborating with people cycling around the country gives her a perspective on streets, traffic, and cyclists' place in them that is different from what transportation professionals bring to the table. Whereas Divya focuses on the way street design gets enmeshed with the politics of the street edge in Indian cities, progressive transportation professionals often see design in apolitical, technical, and universalized terms.

At seminars and lectures on sustainable urbanism in Mumbai, I often heard instances of transportation professionals' perspectives that I contrast with Divya's. For example, in a seminar focused on making Mumbai's streets more pedestrian friendly, the speaker focused on the street redesigns in New York City that slowed traffic there. The speaker started with a slide showing a street that included a single lane of car traffic, a bollard-separated bicycle lane, and a shortened crosswalk. These are familiar street design elements promoted by progressive transportation planners. They are sometimes called "complete streets" and are central to sustainable street design guidelines such as that of the National Association of City Transportation Officials. A central feature of these designs is that motorized traffic is slowed (and therefore pedestrian and cyclist safety improved) by reducing and/or narrowing car lanes and expanding dedicated spaces for walking and cycling.

However, the problem with using New York City's street redesigns to advocate for better walking and cycling conditions in Mumbai is that it ignores the different histories of transportation planning, enforcement, and spatial claim making. For example, New York City "slowed down its streets," as the seminar speaker put it, by redesigning streets that were already characterized by separation. But, as Janette Sadik-Khan and Seth Solomonow document in their book *Streetfight*, the NYC Department of Transportation added bicycle lanes on avenues whose use was clearly defined. Prior to street changes made by Sadik-Khan, New York City already had in a place a system where walking, selling food, and driving took place in clearly delineated spaces. In other words, prior to the implementation of bicycle lanes in New York City, if you stepped off the curb while walking midblock, you inevitably entered a "car-space" and would be met with yelling and curses (or worse) from drivers.

But most of Mumbai's streets—and nearly all Mumbai streets north of the Mithi River—are *not* characterized by the separation of activities or transportation modes. Many do not have curbs or any other clear divide between "car" and "pedestrian" space, and many street edges are used by a mix of people parking cars or motorcycles and street vending. If the goal is to improve walking and cycling conditions by lowering car speeds, as transportation planners argue, then introducing more spatial segregation in Mumbai would *increase* car speed. That is because street edges that are characterized by interaction, overlapping use, and flexibility, such as with street vendors or shops that spill out onto the street, have organic traffic-calming elements (since drivers are forced to go slower due to the narrower lanes and limited space to maneuver).[26] Moreover, these traffic-calming elements enable poorer people such as street vendors to access street space. By contrast, the introduction of a new spatial regime premised on segregation, such as with bicycle lane projects, can further marginalize the poor. Media reports that attribute poor cycling conditions to street vending reflects this tension: "[reporters] saw several stretches of the tracks have been encroached upon by vendors selling fruits and vegetables" and "the freshly painted footpath and cycling tracks have now become haven[s] for hawkers selling vegetables, dry fruits and even sweaters for the winter season."[27] So on one hand, the progressive transportation critique is that the current car-centric model of street building prioritizes moving cars quickly. And on the other hand, the logic of separation implicit in this critique has the potential to further diminish the ability of already marginalized people to access urban space.

By contrast, Divya Tate sees the question of bicycle safety, street design, and infrastructure in terms of different cities' mobility contexts, including the micropractices and everyday political claims people make on the street. For instance, when I asked what she knew about the remnants of the bicycle lanes I had seen on the way to meet her—the yellow- and black-painted concrete blocks that formed partial barriers, the cracked surface of interlocking red tiles and concrete, and the faded green signs that said "Cycle Track" in English—without skipping a beat, she jumped in, irritated by the question: "Reporters ask me about bicycle tracks all the time. I tell them, 'No, it's a scam! To siphon off money from the project. They are a big rip-off!' They made some cycle tracks, but it was a complete scam. Once it was built, then it just lies there. It was proposed as a scheme purely to make money off of executing it." Like Meera, she sees bicycle lane projects first in terms of their political impact and embeddedness in the local context. The rough surfaces, obstacles, and lack of enforcement are not simply technical problems to be overcome but signs of structural problems with the assumption that creating segregated spaces will always benefit people cycling in Indian cities.

"Even if there is a bicycle lane," Divya added, "I'd prefer to be on the street because there are so many obstacles. On the lane, there will be signposts and leaves, and it probably won't have good lighting either. I'd prefer to take my chances among the rickshaw drivers on the street!" The point is not just that bicycle lane projects feed corruption but that their designers seem to ignore the existing informal bicycle infrastructure, as well as the subtle ways traffic in cities like Pune and Mumbai accommodates people on bicycles.

Her comment about reporters asking "about bicycle tracks all the time" highlights the problem mentioned earlier in this chapter: the idea of dedicated bicycle infrastructure in India has a magnetism that narrows the conversation. Divya's observations about bicycle lane projects and traffic draw from her decades of experience cycling in and around Pune, for both practical and recreational reasons, as well as from her work in organizing cycling events and her familiarity with city government. Rather than seeing infrastructure as an abstract technical solution to transportation problems, she interprets projects as they are embedded in the local context. Her perspective thus goes beyond a critique of corruption or of an architect's plans. For over a decade she has expanded cycling in India by organizing inclusive, carefully planned rides that draw hundreds of cyclists at a time, creating a platform for people interested in cycling to interact, share tips and experiences, and simply create a sense of excitement around adult recreational cycling. So her skepticism toward bicycle lanes comes from how people ignore all the other ways to increase ridership or improve cycle safety, so seduced as they are by the idea of large infrastructural solutions to urban problems.[28]

Divya does what so many transportation professionals do not: she distinguishes between the promise of bicycle lane infrastructure and the practical realities of its implementation. She emphasizes the way bicycle lanes' reorganization of space has a particular politics in Indian cities: "I've been vociferously saying we don't need bicycle tracks. We live in cities that are far denser than anywhere else in the world. The moment we say we want segregated space for ourselves—people are going to *hate* us. Tracks take space away from pedestrians, they take space from people trying to park, and take space away from hawkers—they are all a part of the environment too. What we need is respect as users on the street."

Bicycle lanes, when they work, have an element of exclusion. This can be a good thing, when it means excluding cars from sections of streets already overbuilt for them. This is the case in most North American cities, where allocating street space to people on bicycles makes those streets more accessible for everyone. For instance, when they are part of "road diets" (deliberate narrowing of roadways to reduce vehicle speed), bicycle lanes can also improve pedestrian comfort and safety by reducing the number of lanes people on foot have to cross. But Divya points out that the effect is different when street edges are *not* exclusively used by people in cars. In Pune, as in many Mumbai streets, creating exclusive spaces for cycling could also exclude street vendors and others, including many poor people with tenuous claims to the street edge. Firoza similarly cautions against basing bicycle advocacy in terms of spatial claims. As she puts it, "With tracks, or lanes, people will become possessive about them. They will feel, 'This is my space.'"

Moreover, in most Indian cities, creating bicycle lanes does not mean merely taking away parking space. Instead, it means imposing a new spatial regime on the street—a new way of envisioning how *all* spaces are used, regulated, and owned. It means transforming a flexibly used, gray street edge characterized by overlapping uses and claims into a purified, segregated, and homogenous space. By saying "people will hate us" and referring to the "environment," Divya is referring to a total street system that includes how street edges are used, as well as how spatial claims are made—that is, the informal ways people acquire de facto rights to use the street edge. Street edges in Mumbai and Pune are regulated not through a formal city code but through ad hoc arrangements among shopkeepers who use the space to display goods; street vendors who use the space to cook, clean, and sell things; and taxi and autorickshaw drivers and local residents who might use the space to park vehicles. For street vendors and autorickshaw drivers in particular, the ability to use the street edge is a question of survival. Moreover, they maintain access to space on the side of the street practically, through relationships they form with state functionaries fueled by bribe payments, and they assert moral legitimacy to these space through a collective rights–based discourse.[29]

Faisal Thakur's skepticism toward bicycle lanes was similarly rooted in his understanding of the spatial politics of Mumbai's street edge. One day he recalled a bicycle lane project in Thane in 2007 that, like subsequent projects in the Mumbai metropolitan region, never served its intended purpose. "Let's look at the track that was made in Thane in 2007," he said.[30] "When it was built, the cyclists saw that it was occupied by hawkers and autorickshaw drivers who parked there. A few days later the cyclists came back and the hawkers and auto guys said, 'Don't come again or we'll beat you up!'"

Whereas newspaper accounts attribute the project's failure to poor maintenance, its short length, location, and encroachment, Faisal saw its failure as a parable for the perils of middle-class involvement in working-class street politics. The "don't come again" warning that autorickshaw drivers and hawkers delivered (at least in Faisal's account) was not just a threat of violence but was, in the calculus of Mumbai's street politics, a show of political power. It was a message that there are greater forces at play than the individuals physically present in that encounter. Faisal's point was that middle-class people pushing for bicycle lanes are often unaware of the extralegal networks of power that regulate who gets to use the street edge and, despite their privileged class position, do not always have the political savvy to navigate these networks successfully.

Another problem with the Thane cycle lane project was the failure to include in project planning the voices of the street vendors and autorickshaw drivers who had been using the space. By contrast, in Pune, the nonprofit Center for Environmental Education has encouraged street improvements that include the perspectives of multiple street users. Since 2015, the Pune Municipal Corporation (PMC) has attempted to redesign multiple major streets to make them more accessible. For instance, a one-mile stretch of DP Street in Aundh underwent a major transformation in 2017.[31] Store fronts were moved back, extensions and boundary walls were demolished, and some parking was removed, opening up space for a smooth and wide sidewalk with relatively few interruptions. A new three-foot-wide, bright red cycle lane runs parallel to the space for parked cars. There are also designated spaces for street vendors. Designers of the project also included elements to enhance a sense of place, such as fun street furniture, bicycle parking designed by local architecture students, and signs describing the various species of trees in the area.

Sanskriti Menon, who works for the Center for Environmental Education, explained that the DP Street project was successful because it began from the premise that "streets are multifunctional entities" with multiple users and spatial claims. On a walk through the Aundh street project, Sanskriti described her relationship to cycling and how that informed her approach to the street redesign project. As she pushed her bicycle past crowds of pedestrians and a bustling streetside vegetable market she told me,

> In my own experiences of cycling I don't feel particularly unsafe. But I realize that for noncyclists, traffic can be a barrier. Unless you start cycling, you feel that it is dangerous. But you figure out how to deal with traffic. You realize that, actually, traffic is not that fast moving, and you can find your space. On the other hand, as a parent

I do worry about my child cycling on many of these streets. And crossing the street is a problem as well. So I appreciate the need for well worked out design. Good design is a need a lot of people have expressed.

Unlike with so many of the other street design projects I have described in this chapter, the Aundh project's designers recognized from the start that their project intervenes in a space with multiple formal and informal claims by people with very different relationships to power. As Sanskriti said, "We wanted to bring different voices together to craft an idea of what safe streets mean and what comfortable streets should look like." Her organization created what she called a "deliberative forum" to "assemble people's views," bringing together street vendors, solid waste workers, shopkeepers, architects, and city officials. The project coordinators went through multiple iterations of the design to incorporate the needs of shopkeepers and pedestrians and to include the important insights of people doing the day-to-day work of waste management. In contrast to the Carter Road bicycle lane project and the Green Wheels project in Mumbai, which I discussed in the previous chapter, as well as the failed cycle lanes adjacent to the BRT system in Pune, this project worked because it did not conceptually isolate cycling. As Sanskriti put it, the project envisioned "cycling as one element of a multimodal vision for the city."[32]

Grounded Utopianism

Ideally, cities should be designed to accommodate multiple transportation options. I have personally benefited from the successful implementation of this principle. For instance, I find it relaxing, safe, and enjoyable to cycle on the physically separated bicycle paths on my way to work from Cambridge, Massachusetts, where I live, to Brandeis University, where I work. However, after watching how bicycle infrastructure projects get planned, debated, implemented, and maintained in Cambridge, as well as speaking and collaborating with city politicians and planning staff involved in transportation there, I've become even more sensitive to the role of context—governmental, political, and cultural—in determining bicycle lanes' success. I've seen how bicycle lanes can be an effective solution in Cambridge because of the city's particular mobility context, maintenance culture, and enforcement systems.

Creating a clearly demarcated zone for cycling requires a preexisting streetscape that is already divided into discrete zones. But, as I discuss in chapter 4, many Mumbai streets have fluid, flexible street edges where use changes according to time of day. Moreover, I've also seen that good street design is only one of the factors that produces successful bicycle lanes, even if design is the factor on which most people focus. Another factor, one that often gets overlooked, is the enormous amount of maintenance that is required to keep even the most perfectly designed cycle lanes functional. All the elements of bicycle lanes, and the streets they are on, are temporary: painted lines get rubbed away, scratched, and chipped; plastic bollards get bent, crushed, and ripped out; and asphalt crumbles from rain, roots, and trucks. Some white lines on asphalt—such as on areas where cars turn—need to be repainted every year. Even more expensive materials, such as thermoplastic, rub off after three years. Moreover, street edges, where bicycle lanes are often located, are often slightly sloped to allow water to drain from the street, which leads to water pooling and potholes. The edges are also not built to be as structurally sound as the street center since they were not seen as part of the streetway when initially conceived. Maintaining effective bicycle lanes thus requires a robust and well-funded municipal system that monitors and quickly fixes surface elements.[33] Likewise, bicycle lanes without parking enforcement also fail; once drivers realize that they can use the space to park without receiving a fine, demarcated cycle lanes cease to serve their role as offering a dedicated space for people to cycle. Even if the lanes were implemented equitably and in a way attentive to poor people's previously existing spatial claims to the road edge, not all cities have a municipal system with the capacity to keep bicycle lanes functional.[34]

The issues of street edge politics, enforcement, and municipal maintenance capacity show that bicycle lanes are not just technical design but are enmeshed in the messy everyday life of the city. But the idea of dedicated bicycle infrastructure as something separate from the politics and historically accrued spatial practices of the city has a powerful appeal. I also see its attractiveness at work on group rides in Mumbai, when I hear people talk longingly about countries with dedicated cycling infrastructure. People who have traveled in Europe share stories of cycling in cities with beautiful networks of dedicated bicycle infrastructure. I also see the attractiveness at work in the images that get sent around Mumbai cycling WhatsApp groups. A popular post showed the smooth, slightly undulating Shimanami Kaido, a bicycle route that links small islands off the coast of Japan. The image included a bicycle path wrapping around a small hill, bridging expanses of sea, and then cutting through the greenery of another island. The path is well marked, consistent, and maintained. There is nothing adjacent to it except for a railing and, beyond that, blue water and distant green hills. I sometimes also see posted images from the Netherlands or Denmark, such as one image of the famous elevated circular bicycle path in Utrecht. These posts are often accompanied by comments like, "That's my dream," "Where is this?," and "When will Mumbai have this?" Indeed, the images *are* beautiful. I find myself daydreaming of cycling in similar places. I am also drawn in by the charisma of bicycle infrastructure. The problem is when the charisma causes us to ignore the actually existing, implicit systems that support cycling in less photogenic places.

"Cycle tracks—they are very utopian. What's the point of reaching for utopia if we can't even get simple things done?" said Nupur, a Mumbai-based psychiatrist in her forties, as we chatted in a café one afternoon. We were in the midst of a conversation about her experiences cycling in Mumbai, although she accumulates most of her miles outside the city because she often rides sixty miles at a time. In the beginning of our meeting I asked why she cycles. She said she does not cycle to save the environment. Nor does she cycle for fitness—although her taut face and muscled arms suggested otherwise. Instead, she said the appeal of cycling lies in the particular engagement to the surroundings it enables—a "connection" to the street and landscape. This "connection" comes from rolling over street surfaces. It means feeling the street's materiality, sensing it through small vibrations that travel up through the tires, the axle, the fork, the metal of the handlebar, and the rubber grips. "You get to know the place more when you are on a bicycle," Nupur said. "There is a sense of belonging when you are cycling on the street. There is a connection to the street, rather than being cramped up in a car. On the bicycle you are actually connected to the street. You notice the small nuances."

Despite critiquing the "utopianism" of bicycle lanes, Nupur had ideas for future improvements; her view was not a defense of the status quo. Instead, her many hours on the saddle taught her to focus on changing the "simple things," as she put it, like rough street surfaces, potholes, carelessly parked cars, and the lack of trees (which leads to high street temperatures—another obstacle to cycling). These "simple things" lack the spectacular quality or the promise of total social transformation to which bicycle lane infrastructure projects often lay claim. The difference between Nupur's focus on "simple things" and the "utopianism" of bicycle lanes echoes Fredric Jameson's difference between a "utopian project" and a "utopianism that is grounded."[35] Both are visions of the future, but one seeks complete transformation, while the other imagines change rooted in context. In fact, Nupur's comment about the utopianism of bicycle lanes came after a discussion about the sensory experiences that attract her to cycling. Her juxtaposition of the "utopia" of cycle lanes with "simple things" like well-paved streets is an understanding of infrastructure that comes from embodied experience rather than abstract principles. This is a utopianism "without fantasy."[36] It is informed by the experience of actually moving through the city by bicycle and immersing oneself in its streetscapes.

The bicycle lane idea—like that of orderly, segregated streets—has an appeal, a pull, and an aura that make it seem like an inevitability and the necessary solution to current mobility problems regardless of context. It offers the new "passionate promise" of modern urban and sustainable transportation-oriented streetscapes, as modeled by cities like Copenhagen and Amsterdam.[37] By contrast, people active in Mumbai's bicycle community—and especially bicycle lane skeptics like Faisal, Prashant, Ashish, and Firoza—see a promise in the embodied experience of cycling itself. That is why they emphasize, above all, the need to get people out on the streets. They do not deny the genuine safety concerns of a mixed-use street, but they refuse the sense of perpetual deferral that marks many conversations around infrastructure in India—the "not yet" of modernity that marks the postcolonial predicament, which in this case maintains that India is "not yet" ready for sustainable and cyclable cities.[38] In fact, those who cycle are showing that the cities are ready *now*. As one bicycle commuter in Mumbai put it, "Once we start cycling, the infrastructure and environment will adapt. Those who don't cycle to work are the ones making an issue about safety" (Jinko cycle to work nahi karna hai, wohi safety issue ko excuse dete hain).[39]

Conclusion

扰   While cycling to her office at Tata Memorial Hospital during the COVID-19 lockdown in 2020, Dr. Anuprita Dadi noticed that her route coincided with two other people cycling. One was a man who carried a stack of newspapers on the back of his bicycle. The other was a man whose bicycle had a large wicker basket that contained dozens of coconuts. The streets were nearly empty during those weeks, and so encountering other people cycling was rare. After a few accidental meetings, Dr. Dadi would greet them warmly and chat briefly each morning as they rode together. After this went on for a while, the three arranged to meet at a predetermined place and time. Every morning for two months Dr. Dadi met the two men at Sion Circle, a central Mumbai landmark, and they would cycle together to her hospital in Bhoiwada three miles away. They cycled single file, on the leftmost portion of the smoothest part of the street, carefully occupying the thin sliver of space between the rough crumbling street edge and speeding vehicles.

In her years of bicycle commuting, Dr. Dadi did not usually create informal cycling groups with strangers she met on the street, but this was an unusual time. Streets that before the lockdown were perpetually clogged with slow-moving traffic were now empty. Some were so quiet that they were coated with a blanket of red flowers that had fallen from trees the night before. But these empty streets also invited the few people allowed out to drive fast and recklessly. Moreover, the restrictions introduced unprecedented street surveillance. During the first few days of the lockdown, police stopped Dr. Dadi because they assumed she was cycling for recreational purposes. Tired of the incessant questioning, she started cycling in an old white lab coat from her hospital. To make herself look even less sporty, she put a bottle of hand sanitizer in her water bottle cage. When that wasn't enough to convince skeptical police that she really was a doctor, she took the extreme (and to her, absurd) step of draping an old stethoscope around her neck for the duration of her commute.

The informal bicycle group of a newspaper delivery person, a coconut vendor, and a doctor was fun and offered a modicum of protection against the reckless drivers taking advantage of empty roads, said Dr. Dadi. "It is much easier to cycle in traffic," she explained. "When there is traffic, vehicles are bumper to bumper. They are hardly moving 10 miles per hour and there is that side lane for cyclists to move on. But when roads are empty, the cars are fast. And drivers don't expect cyclists." Of course, the "side lane" she referenced was not a physical street element of the kind designed by planners but a de facto lane for two-wheeled vehicles sometimes formed during intense traffic in Mumbai, which I describe in chapter 4. Riding in a group enabled the doctor, newspaper delivery worker, and coconut vendor to regain some of the safety of that "lane" while also offering her added security in the nearly empty lockdown-era road environment. "Riding together was safer. They know the road. And if anything happens, I know they would help me out," she said.

I was struck by the beauty of this story, which Dr. Dadi told me over the phone in June 2020. With the borders effectively closed, I was unable to travel to India during that time, and I was trying to get a sense of how people's cycling experiences were changing because of the pandemic. From afar, I read newspaper reports of the devastating effect the lockdown was having on the millions of low-wage workers and day laborers who, suddenly jobless, were forced to travel home. I was able to stay in touch with some people via WhatsApp. One such contact was Kabir, the food delivery worker I write about in chapter 3, who told me about his experiences during that time. With few orders coming in on his food delivery app, he decided to make the trek home like so many others. He locked his bicycle near the home of a trusted friend and took a train to his family's home in Bihar, where he stayed for three months.

During the 2020 lockdown, many low-wage workers didn't have the option of train travel and went to their villages by whatever means possible. Thousands of people borrowed and bought old, used, and poorly maintained bicycles and rode them to their homes in villages hundreds of miles away. In one widely publicized story, a young woman cycled with her disabled father sitting on the back of her bicycle, covering 745 miles in ten days.[1] A few months later, after the migrant worker crisis receded from the headlines, bicycles were getting attention in a new way. Many people started cycling for exercise because gyms remained closed. New bicycle groups started throughout Mumbai—often with much younger participants than before—because indoor recreational spaces were closed. And more people started cycling to work because the train service was largely shut down. In the Indian media, as around the world, there was more attention to rethinking how street space was being used and whether more could be done to encourage cycling.[2]

The lockdown crisis highlighted major structural inequalities regarding job security and access to food and transportation choices in urban India. The story Dr. Dadi shared also showed how crises can remind us of the inbuilt, implicit relationships, practices, and phenomena that offer moments of hope and possibility. The story of Dr. Dadi's cycling experience during the pandemic reflected some of the themes this book is about— how cycling makes the rider open to people and landscapes and how this openness produces an embodied knowledge of the city. This embodied knowledge can be surprising and challenging and offer a joyful alternative to taken-for-granted transportation planning perspectives or social science critiques. For instance, I found beauty in Dr. Dadi's spontaneous conviviality with two people of very different social and class backgrounds, the joy and fun that she said the three experienced during this dark time, and her recognition of the knowledge of the city the vendors had—her understanding and confidence that "they know the road."

People who cycle in Mumbai do know the road. The key point of this book is that, while moving through the city on two wheels, people are constantly reading the city's streets, traffic, public social worlds, and infrastructure politics. The doctor bicycle commuter, app-based food delivery worker, and small-scale entrepreneurs that make up Mumbai's eclectic cycling communities direct attention to the city as it currently exists. Whereas the technical and professional approach emphasizes how streets should change or what an ideal urban environment looks like, the nonspecialists who cycle show what features of the urban environment already support cycling and what non-design-oriented changes can be made to improve cycling conditions.

I've argued throughout this book that people who cycle in Mumbai reflect a theory of the city, its streets, and its traffic that offers an alternative to ideas considered commonsense by progressive transportation planners. This theory challenges the default planning approach that privileges street design and, in particular, the physically separated bicycle lane. Challenging such default assumptions is not the same thing as saying those assumptions are bad or wrong. I believe that physically separated bicycle lanes can be an excellent way to improve bicycle safety. Bicycle lanes can also make cycling conditions more inclusive for people of all ages and abilities. There is no doubt that many people I write about in this book also appreciate a beautifully designed and well-functioning bicycle lane. However, their embodied expertise also shows other ways to look at bicycle safety and increasing ridership, reminding us of the importance of focusing on the context-specific mobility practices and unwritten rules of traffic and of how people use public space, how people experience the sensory aspects of cycling, how cycling directs attention to the microinfrastructures of cities, the possibilities for empathy and surprising encounters that happen in motion, and the multiple and overlapping meanings bicycles have in people's lives.

With this perspective in mind, what can be done? What are the concrete ways cycling conditions can be improved and ridership increased in Mumbai? The following are some suggestions: emphasize maintenance over starting new projects (for instance, making roads smoother by replacing paver blocks with concrete surfaces and eliminating potholes); give small-scale bicycle mechanics formal rights to occupy street edges; end bicycle bans on highways; install bicycle parking facilities at train stations, the new metro stations, hospitals, schools, and office complexes; start new programs to give out free bicycles and locks; reduce the high import tax on bicycles and bicycle components; normalize practical cycling in the media and government messaging (the "soft aspects" Ashish Agashe suggested [chapter 5]); and financially support programs like the Mumbai-based Smart Commute Foundation's bicycle councilor program and Cycle Chala, City Bacha, a network of bicycle advocates with grassroots connections in neighborhoods throughout the city. This network gives away free bicycles to people who cannot afford them, teaches people practical cycling basics, shows them fun cycling routes throughout the city, and creates a welcoming space for cycling beginners.

As a qualitative and interpretivist researcher based in an academic social science context, I have oriented this book toward showing new ways of seeing cycling, streets, and mobility. But I hope my interpretivist approach complements positivist and policy-oriented research on cycling safety in India and thus might lead to additional practical and design-oriented solutions not mentioned here. Those solutions could include innovative street designs that incorporate the principles I lay out in this book, such as (1) seeing the dense mix of activities, the overlapping claims, and the fluidity of the street edge in Mumbai not as a problem to be eliminated but as a benefit to cities, especially for its traffic-calming effects; (2) minimizing the importance of capital-intensive street improvement projects because of their potential to be used by corrupt officials as revenue-generating sources; (3) recognizing that creating spaces exclusively for cycling is not an apolitical, technical intervention but might take away the rights of marginalized people such as street vendors and autorickshaw drivers to access those spaces; and (4) starting any street improvement project on behalf of people who cycle by basing it on the perspectives and expertise of people who actually cycle.

Every year in Mumbai at most the equivalent of a few hundred thousand dollars is devoted to bicycle-specific projects, compared to the hundreds of millions of dollars devoted to car-oriented infrastructure projects. In light of this vast discrepancy, it might seem strange to argue against capital-intensive bicycle projects. As I write this, a billion-dollar car-oriented infrastructure project is being constructed along the west waterfront of

Mumbai; the Coastal Road project, as it is called, will massively reshape the city's geography by adding an eight-lane limited access highway that connects some of the wealthiest neighborhoods that hug the shoreline. The Coastal Road will be destructive to coastal ecologies and fisher communities and is conceived in a way that ignores the seventy years of failures of similar waterfront road projects built around the world.[3] Unfortunately, as cities around the world are reconnecting people to waterways by removing coastal highways, Mumbai's authorities are disconnecting the city from the sea. And despite the vocal civil society critiquing the project, people in power in Mumbai have not learned the lesson that building more roads, adding lanes, and widening streets do not reduce traffic but increase it.

But the focus of this book is not a critique of car-oriented planning or policies. This is because I believe critiques of car-centric planning need to be accompanied by recognizing, highlighting, and celebrating the people actually enacting the city for which critics of car culture are hoping and planning. Sometimes these alternatives are hard to see because they are implicit in the workings of a city. The expert shows the big picture, describes context, and explains why things are the way they are. But the person cycling might not talk about those things. They demonstrate alternatives through bodily presence, by being on the road and visible to people sitting in cars, showing that it is indeed possible, practical, and fun to cycle in this city.

Highlighting these bicycle worlds does not have to mean ignoring the problems or the vast, powerful forces working in the other direction. Instead, it means representing what persists despite the problems and showing how what persists might offer lessons for the future. Echoing a theme of Kamila Shamsie's novel *Kartography*, it is important to "seek and learn to recognize who and what, in the midst of inferno, are not inferno, then make them endure, give them space."[4] I hope that readers will not take this to mean that they should ignore the inequalities and problems of current patterns of transportation infrastructure development but instead recognize, give space to, and hopefully build on the bicycle worlds that exist on streets that do not seem to have a place for them.

Notes

Introduction

1. See Ghosh and Sharmeen, "Understanding Cycling Regime Transition," for a notable exception to this approach.

2. Lugo argues that the "bike infrastructure strategy had been designed to fit the urban planning process" rather than to reflect the needs of all people who cycle. Lugo, *Bicycle/Race*, 99. She argues for a view of cycling that starts from the diversity of people's experiences, as well as the places and contexts in which people ride. Lugo writes that "bicycling encompassed a pretty wide variety of people, places, and things. Each person brings a particular body to a particular environment on a particular machine. . . . Our feelings of safety are tied to what we know from past experience, what we have heard about a place, what our parents impressed upon us as we walked out the door. In short, *riding a bicycle is deeply perspectival*" (100; emphasis added).

3. Lists of the most bicycle-friendly cities in the world come out regularly and always feature European locations. See Huet, "These Are the 10 Most Bike-Friendly Cities"; *Wired*, "20 Most Bike-Friendly Cities on the Planet, Ranked"; and Copenhagenize Index, "The Most Bicycle-Friendly Cities of 2019." For books that emphasize the importance of street redesign in expanding cycling in cities, see Sadik-Khan and Solomonow, *Streetfight*; Bruntlett and Bruntlett, *Building the Cycling City*; and Colville-Anderson, *Copenhagenize*.

4. Ng, "Top 10 Worst Cities for Cycling."

5. "Perspectival" is from Lugo, *Bicycle/Race*, 100.

6. Lugo, *Bicycle/Race*, 16. For a focus on the historical context of conflicts over bicycle lanes, see Oldenziel and de la Bruhèze, "Contested Spaces." They write, "A singular focus on building bicycle lanes without embedding them in broad-based cycling cultures is likely to lead to technological rather than user-driven designs and solutions" (30).

7. Lugo, *Bicycle/Race*, 114. While Adonia Lugo in *Bicycle/Race* and Luis Vivanco in *Reconsidering the Bicycle* focus on everyday practices of the street as they relate to cycling, other researchers have focused on ordinary or social practices as a kind of infrastructure. For instance, AbdouMaliq Simone writes, "I wish to extend the notion of infrastructure directly to people's activities in the city." Simone, "People as Infrastructure," 407. See also Elyachar, "Phatic Labor"; and Sopranzetti, *Owners of the Map*.

8. Lugo, *Bicycle/Race*, 32. See also Vivanco, *Reconsidering the Bicycle*, 11–13.

9. For critical discussion of the "bikes versus cars" narrative, see Lugo, *Bicycle/Race*, 12–13. For writing on equity and street improvements, see the essays

in Zavestoski and Agyeman, *Incomplete Streets*; and the important report by Brown, with Rose and King, *Arrested Mobility*. Other notable writing on transportation equity includes Butler, "Why We Must Talk about Race"; Davis, *Inclusive Transportation*; Sheller, "Racialized Mobility Transitions in Philadelphia"; Agyeman, *Introducing Just Sustainabilities*; Agyeman, "Poor and Black 'Invisible Cyclists'"; Sulaiman, "Equity 101"; and Roe, "Black Cyclists Are Stopped More Often." See also Untokening Collective, "Untokening 1.0—Principles of Mobility Justice."

10. Spinney, *Understanding Urban Cycling*, 2. Important writing on the relationship between bicycle lanes and gentrification as well as more broadly, equity-oriented sustainable transportation writing include Agyeman, *Introducing Just Sustainabilities*; Hoffman, *Bike Lanes Are White Lanes*; Golub et al., *Bicycle Justice and Urban Transformation*; Meneses-Reyes, "Law and Mobility"; Stehlin, *Cyclescapes of the Unequal City*; Torres-Barragán, Cottrill, and Beecroft et al., "Spatial Inequalities"; and Zavestoski and Agyeman, *Incomplete Streets*. For an account of the way bicycle lane battles are enmeshed in gentrification debates, see T. Miller and Lubitow, "Politics of Sustainability." This literature shows that bicycle lanes are often the *result* of gentrification, rather than the cause of it. By the time bicycle lanes are planned in US cities like Portland, San Francisco, or Cambridge, the processes leading to displacement, such as the increase in property values, are often over a decade old. The authors of the literature on bicycle lanes and gentrification in the US urge sustainable transportation advocates to move beyond bicycle-versus-cars thinking and see potential connections between street improvement projects and exclusionary processes related to real estate development, as well as legacies of racist planning in cities.

11. While there has been little writing on transportation equity in India, there has been a lot of research on the equity impact of environmental discourses and the creation of open, or "green" spaces. Notable books on this topic include Anantharaman, *Recycling Class*; Baviskar, *Uncivil City*; and Rademacher, *Building Green*.

12. The vocabulary for describing bicycle infrastructure varies according to place and type of publication. In India, the terms "bicycle track" and "bicycle lanes" are used interchangeably in media, technical reports, and casual conversation; see, for example, India Cycles 4 Change, "Design Guidelines," ITDP India, accessed October 4, 2023, https://smartnet.niua.org/indiacyclechallenge /design-guidelines/. In North American technical contexts, bicycle lanes are painted spaces for bicycle use, whereas bicycle tracks denote space for bicycle movement that is physically separated from other forms of traffic; see NACTO, *Urban Bikeway Design Guide*. These designated spaces are created using such measures as raised concrete pathways, bollards, or parked cars (in what are

called "parking separated" bicycle lanes, in which the space for parking is shifted into the roadway and people on bicycles ride between the curb and the cars). For the sake of readability, in this book I use the term "bicycle lanes" to refer to any segregated space for cycling, regardless of whether it is physically separated from the rest of traffic.

13. Sur, "Ambient Air," 68. See also Sur, "Cultures of Repair."

14. The spatial features I describe here are typically associated with the concept of "automobility," a term that refers to the complete re-ordering of urban space, law, politics, economics, and cultural norms to accommodate driving. Colloquially, the term "car culture" is used to refer to a similar phenomenon. For a thorough historical account of the way US cities were transformed in order to facilitate driving, see Norton, *Fighting Traffic*. For an account of attempts to re-order streets in India, see Arnold, "Problem of Traffic." Notable writings on the automobility concept include Urry, *Sociology beyond Societies*; Sheller and Urry, "City and the Car"; Urry, "'System' of Automobility"; and Edensor, "Automobility and National Identity." In anthropology, notable work on automobility includes Bedi, *Mumbai Taximen*; Lutz, "U.S. Car Colossus"; Lutz and Fernandez, *Carjacked*; Khan, "Flaws in the Flow"; and Menoret, "Learning from Riyadh."

15. To be more precise, in the particular case of parking-protected bicycle lanes, a bicycle lane would entail shifting, rather than replacing, most parking spots. However, the point remains; in cities like Cambridge, Massachusetts, bicycle lane installation involves at least a partial reclamation of space that had been designated for parking in the early twentieth century.

16. Gupte and Shetty, "It Takes So Much for a City to Happen."

17. For a history of efforts to re-order and control Indian streets, which often means controlling how the poor use the streets, see Arnold, "Problem of Traffic." For a detailed account of government and elite discourses of unruly traffic in India, see Annavarapu, "Moving Targets."

18. I am inspired by conversations with anthropologist Melissa Cefkin, who helped me see cycling in Mumbai in terms of the mobility contexts that all cities have. See also Cefkin, "Dr. Melissa Cefkin, Nissan's Autonomous Car Anthropologist."

19. The bicycle mode share (the percentage of trips done by bicycle) in Mumbai ranges from 2.3 percent (Pucher et al., "Cycling in China and India," 283) to 6 percent ("Passenger Transport Mode Shares in World Cities," *Journeys*, November 2011, accessed April 10, 2024, https://web.archive.org/web/20140715001906/http://app.lta.gov.sg/ltaacademy/doc/J11Nov-p60PassengerTransportModeShares.pdf, depending on the source. Relative to other major cities worldwide, this percentage is high. According to the 2011 census, across India the mode share for trips by bicycle is roughly 10 percent.

Tiwari and Nishant, *Travel to Work in India*, 2. It is also important to note that in Mumbai, only 10 percent of all trips are done by car (1); most trips in Mumbai are on foot. The second most common way of traveling is by commuter train.

20. Important writing on the car-centric and elitist approaches to transportation development in urban India include Gopakumar, *Installing Automobility*; and Joshi and Joseph, "Invisible Cyclists."

21. Other researchers who have utilized cycling as a field method include Hammer, "Pedaling in Pairs"; Lugo, *Bicycle/Race*; Vivanco, *Reconsidering the Bicycle*; Cox, "Cycling Cultures and Social Theory"; and Spinney, "Place of Sense." In particular, Justin Spinney writes about mobile interviews, or talking with people about cycling while cycling: "I wanted to know what the rider, the hybrid subject-object, felt and experienced, not simply the person. In order to talk to riders, as opposed to talking to people, about cycling, I needed to keep the context of riding and therefore talk to bikers whilst cycling" (716).

22. This phrase is inspired by the title of the book *What Can a Body Do?*, by Sara Hendren.

23. Rashmi Sadana, in her ethnography of the New Delhi metro, similarly observed that "people were making individual journeys . . . [and] also understanding their city and themselves in a new way." Sadana, *Moving City*, 10. Adonia Lugo also emphasizes how the understanding of cycling and infrastructure is partly based on "the context of [people's] own lives." Lugo, *Bicycle/Race*, 130.

24. Ride-alongs enable "performance-sensitive ethnography"; see Conquergood, *Cultural Struggles*, 93. See also Dwight Conquergood's discussion about the relationship between ethnography and performance (96).

25. Jones, "Performing the City," 814. See also Jeffery Kidder's ethnography of bicycle messengers in North America, *Urban Flow*, which discusses the "tacit knowledge of urban cycling" (78).

26. Cefkin, "Dr. Melissa Cefkin, Nissan's Autonomous Anthropologist," offers a model of how anthropologists can research the subtle ways road users "read" nonverbal cues and anticipate each other's movements. Cefkin shows the importance of ethnography in understanding questions about traffic movement that have traditionally been the domain of traffic engineers and planners.

27. Phil Jones, writing on the embodied experience of cycling in Birmingham, England, describes a similar tension between "the sheer physicality of the cyclist's city and the rather abstract, policy notions of a transport policy promoting a sustainable city." He calls this tension an "uneasy alliance." Jones, "Performing the City," 814.

28. Conquergood, *Cultural Struggles*, 96.

29. Helphand, "Bicycle Kodak," 25. In this article, Helphand expands on the historical understanding of bicycle riders' relationships to the surrounding

environment in the 1880s. He begins with the 1880s; however, it is important to note that the earliest version of the bicycle was the draisine, developed in the 1810s and circulated in France, England, and Germany. The draisine was seen as impractical and not widely adopted. Herlihy, *Bicycle*, 29. The first bicycles that were pedal-powered and enabled riders to go long distances reliably were developed in the 1860s in France. It was not until the 1880s that the bicycle form and technology seen today were developed. For a thorough account of the history of bicycle technology and what this technology meant for early users, see Herlihy, *Bicycle*. See Reid, *Roads Were Not Built for Cars*, for an account of how cyclists in the 1890s pushed for smooth, paved roads in the United States. Ironically, those smooth roads also enabled the car dominance that US bicycle advocates oppose.

30. Spinney, "Cycling the City," 29. Numerous researchers have written on the exposure of cycling, as well as its simultaneous positive and negative effects. Katrina Jungnickel and Rachel Aldred have documented how "cycling offers unique embodied experiences of urban travelscapes (or 'views from the saddle')." Jungnickel and Aldred, "Cycling's Sensory Strategies," 238. Luis Vivanco writes, "While bicycles are always symbolic, they are not simply symbols. Their materiality—that is, their physical properties and temporal dimensions—contributes to the experience and perceptions of the user, as well as the social relations surrounding the object." Vivanco, *Reconsidering the Bicycle*, 130. John Stehlin adds, "Cycling produces space, and acts as a lens into it. The material qualities of bicycles themselves elicit this orientation. They do not shield the rider from the weather, from injury due to collisions, or from the gaze of other road users," and cycling also enables "exposure to place." Stehlin, *Cyclescapes of the Unequal City*, 71. Of course, cycling is not the only form of movement that makes people open to the landscape. For instance, see Ingold, *Perception of the Environment*, for a discussion of the sensory experiences of walking.

31. Vivanco, *Reconsidering the Bicycle*, 12.

32. Urry, *Sociology beyond Societies*, 63.

33. See Stehlin, *Cyclescapes of the Unequal City*; and Edensor, "Automobility and National Identity."

34. Jones, "Performing the City," 814.

35. I am not the first to emphasize the interactions among bodies, bicycles, and landscapes. For excellent discussions of this topic, see Lugo, "Body-City-Machines"; and Vivanco, *Reconsidering the Bicycle*. For instance, Vivanco writes, "The result is a relationship, even a temporal fusion or assemblage, between human and machine that is distinctive from other vehicles in what it requires, enables, and effects" (11–12). See also Pinch and Reimer, "Moto-mobilities," for a related discussion of the relationships between bodies and motorcycles.

36. Vivanco, *Reconsidering the Bicycle*, 12.

37. Quoted in Vivanco, *Reconsidering the Bicycle*, 11. Versions of this also appear on T-shirts and memes. An image shared with a Mumbai WhatsApp cycling group showed a man next to a bicycle with the caption, "I am the engine of my own machine."

38. Hendren, *What Can a Body Do?*, 40. See also Hendren's useful discussion of prosthesis use, as well as the difference between "assistive technology" and "adaptive technology" (40).

39. Borden, *Skateboarding and the City*, 173. Borden writes about skateboarders' relationship to the urban environment, and there are significant overlaps with bicycle riding.

40. Herlihy, *Bicycle*, 23; Rosen, "Bicycle as a Vehicle of Protest." See also the 1895 article by Jean Porter Rudd titled "My Wheel and I," for a vivid account of the affective relationship between the rider and bicycle.

41. Vivanco, *Reconsidering the Bicycle*, 12. On the idea of seeing bicycles (and tricycles) as mobility assistive devices, see Laura Laker, "'A Rolling Walking Stick': Why Do So Many Disabled People Cycle in Cambridge?," *The Guardian*, January 2, 2018, https://www.theguardian.com/cities/2018/jan/02/cambridge-disabled-people-cycling-rolling-walking-stick; and Wilson, "On the ADA's 30th Anniversary."

42. Vivanco writes, "The very materiality of the machine contributes to the experience and perceptions of its users." Vivanco, *Reconsidering the Bicycle*, xx.

43. Joshi and Joseph, "Invisible Cyclists."

44. Sometimes mopeds and scooters are referred to as Activas; Activa is the name of a popular brand. In Mumbai, bicycles are referred to as "cycles" and the term "bikes" refers to motorized two-wheeled vehicles.

45. I use a mix of pseudonyms and real names in this book. I use real names when people tell me that they want me to include their names in this book, when writing about public figures, or when describing information that is publicly available (for instance, in magazine articles, radio interviews, and newspaper articles). For everyone else, I use pseudonyms. I balance referring to people by a first name or full name based on whether I am using a pseudonym or not, and also for readability. The quotes I include in this book are taken from a mix of audio recordings and conversations I re-created from memory when I was first able to write them down. Moreover, following Philippe Bourgois and Jeff Schonberg's practice in *Righteous Dopefiend*, I occasionally change or slightly add phrasing to keep the quotes readable, rather than use ellipses or brackets. These changes are meant to facilitate readability and are not intended to alter the meaning of what people said.

46. According to the 2019 National Family Health Survey, 43 percent of urban

households and 54 percent of rural households in India own a bicycle. Government of India, *National Family Health Survey*, 5.

47. The race was founded by the Custom Point Welfare Society in 1981. Tarfe, "Custom Point Race."

48. "Defunct Bicycle Factory," *Pedal and Tring Tring*. Mumbai was never a major bicycle manufacturing hub, instead serving primarily as a distribution center. According to the owners of bicycle shops in Kalbadevi, the historic center of the bicycle trade in Mumbai, through the mid-twentieth century bicycles were imported via Mumbai, from where they were delivered to cities throughout the subcontinent by train. For an account of the history of bicycle manufacturing in India, see Kannan, "Journey since 1947."

49. The first bicycles were ridden in Bombay in the 1880s by Europeans and wealthy Indians, primarily Parsis. Kannan, "Journey since 1947." Others note that "bicycles began to enter India in substantial numbers in the 1890s and by 1913–14 nearly thirty-five thousand were imported annually." Arnold and DeWald, "Cycles of Empowerment?" 974. Moreover, middle class-oriented "cycling clubs" existed in Bombay as early as the 1890s (983). In 1908, there were three times as many bicycles as motor vehicles on Bombay's streets. Arnold, "Problem of Traffic," 124.

50. See Kuroda, "Shankar," for an account of following a dabbawala while he makes deliveries in Mumbai.

51. I am indebted to Sara Hendren for articulating categorizations in terms of shorthand value versus precision; see Hendren, *What Can a Body Do?*, 40.

52. The literature on urban middle-class India's retreat from public spaces and simultaneous desire for sanitizing those public spaces of the visible presence of the poor is vast. See Anantharaman, "Elite and Ethical"; Brosius, *India's Middle Class*; Fernandes, "Politics of Forgetting"; Kaviraj, "Filth and the Public Sphere"; Mathur, "Shopping Malls, Credit Cards and Global Brands"; and S. Srivastava, "National Identity, Kitchens and Bedrooms."

53. Tate, "Retrospective—1992–2022."

54. Middle-class cyclists in Mumbai also challenge a prevailing self-stereotype that people in India do not exercise or willingly engage in physical activity. Examples of this view abound: "middle-class or affluent people who engage easily and happily in physical labour," writes the novelist Ruchir Joshi, constitute a "category" he finds "mostly missing in India. These are people you find much more easily abroad, specifically in the West." Ruchir Joshi, "Brain against Muscle," *Telegraph Online*, July 28, 2016, https://www.telegraphindia.com/opinion/brain-against-muscle/cid/1451628. Similarly, the columnist Sanjay Austa writes that in the United States he "saw the young and the old jogging, walking and cycling. . . . They were sweating on bridges, pavements, in downtowns and

on beaches, . . . [but] in India . . . you hardly see anyone jogging on the road unless they are catching a bus." Sanjay Austa, "Why We Don't Exercise," *Deccan Herald*, January 25, 2014, https://www.deccanherald.com/content/382671 /why-we-dont-exercise.html.

55. The full name of the organization is Audax India Randonneurs. In India, it is officially a representative of Audax Club Parisien and is responsible "for conducting and overseeing all Brevet de Randonneurs Mondiaux (BRMs) and Audax events in India." Audax India Randonneurs, accessed October 5, 2023, https://www.audaxindia.in/. BRMs are timed endurance events. For instance, participants must complete two hundred kilometers in thirteen and a half hours, three hundred in twenty hours, six hundred in forty hours, and so forth.

56. Divya Tate also observed that in Pune and Bengaluru following the 2008 stock market crash, IT tech workers returning from the bicycle-friendly Bay Area in the United States also helped make cycling "cool" among urban professionals in those cities. Tate, "Retrospective—1992–2022."

57. Archambault, "Sweaty Motions," 333.

58. Archambault, "Sweaty Motions," 333.

59. Here I am paraphrasing Clifford Geertz. See Geertz, *Interpretation of Cultures*, 9.

60. For a sampling of published interviews with Firoza Dadan, see Roach, "Honk Honk"; Jamwal, "Why Firoza Came to Be Known as Mulund ki Cyclewali"; and Ismat Tahseen, "Meet the First Bicycle Mayor from Mumbai," *Times of India*, February 17, 2019, https://timesofindia.indiatimes.com/city/mumbai /meet-the-first-bicycle-mayor-from-mumbai/articleshow/68024070.cms.

61. Chakrabarty, *Provincializing Europe*, 8–9.

62. Phil Jones frames this as "the city I perform into being as I ride around it." Jones, "Performing the City," 828.

1. Starting with the Surface

1. For example, during community outreach for the Oakland Bicycle Plan in California, residents and community activists emphasized street surface conditions as one element of bicycle safety, in addition to other noninfrastructural issues like police violence on Black and brown people cycling. As Roger Rudick reports: "'You have to make up for deep disinvestment in East Oakland' said Keta Price of the East Oakland Collective. . . . when people live on neighborhood streets where the pavement is so bad they have to get mountain bikes, they have a different sense of what bike safety means. 'Yeah, it's cool that you have the main bikeways, but to get to that main bikeway it can be impossible because of all the potholes.'" Rudick, "SPUR Talk." "Protected bike infrastructure can seem pretty ridiculous in neighborhoods where the pavement is so broken

up it's all but impossible to bike in the first place." Rudick, "SPUR Talk," caption text, n.p.

2. Lugo, *Bicycle/Race*, 12.

3. Felski, *Limits of Critique*, 1. Drawing from Paul Ricoeur, Rita Felski argues for an approach based on a "hermeneutics of trust" rather than suspicion. Although Felski's writing focuses on literary reading methods, her argument is relevant to anthropologists and other social scientists. Going beyond the question of trust versus suspicion, Felski's writing could enable anthropologists to rethink our relationship to our research topics, and to what we observe and what people say during fieldwork. Daniel Miller and Sophie Woodward also write about identifying meaning that's *on* the surface, "pitched against the established philosophical sense of ontology that assumes being always resides in depth, and that things of the surface, such as clothes, are intrinsically superficial." Miller and Woodward, "Manifesto for the Study of Denim."

4. Best and Marcus, "Surface Reading," 9. Felski identifies a tradition of interpretation that relies on a "division between surface illusion and deeper truth." Felski, *Limits of Critique*, 67.

5. Felski, *Limits of Critique*, 107.

6. Since the early 2010s, anthropologists and geographers in particular have emphasized the everyday life of infrastructure. Notable writing on this topic includes Björkman, *Pipe Politics*; Graham and McFarlane, *Infrastructural Lives*; Anand, Gupta, and Appel, *Promise of Infrastructure*; Fennell, "'Project Heat'"; and Von Schnitzler, "Traveling Technologies."

7. Lowrie, "Dominic Boyer on the Anthropology of Infrastructure"; Larkin, "Politics and Poetics of Infrastructure," 328.

8. Lee, "Absolute Traffic"; Appel, *Licit Life of Capitalism*. Hannah Appel writes against the critical impulse that focuses on "'uncovering' local complexity beneath the smooth surface that the industry was laboring to create." Appel, *Licit Life of Capitalism*, 25–26.

9. Larkin, *Signal and Noise*.

10. Arnold, "On the Road," 8.

11. Lowrie, "Dominic Boyer on the Anthropology of Infrastructure." Recent writings on infrastructure in geography and anthropology have emphasized embodied experiences; see Doshi, "Embodied Urban Political Ecology." See Ramakrishnan, O'Reilly, and Budds, "Between Decay and Repair," for a discussion of this shift toward a more corporeal approach and how it connects with prior focus on the political economy of infrastructure. See also Trovalla and Trovalla, "Infrastructure Turned Suprastructure," on what happens when previously hidden infrastructure becomes visible.

12. Kathleen Stewart's *Space on the Side of the Road* is an early example of road

ethnography that emphasizes the tactile. Writing about a very different context, Justin Spinney emphasizes the importance of feeling the road: "An experience that is felt rather than seen comes to the fore. Exertion pulls the gaze inwards ... onto only what is directly useful to the ride: the road surface, the gradient, the shade, the rider in front." Spinney, "Place of Sense," 726. Spinney writes that the cyclist's surface-attention is ultimately directed inward; however, like Gili Hammer, I emphasize how this gaze also has significance beyond the individual rider. Hammer writes, "I argue that tandem cycling also draws the gaze outwards, creating intimate relations with other people and with the other senses." Hammer, "Pedaling in Pairs," 511. Whereas Hammer emphasizes empathy among riders that gets created while cycling and sensing surfaces together, I show how the focus on road surfaces can provide a model for a more equitable approach to bicycle-oriented transportation planning.

13. Hammer, "Pedaling in Pairs," 511. Katrina Jungnickel and Rachel Aldred similarly write about how people on bicycles "feel the city via the smells, sights and sounds." Jungnickel and Aldred, "Cycling's Sensory Strategies," 247. See also Solomon, "Death Traps," for a discussion of the relationship between broken infrastructure and embodiment.

14. Hammer, "Pedaling in Pairs," 511.

15. Furness, *One Less Car*, 5.

16. Spinney, "Cycling the City," 29.

17. See Solomon, "Death Traps."

18. Mumbai has 24 wards and 227 corporators (elected at the neighborhood level). These corporators make up the BMC legislature. See Puranik, "Understanding Mumbai's Municipal Corporation."

19. Jeet Mashru (@mashrujeet), post on Twitter, August 12, 2022.

20. "No Phasing Out, Paver Blocks to Be Used for Lanes," *Times of India*, February 22, 2015, https://m.timesofindia.com/city/mumbai/no-phasing-out-paver -blocks-to-be-used-for-lanes/articleshow/46328907.cms.

21. Mhaske, "Mumbai Rides on Paver Blocks."

22. "No More Paver Blocks, Only Concrete on Footpaths Now," *The Hindu*, November 15, 2018, https://www.thehindu.com/news/cities/mumbai/no-more -paver-blocks-only-concrete-on-footpaths-now/article25499938.ece/amp/.

23. At various historical moments, street surface conditions became a pressing concern for the authorities in India. For instance, as Bandyopadhyay shows in the book *Streets in Motion*, in the late nineteenth and early twentieth centuries, colonial officials searched for the most appropriate surface for urban Indian streets. This was partly triggered by the arrival of motorized vehicles, which were replacing bullock carts and pedestrians. Cars required new street surfaces that could withstand their speed and weight. See Bandyopadhyay, *Streets in Motion*,

for an exhaustive account of colonial authorities' experiments with gravel, tar, and asphalt in Calcutta. This analysis emphasizes authorities' attention to street surfaces. Bandyopadhyay writes, "With the beginning of the automobile age, vital to the realization of this modern city of motion, a preoccupation with the street 'surface' became distinctly pressing" (43). See also Kidambi, *Making of an Indian Metropolis*. It is important to note that in the United States, by contrast, the push for good, smooth roads *preceded* the automobile age. In *Roads Were Not Built for Cars*, Carlton Reid describes the surprising relationship between cycling and smooth road surfaces in the United States. Contrary to commonly held beliefs, many roads in the United States were given smooth surfaces during the height of the 1890s bicycle boom *prior* to the advent of motor vehicles. The Good Roads movement involved elite white male cyclists successfully organizing for concretized roads. Ironically, these smooth roads *also* had the effect of "paving the way for cars." Guroff, *Mechanical Horse*, chap. 4. Of course, smooth roads are not the only reason for car dominance in the United States. Defunding public transit and changing policies, like the invention of the "jaywalker," had a greater impact, as thoroughly documented in Norton, *Fighting Traffic*. However, my point is that there is no *inherent* politics of smooth streets. Making smooth streets can be good for cycling in one context and might hurt it in others.

24. See Solomon, "Death Traps."

25. Helphand, "Bicycle Kodak," 25. Cycling is not the only way people acquire a sense of intimacy with the road. For instance, an article on motorcycle touring describes a relationship with the landscape that is strikingly similar to what I observed with cycling: "By closer I mean more intimate with. The surface of the road, for instance. You are conscious of all its possible variations, whether it offers grip or is smooth, whether it's new or used, wet, damp or dry." Berger, *Keeping a Rendezvous*, 194–95, cited in Pinch and Reimer, "Moto-mobilities," 443. Another mode of transport that makes the user most intimate with the subtleties of road surfaces is skateboarding. Iain Borden writes, "*Smoothness* of surface contributes dramatically to the skater's micro-experience, affecting speed, noise, grip and predictability. . . . [Surface can also be] translated into gesture and attitude." Borden, *Skateboarding and the City*, 181.

26. Helphand, "Bicycle Kodak," 25.

27. Rudd, "My Wheel and I," cited in Helphand, "Bicycle Kodak," 25. See also Reid, *Roads Were Not Built for Cars*; and Spinney, "Place of Sense," 727.

28. Since the 2010s, authors have highlighted how sensing landscapes is a central part of cycling. Hammer writes, "Alongside hearing and smell, blind and visually impaired riders addressed rich tactile and haptic experiences within cycling, noticing sensations of temperature (riding on a hot/cold day, in the sun/the shade), sense of direction (when turning right or left, descending/ascend-

ing), and vibration (the actual movement of the cycle)." Hammer, "Pedaling in Pairs," 509.

29. These rides occurred in 2015 and 2016. Access to the Sewri jetty has since been closed due to the construction of the Mumbai-Trans-Harbour Link, a bridge connecting Mumbai with Navi Mumbai.

30. Bicycle literature abounds with references to affective and intimate relationships to bicycles, as in: "My wheel is a sentient thing responding to the mood of the rider almost like a thoroughbred." Rudd, "My Wheel," 124. Another example: "The great Brambilla was a courageous racer who didn't pamper himself. When he felt that he hadn't been up to the job, he put his cycle in his bed and slept on the floor." Fournel, *Need for the Bike*, 35–36. See also Krabbé, *The Rider*; and Battista, *Bicycle Love*.

31. My use of "vibrant" references Bennett, *Vibrant Matter*.

32. See also Jungnickel and Aldred, "Cycling's Sensory Strategies."

33. My conversation with Custom Point's founders was in Hindi, although their primary language is Marathi.

34. See Finkelstein, *Archive of Loss*.

35. Gupte and Shetty, "It Takes So Much for a City to Happen."

36. See Tsing, *Mushroom at the End of the World*, 253–55. My use of the term "latent commons" is similar to Katherine Sacco's articulation of the concept: "Latent commons do not seek or offer visions of progress; they are founded upon collaborations. They offer alternative futures." Sacco, "Latent Commons in the City."

37. "Seeing" is a reference to Scott, *Seeing Like a State*. For a thorough account of Indian urban governments' attempts to control populations, as well as analyses of elite discourses of the unruly Indian city, see Kaviraj, "Filth and the Public Sphere"; and Chakrabarty, "Of Garbage, Modernity, and the Citizen's Gaze." See also Annavarapu, "Moving Targets," for an account of the urban government's views toward traffic, as well as state discourses of the "unruly" Indian driver. See Arnold, "Problem of Traffic," on the colonial and postcolonial obsession with the ordering of India's disorderly traffic. Arnold writes, "The longed-for orderliness of Indian street-life in general, and its traffic in particular, thus became indicative of the regulatory needs of the modern nation" (123).

38. On the 2017 proposed track along a water pipeline, see Sujit Mahamulkar, "CM Devendra Fadnavis Approves BMC's Proposal for Cycle Track," *Times of India*, September 2, 2017, https://timesofindia.indiatimes.com/city/mumbai/cm-devendra-fadnavis-approves-bmcs-proposal-for-cycle-track/articleshow/60341005.cms.

39. Best and Marcus, "Surface Reading," 9.

40. Best and Marcus, "Surface Reading," 9.

41. See Felski, *Limits of Critique*, for a discussion of surface/depth metaphors in scholarly writing and the assumed politics of those metaphors.

42. Felski, *Limits of Critique*; Best and Marcus, "Surface Reading."

2. Mumbai's Cycling Landscape

1. I use the word "slum" in this book despite its negative connotation in English because it is commonly used in Mumbai regardless of the speaker's language. Hindi speakers discussed in this chapter use the terms "jhopadpatti," "basti," and "slum." "Jhopadpatti" refers to clusters of small huts, and "basti" means settlement. As Lisa Björkman writes, "While it is tempting to treat *slum* as a foreign word with a clearly negative valence and to celebrate others like *bustee* and *jhopadpatti* as value-neutral native categories, neither is it the case that native categories are value neutral (*jhopadpatti* is sometimes used . . . as an epithet . . .), nor does *slum* carry an unequivocally negative connotation." Björkman, *Pipe Politics*, 253–54n13.

2. Here, Mohan's personal focus on the embodied quality of cycling over its social and symbolic value echoes Luis Vivanco's writing on the meaning of bicycles: "Their materiality—that is, their physical properties and temporal dimensions—contributes to the experience and perceptions of the user." Vivanco, *Reconsidering the Bicycle*, 130.

3. [The] Energy and Resources Institute (TERI) and All India Cycle Manufacturers' Association (AICMA), *Benefits of Cycling in India*, 3.

4. Shakti: Sustainable Energy Foundation (SSEF), *Planning and Design Guideline for Cycle Infrastructure*, 8. Here is another example: "What is difficult to combat is the low image of the bicycle. Bicycles are the mode of the poor; bicyclists are captive riders in India; that is, they have no choice." Arora, "Gendered Perspective on Bicycling," 133. See also Tiwari, Arora, and Jain, *Bicycling in Asia*, 14.

5. Anantharaman, "Elite and Ethical," 2. See also S. Srivastava, "Meaning of the Sports Bicycle."

6. Rachel Aldred also mentions the need to go beyond commonsense binaries when describing cyclists: "In this research, participants' descriptions of diverse cycling practices challenged the easy split of cycling into 'utility' and 'leisure.'" Aldred, "'On the Outside,'" 37.

7. Millar, *Reclaiming the Discarded*, 3, 4.

8. Demetriou, "Reconsidering the Vignette as Method," 210.

9. All quotes in this paragraph are from Logan Hollarsmith's "The Cargo Bike," unpublished manuscript, presented at Bard College, May 2012. Quotes used with permission.

10. For a thorough account of the cultures of cargo cycles in Kolkata, see Sur, "Cultures of Repair." If you search online for "cargo cycle," you will not see an image of a ghoda cycle; instead, you might see a tricycle with a bucket-like cargo bay in front. This is what gas cylinder delivery workers in Mumbai commonly use. Or you will see a tricycle with a cargo bay in the back, which is used to carry large boxes or plastic containers. Cargo bicycles in Europe and North America are also associated with unusual frames, such as the "longtail," which has a significant distance between the front and back wheels to enable extra carrying capacity in the back, or the Dutch-style *bakfiets*, which has a long wheelbase to support a cargo bay in the front capable of holding two small children. Cargo bicycles with front or back bays or long frames are uncommon in Mumbai, with the exception of the tricycles used by gas cylinder delivery workers.

11. See Sur, "Cultures of Repair."

12. Sur, "Cultures of Repair"; Anwar and Sur, "Keeping Cities in Motion." Simone, "People as Infrastructure," makes a similar point.

13. Sur, "Cultures of Repair."

14. Aggarwal and Bedi, "*Dhandha*, Accumulation and the Making of Valuable Livelihoods," 711.

15. Aggarwal and Bedi, "*Dhandha*, Accumulation and the Making of Valuable Livelihoods," 711–12. For additional examples that show how dhandha "animate[s] projects of self-fashioning" in Mumbai, see Björkman, *Bombay Brokers*, 34.

16. Joshi, "Mobility Practices of the Urban Poor," 167.

17. Joshi, "Mobility Practices of the Urban Poor," 168.

18. R. Srivastava and Echanove, "Tool-House Case Study."

19. In order to maintain anonymity, on occasion I have mixed details like ride destinations, as well as interactions, from various group rides in which I participated. So while this account is all based on firsthand observations and I include direct quotes, the timeline and context have been rearranged slightly.

20. Krishnendu Ray, personal communication, March 23, 2018.

21. "Despite the fact that our interlocutors live with immense uncertainty in a changing city, they refer to their *dhandhas* with such pride and dignity that it became impossible to not take this conception of *dhandha* as seriously as they did." Aggarwal and Bedi, "*Dhandha*, Accumulation and the Making of Valuable Livelihoods," 707.

3. Embodied Freedoms

1. ₹1 lakh means ₹100,000. That was roughly the equivalent of $1,400 in 2019, when I had this conversation.

2. Incorporating English words into conversations conducted in Hindi, even

among non-English speakers, is very common in Mumbai and in most Indian cities.

3.   The association of the bicycle with freedom can be seen historically not just in India but also in Japan and China as well. See Arnold and DeWald, "Cycles of Empowerment?"; Maini, "Dressed Up and on the Go"; and Rhoads, "Cycles of Cathay."

4.   Sainath, "Where There Is a Wheel." See also Date, "Bicycle Treated as a Party Symbol."

5.   This quote is from an interview Susan B. Anthony gave to the journalist Nellie Bly that was published in the *New York World* on February 2, 1896. For a full transcription of Nellie Bly's interview, see "Champion of Her Sex," Ignorance Is Blixt, https://ignoranceisblixt.com/2020/08/champion-of-her-sex-nellie-bly -interviews-susan-b-anthony/. See also Louise Dawson, "How the Bicycle Be- came a Symbol of Women's Emancipation," *The Guardian*, November 4, 2011, https://www.theguardian.com/environment/bike-blog/2011/nov/04 /bicycle-symbol-womens-emancipation. Kat Jungnickel, in *Bikes and Bloomers*, meticulously documents how nineteenth-century women developed new types of clothing that made cycling possible for women in that era. For a discussion on the relationship between bicycles and changing gender norms in early twentieth-century India, see Arnold and DeWald, "Cycles of Empowerment?"

6.   Lino e Silva, *Minoritarian Liberalism*, 19. This framing is inspired by the anthro- pologist Moisés Lino e Silva's nuanced examination of writings on freedom and especially his analysis of the implicit Eurocentrism in political theorists' writ- ings on the concept.

7.   The idea of freedom to take risks, freedom to have fun, or freedom to do noth- ing in public is a key theme of the groundbreaking book *Why Loiter? Women and Risk on Mumbai Streets*, by Shilpa Phadke, Sameera Khan, and Shilpa Ranade.

8.   Phadke, Khan, and Ranade, *Why Loiter?*

9.   Gamble, "Playing with Infrastructure Like a Carishina."

10.   Brunson, "'Scooty Girls,'" 611. See also Truitt, "On the Back of a Motorbike."

11.   Visakha (with Annavarapu), "Where Are Women Drivers?" See also Anna- varapu, "Risky Routes, Safe Suspicions."

12.   My interpretation of this interaction with Anil is inspired by Snigdha Poonam's *Dreamers*, which offers a vivid account of young men in India who, with little access to education or capital, create or seek out jobs that have freedom—and not necessarily professional advancement—built into them.

13.   The exploitation and precarious working conditions of gig workers in India have been well documented. See Kaveri Medappa, "Bengaluru Zomato Worker Kamaraj Got a Chance to Defend Himself; Others Are Not as Lucky," *Indian*

Express, March 24, 2021, https://indianexpress.com/article/opinion/columns/zomato-delivery-partner-suspension-food-app-7240416/; and Naraharisetty, "In the Gig Economy." Various social media accounts also focus on the harsh working conditions of app-based delivery workers in urban India—for instance, the account of the Indian Federation of App Based Transport Workers on Facebook (and @connectifat on X/Twitter).

14. Lino e Silva, *Minoritarian Liberalism*, 13.

15. Ang, *Watching Dallas*, 18.

16. Hall quoted in Ang, *Watching Dallas*, 18.

17. See Paxson, *Life of Cheese*; and Sennett, *The Craftsman*.

18. Spinney, "Cycling the City," 29.

19. Freudendal-Pedersen, "Cyclists as Part of the City's Organism," 37.

20. In their interviews with cyclists in London, Katrina Jungnickel and Rachel Aldred similarly observed that "cycling can operate as a catalyst for reawakening dormant senses," such as "feeling the texture of the road." Jungnickel and Aldred, "Cycling's Sensory Strategies," 246. Moreover, respondents in their study reported that "they *feel* the city via the smells, sights and sounds" (247).

21. Furness, *One Less Car*, 89.

22. Hendren, *What Can the Body Do?*, 15.

23. Hendren, *What Can the Body Do?*, 15.

24. Tandems are just one type of cycle that serves as mobility assistive devices for people with disabilities. For instance, hand-operated tricycles are fairly common in urban India. Friedner and Osborne, "New Disability Mobilities."

25. Adventures beyond Barriers Foundation, accessed October 30, 2022, https://abbf.in/.

26. Hammer, "Pedaling in Pairs," 508.

27. Vicki Balfour, "Tandem Bicycles Explained, from How to Ride Them to All the Different Types," *Bike Radar*, October 16, 2023, https://www.bikeradar.com/advice/buyers-guides/tandem-cycles-explained/#:~:text=Only%20one%20of%20the%20riders,together%20with%20a%20timing%20chain.

28. Hammer writes, "tandem cycling requires collaboration . . . engendered by the need to coordinate technicalities such as balance, cadence, and force, as well as to consider each other's physical and emotional needs." Hammer, "Pedaling in Pairs," 513.

29. I participated in the Deccan Cliffhanger as an observer twice. In 2018, I rode the route in a race marshal vehicle. In 2019, I rode the route in an ABBF support truck that accompanied the cyclists throughout the event.

30. On bicycles as mobility assistive devices for people with low vision, see Wilson, "On the ADA's 30th."

31. Phadke, Khan, and Ranade, *Why Loiter?*, 181. The authors argue against "ideol-

ogies that privilege *safety* over *access* to public space" (67), while also recognizing the violence and dangers of public space and the state's culpability in not reducing them. Prioritizing access also emphasizes the importance of women "engaging city spaces on our own terms" (181).

32. Bunte, "Randonneurship," 160.

33. Tsui, *Why We Swim*, 111. I am inspired by Bonnie Tsui's writing on the embodied experience of swimming. Her book resonates with how I approach cycling because it centers embodied experience and materiality while also recognizing the symbolic significance of swimming in particular contexts.

34. Geertz, *Interpretation of Cultures*, 9.

4. Navigating Traffic

1. The journalist Mary Roach similarly writes that Mumbai's traffic, despite the outward appearance of chaos, can be surprisingly accommodating to cycling: "From the perspective of the cyclist, Mumbai traffic can move with a surprising, almost balletic fluidity. For long stretches of road, everyone—cars, bicycles, autorickshaws, motorbikes—moves at the same 15 miles per hour. . . . In India, drivers are accustomed to sharing the road with bicycles. They've been doing it for a century," unlike in the United States, where "drivers tend to view bicycles as interlopers, nuisances." Roach, "Honk Honk."

2. Lugo, *Bicycle/Race*, 45–46.

3. Tanushree Venkatraman, "Poor Infra Poses a Speed Bump as Mumbai Aims to Become Bicycle Capital of India," *Hindustan Times*, February 18, 2021, https://www.hindustantimes.com/cities/mumbai-news/poor-infra-poses-a-speed-bump-as-mumbai-aims-to-become-bicycle-capital-of-india-101613670764082.html.

4. Datey et al., "Walking and Cycling," 3.

5. Tiwari, Arora, and Jain, *Bicycling in Asia*, 23.

6. Pucher et al., "Cycling in China and India," 290–91.

7. Adonia Lugo calls this the "bike infrastructure strategy." Lugo, *Bicycle/Race*, 39. See Sadik-Khan and Solomonow, *Streetfight*; Colville-Anderson, *Copenhagenize*; and Bruntlett and Bruntlett, *Building the Cycling City*, for examples of this infrastructure-oriented perspective, which is also evident in the literature on creating a "bicycle level of service" metric (which complements the much older car-specific level of service metric for evaluating road and highway quality by measuring speed and traffic volume). Bicycle level of service typically focuses on the amount of heavy vehicle traffic, overall traffic speed, lane width, and pavement quality. See Sprinkle Consulting Inc., *Bicycle Level of Service*; and Landis, Vattikuti, and Brannick, "Real-Time Human Perceptions."

8. Edensor, "Automobility and National Identity." The documentary film *Why We Cycle*, directed by Arne Gielen and Gertjan Hulster, also contains a vivid representation and narration of the nonverbal ways people on bicycles communicate in complex traffic environments. I am also indebted to the anthropologist Melissa Cefkin for this framing of the traffic behaviors and mobility contexts that all cities contain. See Cefkin, "Dr. Melissa Cefkin, Nissan's Autonomous Car Anthropologist."

9. Edensor, "Automobility and National Identity," 116.

10. Edensor, "Automobility and National Identity," 112.

11. Writings that pay close attention to how people interact in different traffic environments include Vanderbilt, *Traffic*, 211–43; Bedi, *Mumbai Taximen*; and Annavarapu, "Moving Targets." Sneha Annavarapu in particular provides a vivid account of implicit driving knowledge in Hyderabad. Geetam Tiwari, in *Road Designs for Improving Traffic Flow*, offers a discussion of road use and traffic behavior in New Delhi, especially the tendency of people on bicycles and in slow-moving vehicles to move to the right. Vanderbilt, drawing from Tiwari's research, calls this phenomenon an example of the "logic" of traffic that might otherwise look like "anarchy in the eyes of conventional traffic engineering." Vanderbilt, *Traffic*, 217. Moreover, Alison Truitt provides an insightful discussion of the social conventions that "structure the movement of traffic" in Ho Chi Minh City, Vietnam. Truitt, "On the Back of a Motorbike," 13. See also Pinch and Reimer, "Moto-mobilities."

12. Truitt, "On the Back of a Motorbike," 4.

13. Lugo, *Bicycle/Race*, 36.

14. Shamsie, *Kartography*, 296. The concept of the ephemeral, unmapped city in *Kartography* is inspired by the book *Invisible Cities*, by Italo Calvino.

15. Shamsie, *Kartography*, 296.

16. Sheller and Urry, "City and the Car," 739. See also Urry, "'System' of Automobility."

17. For further discussion on heterogenous traffic in Indian cities, see Tiwari, *Road Designs for Improving Traffic Flow*.

18. Norton, *Fighting Traffic*.

19. Menoret, "Learning from Riyadh," 131. Catherine Lutz similarly describes a "car system" (a term used in place of automobility) as a "complex that includes the quasi-private and embodied technology of the car, governance practices, changed time-space conceptions, and landscapes of affordance to the car." Lutz, "U.S. Car Colossus," 232.

20. Quoted in Edensor, "Automobility and National Identity," 114.

21. Bedi, *Mumbai Taximen*.

22. Gupte and Shetty, "It Takes So Much."

23. The door zone refers to the three to four feet adjacent to parked cars where drivers opening a door can potentially hit passing cyclists and/or push them into oncoming traffic, severely injuring or killing them. See "Avoid the Door Zone," Active Transportation Alliance, accessed December 9, 2023, https://activetrans.org/resources/bike-to-work/avoid-the-door-zone.
24. Edensor, "Automobility and National Identity," 110.
25. Bedi, *Mumbai Taximen*, 71.
26. Sadik-Khan and Solomonow, "Mean Streets."
27. Sadik-Khan and Solomonow, "Mean Streets."
28. Sadik-Khan and Solomonow, "Mean Streets."
29. For an example of the writing emphasizing the danger of traffic friction, see Pucher et al., "Cycling in China and India." For an example of writing emphasizing the safety benefits of traffic friction, see Goel, Jain, and Tiwari, "Correlates of Fatality Risk."
30. Rajanbir Singh, "Chandigarh 4th Most Dangerous City for Cyclists in India," *Hindustan Times*, August 31, 2022, https://www.hindustantimes.com/cities/chandigarh-news/chandigarh-4th-most-dangerous-city-for-cyclists-in-india-101661896177263.html.
31. See, Goel, Jain, and Tiwari, "Correlates of Fatality Risk," 91.
32. Gopakumar, *Installing Automobility*, 5.
33. This phrasing is borrowed from the title of Ranajit Guha's book *Dominance without Hegemony*. Guha distinguishes a politically powerful entity, set of ideas, or people (i.e., dominance) that might not necessarily be normalized across society (i.e., hegemony). I am inspired by Dipesh Chakrabarty's way of putting it: "it was capitalist dominance without a hegemonic bourgeois culture—or, in Guha's famous terms, 'dominance without hegemony.'" Chakrabarty, *Provincializing Europe*, 15.
34. Bhatt and Basu, "How India Missed the Bus."
35. A driving instructor in Hyderabad told the sociologist Sneha Annavarapu that honking is about communication. He said that it is a way to stay safe and tell people you are nearby: "Sravan said, 'It is very risky if you don't honk. How else will someone know you are behind them?'" Annavarapu, "Moving Targets," 105.
36. The use of the English term "adjust" is common in many parts of India. Just as Hindi speakers use the phrase "adjust kar lo," Kannada speakers, for instance, often say "swalpa adjust maadi." Gowthaman Ranganathan, personal communication, August 30, 2021. Moreover, Harris Solomon focuses on adjustment in the context of triage in Mumbai hospitals: "I have argued for closer attention to adjustment that triage demands." Solomon, "Shifting Gears," 361. However, Solomon's use of "adjustment" does not have the connotation of "accommodation" evident in the phrase "adjust kar lo."

37. Walljasper, "Ten Ways Bicycle-Friendly Streets Are Good for People Who Don't Ride Bikes" (emphasis added).

38. Dinesh Mohan and Geetam Tiwari similarly observe that in New Delhi, "on two and three lane roads, bicycle traffic will always segregate itself into the curb sidelane even without any direction for the same." Mohan and Tiwari, "Sustainable Transport Systems," 5. Geetam Tiwari makes this point in numerous publications. In particular, see Tiwari, "Traffic Flow and Safety," for a discussion of heterogenous traffic interactions in Delhi. Moreover, Vanderbilt, summarizing Tiwari's research, writes, "Bicycles tend to form an impromptu bike lane in the curb lane; the more bikes, the wider the lane." Vanderbilt goes on to add that "lane discipline makes sense" in urban contexts with "homogenous traffic flows" but not necessarily in the contexts Tiwari describes. Vanderbilt, *Traffic*, 217. Allison Truitt describes similar self-segregating traffic in Ho Chi Minh City: "The vehicles that travel on the far right-hand side of the street are 'primitive vehicles' . . . —bicycles, cycles, and food carts. The vehicles that travel on the left-hand side are the mightier motorized vehicles with four or more wheels—private cars, passenger vans, and commercial trucks." Truitt, "On the Back of a Motorbike," 7. See also Edensor, "Automobility and National Identity," 115.

39. Various researchers have shown that streets with these de facto lanes for slower-moving vehicles are considerably safer for people walking and cycling. This is partly because the density and variety of vehicle types translates to lower motorized vehicle speeds. For example, "high density locations are more likely to have higher number[s] of pedestrians. In the absence of dedicated facilities for pedestrians and cyclists, the two slow-moving road users occupy the curb-side lane of the roads. This effectively slows down the traffic and makes roads safer." Here, "dedicated facilities for pedestrians and cyclists" refers to sidewalks and bicycle lanes or tracks. Goel, Jain, and Tiwari, "Correlates of Fatality Risk," 91.

40. Thanks to David Falcioni and Ulka Anjaria for sharing their firsthand observations on driving practices in India, which have informed this section of the chapter.

41. Annavarapu, "Moving Targets."

42. Annavarapu, "Moving Targets," 105. For a thorough discussion of embodied driving practices in Hyderabad, see Annavarapu, "Moving Targets," 85–107.

43. Tiwari, *Road Designs for Improving Traffic Flow*.

44. Tarini Bedi writes that driving in Mumbai is "characterized by congregational and entangled movement rather than the linearity one finds in Western driving contexts and where cars move in straight lines along straight roads." Bedi, *Mumbai Taximen*, 71.

45. The geographer Tim Edensor similarly observes that "because of the varied speeds and multi-directional routes adopted by road-users, pedestrians and an-

imals, car drivers in India have to be constantly aware of the flow of bodies and vehicles which crisscross the street, veering into and emerging out of courtyards, alleys and culs-de-sac." Edensor, "Automobility and National Identity," 114.

46. Annavarapu, "Moving Targets," 105.

47. Sennett, *Flesh and Stone*, 18.

48. See also Tiwari, *Road Designs for Improving Traffic Flow*, for a discussion of heterogenous traffic in India.

49. Edensor, "Automobility and National Identity," 112.

50. Chakrabarty, *Provincializing Europe*.

5   Are Bicycle Lanes the Future?

1. Ranjeet Jadhav, "Mumbai: 3 Years and Rs 6.5 cr Later, BKC Cycle Track to Go," *Mid-Day*, November 14, 2014, https://www.mid-day.com/mumbai /mumbai-news/article/mumbai—3-years-and-rs-6.5-cr-later—bkc-cycle -track-to-go-15765171.

2. In 2021, the MMRDA decided to implement a new bicycle network in Bandra Kurla Complex, this time using bollards to distinguish the bicycle lanes from sidewalks. Tanushree Venkatraman, "MMRDA's Cycle Vision Back on Track in BKC," *Hindustan Times*, February 9, 2021, https://www.hindustantimes .com/cities/mumbai-news/mumbai-mmrda-s-cycle-vision-back-on-track-in -bkc-101612894378360.html.

3. Chandigarh is notable for its large system of physically segregated bicycle lanes. However, lack of maintenance of these lanes also leads people to cycle on the roadway instead. See Barinderjit Saluja, "It's a Bumpy Ride on Chandigarh's Bicycle Tracks," *Times of India*, December 30, 2019, https:// timesofindia.indiatimes.com/city/chandigarh/its-a-bumpy-ride-on -chandigarhs-bicycle-tracks/articleshow/73025632.cms.

4. Thanks to Ashish Agashe (personal communication, July 2022) for the useful description of disconnected, impractical bicycle lanes as "islands."

5. Riyan Ramanath, "City's Much-Vaunted Cycle Tracks Become Parking Lots," *Times of India*, January 23, 2019, https://timesofindia.indiatimes.com/city /bhubaneswar/citys-much-vaunted-cycle-tracks-become-parking-lots/article show/67647063.cms; "Mulund Cycle Track or 'Adda' of Romance and Crime?," *Home Times*, last modified January 13, 2019, http://www.hometimes.in /mulund-cycle-track-or-adda-of-romance-and-crime/; Saswat Singh Deo, Shruti Zende, and Priyanka Kumari, "Pune Cycle Tracks Not for Cyclists for Sure," *DNA India*, May 26, 2014, https://www.dnaindia.com/pune/report -pune-cycle-tracks-not-for-cyclists-for-sure-1991313; Aditi R., "Chennai's First Cycling Track Taken Over," *Times of India*, February 10, 2020, https://times ofindia.indiatimes.com/city/chennai/chennais-first-cycling-track-taken-over

/articleshow/74059389.cms; Ojas Mehta, "Cyclists on Rise Even as Bicycle
Lanes Shrink," *Ahmedabad Mirror*, June 3, 2022, https://ahmedabadmirror
.com/cyclists-on-rise-even-as-bicycle-lanes-shrink/81834286.html.

6. Harvey and Knox, "Enchantments of Infrastructure," 523.

7. Schwenkel, "Spectacular Infrastructure," 520. Christina Schwenkel argues that
    infrastructure is framed as "spectacular socialist achievements that stood as em-
    blems of progress" (521).

8. For a discussion of spectacularizing water infrastructure, see Rawson, *Eden on
    the Charles*. For a related discussion of waste disposal and sanitation, see Nagle,
    Picking Up. Likewise, Rashmi Sadana's ethnography of the Delhi Metro de-
    scribes the everyday experience of the "mega-ness" of public transport. Sadana,
    Moving City, 10.

9. Sadana, *Moving City*, 10.

10. For a notable example of anthropological writing on the relationship between
    highways and power, see Khan, "Flaws in the Flow."

11. Furness, *One Less Car*.

12. Jungnickel and Aldred, "Cycling's Sensory Strategies," 239.

13. See Untokening Collective, "Untokening 1.0—Principles of Mobility Justice."

14. Hoffman, *Bike Lanes Are White Lanes*, 84.

15. @Jostehlin, post on Twitter, February 27, 2020.

16. Stehlin, *Cyclescapes of the Unequal City*, 107.

17. @Ashish.Agash.12, Facebook post, July 6, 2022. The quote is shared with per-
    mission and has been lightly edited for readability.

18. "Mumbai: BMC's Cycle Track at Carter Road Used by All but Cyclists," *Free
    Press Journal*, May 30, 2019, https://www.freepressjournal.in/cmcm/mumbai
    -bmcs-cycle-track-at-carter-rd-used-by-all-but-cyclists. See also Aparna Shukla,
    "Runner Injured by Shoddy Carter Road Divider to Sue BMC," *Mid-Day*, Janu-
    ary 13, 2017, https://www.mid-day.com/mumbai/mumbai-news/article
    /Mumbai-news-Mumbai-runner-injured-shoddy-Carter-Road-divider-BMC
    -lawsuit-Natasha-Tuli-17907152; and "Is Mumbai Ready for Cycle Tracks? Ban-
    dra Tells a Different Story," *Hindustan Times*, February 1, 2017, https://www
    .hindustantimes.com/mumbai-news/is-mumbai-ready-for-cycle-tracks
    -bandra-tells-a-different-story/story-Q25wkZNmecErpvEtW5akOM.html.

19. See Rademacher, *Building Green*, for a thorough account of aestheticized de-
    sign approaches to creating open or "green" spaces in Mumbai. In her book,
    Rademacher documents numerous examples of designs for open space creation
    in Mumbai that overlook how these spaces historically marginalize the poor.
    Moreover, it is important to note that the Green Wheels along Blue Lines project
    was not the first time Mumbai's water pipelines were imagined as sites for poten-
    tial design innovation. At the BMW Guggenheim Urban Lab held in Mumbai in

2011, the architect Neville Mars proposed creating a multimodal space above the Tansa pipeline: "The Landlink eventually combines an auto rickshaw highway and a pedestrian connection between several neighborhoods, while simultaneously providing a large public domain located right at the geographic heart of Greater Mumbai." BMW Guggenheim Lab, "Landlink Design Prototype."

20. For an account of the ways people in Mumbai slums organize and resist municipal demolition efforts, see Weinstein, *Durable Slum.*

21. "Mulund Cycle Track or 'Adda' of Romance and Crime?," *Home Times.*

22. Sonia Dutta, "Bengaluru: Now, Pop-Up Bicycle Lane on Outer Ring Road Disappears," *Times of India*, September 26, 2022, https://timesofindia.indiatimes .com/city/bengaluru/bengaluru-now-pop-up-bicycle-lane-n-outer-ring-road -disappears/articleshow/94441321.cms.

23. "Pune's Attempts to Become 'City of Cycles' Again Punctured Many Times," *Indian Express*, June 3, 2017, https://indianexpress.com/article/cities/pune/punes-attempts-to-become-city-of-cycles-again-punctured-many-times-4686622/.

24. Ranjit Gadgil, personal communication, February 2019, Pune.

25. Deo, Zende, and Kumari, "Pune Cycle Tracks Not for Cyclists for Sure," *DNA India.*

26. On one hand, traffic calming in dense urban areas is considered an ideal by transportation planners. One kind of traffic calming would be narrow streets that have a lot of non-car-based activity along the edge, including people walking. On the other hand, however, bicycle lanes are also justified because they *reduce* conflicts. So in theory, bicycle lanes installed in places that previously had eclectically used edges would remove the already existing traffic-calming features, which would make those streets less safe. I say "in theory" because I do not know of an example where a successful bicycle lane has been implemented this way in India. For research on traffic crashes in India and their relationship to density and mixed-use streets, see Goel, Jain, and Tiwari, "Correlates of Fatality Risk."

27. Snehal Sengupta, "New Town: Cycle Tracks Get Blocked by Vendors," *Telegraph*, January 7, 2022, https://www.telegraphindia.com/my-kolkata /news/new-town-cycle-tracks-get-blocked-by-vendors/cid/1846560; Prachi Bari, "Hawkers Encroach Footpaths, Cycle Tracks of Newly Constructed Roads, Cause Inconvenience," *Hindustan Times*, December 12, 2017, https:// www.hindustantimes.com/pune-news/hawkers-encroach-footpaths-cycle -tracks-o-newly-constructed-roads-cause-inconvenience/story-djL7imalxIja G5iKU1dc1M_amp.html.

28. On the significance of community building over infrastructure-oriented approaches to promoting cycling, see Lugo, *Bicycle/Race*; and Hoffman, *Bike Lanes Are White Lanes.*

29. How street vendors maintain informal ownership over space on the side of the street is the subject my book *The Slow Boil: Street Food, Rights, and Public Space in Mumbai*. See Bedi, *Mumbai Taximen*, for an account of how taxi drivers assert and retain informal rights to use the street edge in order to maintain, repair, and store their vehicles. Another notable book on this topic is Bandyopadhyay, *Streets in Motion*.

30. See Susamma Kurian, "Thane Cycling Lane Changes Track," *Hindustan Times*, March 18, 2010, https://www.hindustantimes.com/india/thane-cycling-lane -changes-track/story-M36ONLdXqfXMu4pMjqBM7I.html.

31. Naushad, "Vibrant Pune."

32. Pune Municipal Corporation, "Aundh Street Programme."

33. Thanks to Joe Barr, director of traffic and parking for the City of Cambridge, for his accounts of how street surface markings are maintained.

34. For an account of the effect regulatory and policing contexts have on the effectiveness of segregated bicycle lanes, see Meneses-Reyes, "Law and Mobility."

35. Jameson, "Realism and Utopia."

36. Jameson, "Realism and Utopia."

37. Harvey and Knox, "Enchantments of Infrastructure," 521.

38. Chakrabarty, *Provincializing Europe*.

39. The full comment is slightly edited for readability and to maintain the confidentiality of the author.

Conclusion

1. "Fifteen Year Old in India Cycles 745 Miles Home with Disabled Father on Bike," *The Guardian*, May 24, 2020, https://www.theguardian.com/world /2020/may/24/fifteen-year-old-in-india-cycles-745-miles-home-with-disabled -father-on-bike.

2. For examples of media coverage on the increase in cycling during the COVID-19 pandemic, see Ajita Shashidhar, "Cycling Becomes Popular Lockdown Past Time; Bicycle Demand Surges by 20 Per Cent," *Business Today*, May 31, 2021, https://www.businesstoday.in/latest/economy-politics/story/cycling -becomes-popular-lockdown-past-time-bicycle-demand-surges-by-20-per-cent -297454-2021-05-31; and Amrit Dhillon, "Two Wheels Good: India Falls Back in Love with Bikes," *The Guardian*, July 24, 2020, https://www.theguardian.com /global-development/2020/jul/24/two-wheels-better-than-four-india-falls -in-love-with-cycling-lockdown-coronavirus.

3. See Wagh, Indorewala, and Patel, "Mumbai's Coastal Road."

4. Calvino, *Invisible Cities*, quoted in Shamsie, *Kartography*, 296..

Bibliography

Aggarwal, Aditi, and Tarini Bedi. "*Dhandha*, Accumulation and the Making of Valuable Livelihoods in Contemporary Mumbai." *South Asia: Journal of South Asian Studies* 45, no. 4 (2022): 706–22. https://doi.org/10.1080/00856401.2022.2073711.

Agyeman, Julian. *Introducing Just Sustainabilities: Policy, Planning, and Practice.* London: Zed Books, 2013.

———. "Poor and Black 'Invisible Cyclists' Need to Be Part of Post-Pandemic Transport Planning Too." *The Conversation.* Last modified May 27, 2020. https://theconversation.com/poor-and-black-invisible-cyclists-need-to-be-part-of-post-pandemic-transport-planning-too-139145.

Aldred, Rachel. "'On the Outside': Constructing Cycling Citizenship." *Social & Cultural Geography* 11, no. 1 (2010): 35–52. https://doi.org/10.1080/14649360903414593.

Anand, Nikhil, Akhil Gupta, and Hannah Appel, eds. *The Promise of Infrastructure.* Durham, NC: Duke University Press, 2018.

Anantharaman, Manisha. "Elite and Ethical: The Defensive Distinctions of Middle-Class Bicycling in Bangalore, India." *Journal of Consumer Culture* 17, no. 3 (2016): 1–23. https://doi.org/10.1177/1469540516634412.

———. *Recycling Class: The Contradictions of Inclusion in Urban Sustainability.* Cambridge, MA: MIT Press, 2024.

Ang, Ien. *Watching Dallas: Soap Opera and the Melodramatic Imagination.* London: Routledge, 1985.

Angus, Hilary. "Three Women Who Changed the Course of History on Bicycles." *Momentum Magazine,* September 22, 2022. https://momentummag.com/three-women-changed-course-history-bicycle/.

Anjaria, Jonathan Shapiro. "Mumbai Has the Makings of a Great Cycling City—But It Needs to Set the Wheels in Motion." Scroll.in, September 16, 2017. https://scroll.in/article/844975/why-mumbai-has-the-makings-of-a-great-cycling-city.

———. *The Slow Boil: Street Food, Rights, and Public Space in Mumbai.* Stanford, CA: Stanford University Press, 2016.

Anjaria, Ulka. *Reading India Now: Contemporary Formations in Literature and Popular Culture.* Philadelphia: Temple University Press, 2019.

Annavarapu, Sneha. "Moving Targets: Traffic Rules, State Authority and Road Safety in Hyderabad, India." PhD diss., University of Chicago, 2020.

———. "Risky Routes, Safe Suspicions: Gender, Class, and Cabs in Hyderabad,

India." *Social Problems* 69, no. 3 (2022): 761–80. https://doi.org/10.1093/socpro
/spab008.

Anwar, Nausheen, and Malini Sur. "Keeping Cities in Motion: An Introduction to
the Labours of Repair and Maintenance in South Asia." *Economic and Political
Weekly* 55, no. 51 (December 26, 2020): 31–33. https://www.proquest.com
/docview/2473358879?accountid=9703.

Appel, Hannah. *The Licit Life of Capitalism: US Oil in Equatorial Guinea.* Durham,
NC: Duke University Press, 2019.

Archambault, Julie. "Sweaty Motions: Materiality, Meaning, and the Emerging
Workout Ethic in Mozambique." *American Ethnologist* 49, no. 3 (2022): 332–44.
https://doi.org/10.1111/amet.13086.

Arnold, David. "On the Road: A Social Itineration of India." *Contemporary South
Asia* 22, no. 1 (2014): 8–20. https://doi.org/10.1080/09584935.2013.870977.

———. "The Problem of Traffic: The Street-Life of Modernity in Late-Colonial
India." *Modern Asian Studies* 46, no. 1 (2012): 119–41.

Arnold, David, and Erich DeWald. "Cycles of Empowerment? The Bicycle and
Everyday Technology in Colonial India and Vietnam." *Comparative Studies in
Society and History* 53, no. 4 (2011): 971–96. https://doi.org/10.1017/S00104
17511000478.

Arora, Anvita. "A Gendered Perspective on Bicycling." In *Bicycling in Asia,* edited by
Geetam Tiwari, Anvita Arora, and Himani Jain, 131–38. N.p.: Interface for Cycling
Expertise (ICE), The Netherlands, and Transport Research & Injury Prevention
Programme, IIT Delhi, 2008.

Bandyopadhyay, Ritajyoti. *Streets in Motion: The Making of Infrastructure, Property
and Political Culture in Twentieth-Century Calcutta.* Cambridge: Cambridge
University Press, 2022.

Battista, Garth, ed. *Bicycle Love: Stories of Passion, Joy, and Sweat.* New York:
Breakaway Books, 2004.

Baviskar, Amita. *Uncivil City: Ecology, Equity and the Commons in Delhi.* New Delhi:
SAGE, 2020.

Bedi, Tarini. *Mumbai Taximen: Autobiographies and Automobilities in India.* Seattle:
University of Washington Press, 2022.

Bennett, Jane. *Vibrant Matter: A Political Ecology of Things.* Durham, NC: Duke
University Press, 2009.

Berger, John. *Keeping a Rendezvous.* New York: Vintage International, 1992.

Best, Stephen, and Sharon Marcus. "Surface Reading: An Introduction."
Representations 108, no. 1 (Fall 2009): 1–21. https://doi.org/10.1525/rep.2009.108.1.1.

Bhatt, Sarika Panda, and Akash V. Basu. "How India Missed the Bus—and Why We
Must Catch Up Now." Scroll.in, June 26, 2022. https://scroll.in/article/1025106
/how-india-missed-the-bus-and-why-we-must-catch-up-now.

Bishara, Amahl. "Driving While Palestinian in Israel and the West Bank: The Politics of Disorientation and the Routes of a Subaltern Knowledge." *American Ethnologist* 42, no. 1 (2015): 33–54. https://doi.org/10.1111/amet.12114.

Björkman, Lisa, ed. *Bombay Brokers*. Durham, NC: Duke University Press, 2021.

———. *Pipe Politics, Contested Waters: Embedded Infrastructures of Millennial Mumbai*. Durham, NC: Duke University Press, 2015.

BMW Guggenheim Lab. "Landlink Design Prototype." Accessed October 30, 2022. http://www.bmwguggenheimlab.org/where-is-the-lab/mumbai-lab/mumbai -lab-city-projects/landlink-design-prototype.

Borden, Iain. *Skateboarding and the City: A Complete History*. London: Bloomsbury, 2019.

Bourgois, Philippe, and Jeff Schonberg. *Righteous Dopefiend*. Berkeley: University of California Press, 2009.

Brosius, Christiane. *India's Middle Class: New Forms of Urban Leisure, Consumption and Prosperity*. London: Routledge, 2010.

Brown, Charles T. "Mobility & Equity with Charles T. Brown, Equitable Cities." *Govlove: A Podcast about Local Government*, May 21, 2021. https://elgl.org/ podcast-mobility-equity-with-charles-t-brown-equitable-cities/.

Brown, Charles T., with J'Lin Rose and Samuel King. *Arrested Mobility: Barriers to Walking, Biking and e-Scooter Use in Black Communities in the United States*. Report from Equitable Cities, March 2023.

Brunson, Jan. "'Scooty Girls': Mobility and Intimacy at the Margins of Kathmandu." *Ethnos* 79, no. 5 (2014): 610–29. https://doi.org/10.1080/00141844.2013.813056.

Bruntlett, Melissa, and Chris Bruntlett. *Building the Cycling City: The Dutch Blueprint for Urban Vitality*. Washington, DC: Island Press, 2018.

Bunte, Heike. "Randonneurship—a Modern Cycling Construction." In *Cycling Cultures*, edited by Peter Cox. Chester, UK: University of Chester Press, 2015.

Butler, Tamika. "Why We Must Talk about Race When We Talk about Bikes." *Bicycling Magazine*, June 9, 2020. https://www.bicycling.com/culture/a32783551 /cycling-talk-fight-racism/.

Calvino, Italo. *Invisible Cities*. Translated by William Weaver. London: Harcourt, 1974.

Cefkin, Melissa. "Dr. Melissa Cefkin, Nissan's Autonomous Car Anthropologist." *Autonocast: The Future of Transportation* (podcast), February 8, 2018. http:// www.autonocast.com/blog/2018/2/8/52-dr-melissa-cefkin-nissans-autonomous -car-anthropologist.

Chakrabarty, Dipesh. *Habitations of Modernity: Essays in the Wake of Subaltern Studies*. Chicago: University of Chicago Press, 2002.

———. "Of Garbage, Modernity, and the Citizen's Gaze." *Economic and Political Weekly* 27, no. 10–11 (1992): 541–47.

————. *Provincializing Europe: Postcolonial Thought and Historical Difference.*
Princeton: Princeton University Press, 2000.

Colville-Anderson, Mikael. *Copenhagenize: The Definitive Guide to Global Bicycle Urbanism.* Washington, DC: Island Press, 2018.

Conquergood, Dwight. *Cultural Struggles: Performance, Ethnography, Praxis.* Ann Arbor: University of Michigan Press, 2013.

Copenhagenize Index. "The Most Bicycle-Friendly Cities of 2019." 2019. https://copenhagenizeindex.eu/about/the-index.

Cox, Peter. "Cycling Cultures and Social Theory." In *Cycling Cultures,* edited by Peter Cox. Chester, UK: University of Chester Press, 2015.

Date, Vidyadhar. "Bicycle Treated as a Party Symbol, Not a Vehicle of Democracy." *Counter Currents,* March 10, 2012. https://www.countercurrents.org/date100312.htm.

Datey, Abhijit, Vishal Darji, Tejas Patel, and Darshini Mahadevia. "Walking and Cycling in Indian Roads: A Struggle for Reclaiming Edges." Working paper 18, Centre for Urban Equity, CEPT University, Ahmedabad, 2012.

Davis, Veronica O. *Inclusive Transportation: A Manifesto for Repairing Divided Communities.* Washington, DC: Island Press, 2023.

"A Defunct Bicycle Factory." *Pedal and Tring Tring,* December 13, 2019. https://pedalandtringtring.com/2019/12/13/a-defunct-bicycle-factory/#more-4001.

Demetriou, Olga. "Reconsidering the Vignette as Method: Art, Ethnography, and Refugee Studies." *American Ethnologist* 50, no. 2 (2023): 208–22. https://doi.org/10.1111/amet.13145.

Doshi, Sapana. "Embodied Urban Political Ecology: Five Propositions." *Area* 49, no. 1 (2017): 125–28. https://doi.org/10.1111/area.12293.

Edensor, Timothy. "Automobility and National Identity: Representation, Geography and Driving Practice." *Theory, Culture and Society* 21, no. 4–5 (2004): 101–20. https://doi.org/10.1177/0263276404046063.

Elyachar, Julia. "Phatic Labor, Infrastructure, and the Question of Empowerment in Cairo." *American Ethnologist* 37, no. 3 (2010): 452–64. https://doi.org/10.1111/j.1548-1425.2010.01265.x.

————. "The Political Economy of Movement and Gesture in Cairo." *Journal of the Royal Anthropological Institute* 17, no. 1 (2011): 82–99. https://doi.org/10.1111/j.1467-9655.2010.01670.x.

[The] Energy and Resources Institute (TERI) and All India Cycle Manufacturers' Association (AICMA). *Benefits of Cycling in India: An Economic, Environmental, and Social Assessment.* New Delhi: TERI, 2018.

Felski, Rita. *The Limits of Critique.* Chicago: University of Chicago Press, 2015.

Fennell, Catherine. "'Project Heat' and Sensory Politics in Redeveloping Chicago Public Housing." *Ethnography* 12, no. 1 (2011): 40–46. https://doi.org/10.1177/1466138110387221.

Ferguson, James. *The Anti-Politics Machine: Development, Depoliticization, and Bureaucratic Power in Lesotho*. Minneapolis: University of Minnesota Press, 1994.

Fernandes, Leela. "The Politics of Forgetting: Class Politics, State Power and the Restructuring of Urban Space in India." *Urban Studies* 41, no. 12 (2004): 2415–30. https://doi.org/10.1080/00420980412331297609.

Finkelstein, Maura. *The Archive of Loss: Lively Ruination in Mill Land Mumbai*. Durham, NC: Duke University Press, 2019.

Fournel, Paul. *Need for the Bike*. Lincoln: University of Nebraska Press, 2003.

Friedner, Michele, and Jamie Osborne. "New Disability Mobilities and Accessibilities in Urban India." *City & Society* 27, no. 1 (2015): 9–29. https://doi.org/10.1111/ciso.12054.

Freudendal-Pedersen, Malene. "Cyclists as Part of the City's Organism: Structural Stories on Cycling in Copenhagen." *City & Society* 27, no. 1 (2015): 30–50. https://doi.org/10.1111/ciso.12051.

Furness, Zack. *One Less Car: Bicycling and the Politics of Automobility*. Philadelphia: Temple University Press, 2010.

Gamble, Julie. "Playing with Infrastructure Like a Carishina: Feminist Cycling in an Era of Democratic Politics." *Antipode* 51, no. 4 (2019): 1166–84. https://doi.org/10.1111/anti.12533.

Geertz, Clifford. *Interpretation of Cultures*. New York: Basic Books, 1973.

Ghosh, Bipashyee, and Fariya Sharmeen. "Understanding Cycling Regime Transition and Inequality in the Global South: Case Study of an Indian Megacity." In *Cycling Societies: Innovations, Inequalities and Governance*, edited by Dennis Zuev, Katerina Psarikidou, and Cosmin Popan, 201–18. London: Routledge, 2021.

Gielen, Arne, and Gertjan Hulster, dirs. *Why We Cycle*. Nieuw & Verbeterd, 2018.

Goel, Rahul, Parth Jain, and Geetam Tiwari. "Correlates of Fatality Risk of Vulnerable Road Users in Delhi." *Accident: Analysis and Prevention* 111 (February 2017): 86–93. https://doi.org/10.1016/j.aap.2017.11.023.

Golub, Aaron, Melody L. Hoffman, Adonia E. Lugo, and Gerardo F. Sandoval, eds. *Bicycle Justice and Urban Transformation: Cycling for All?* London: Routledge, 2017.

Gopakumar, Govind. *Installing Automobility: Emerging Politics of Mobility and Streets in Indian Cities*. Cambridge, MA: MIT Press, 2020.

Government of India. *National Family Health Survey* (NFHS-5), 2019–21. India: Volume 1. Mumbai: International Institute for Population Sciences (IIPS) and ICF, 2021. https://dhsprogram.com/pubs/pdf/FR375/FR375.pdf.

Graham, Stephen, and Colin McFarlane, eds. *Infrastructural Lives: Urban Infrastructure in Context*. London: Routledge, 2016.

Guha, Ranajit. *Dominance without Hegemony: History and Power in Colonial India*. Cambridge, MA: Harvard University Press, 1998.

Gupte, Rupali, and Prasad Shetty. "It Takes So Much for a City to Happen."
    Supercommunity e-flux, August 7, 2015. http://supercommunity.e-flux.com/texts
    /it-takes-so-much-for-a-city-to-happen/.

Guroff, Margaret. *The Mechanical Horse: How the Bicycle Reshaped American Life.*
    Austin: University of Texas Press, 2016.

Hammer, Gili. "Pedaling in Pairs toward a 'Dialogical Performance': Partnerships
    and the Sensory Body within a Tandem Cycling Group." *Ethnography* 16, no. 4
    (2014): 503–22. https://doi.org/10.1177/1466138114552950.

Harvey, Penny, and Hannah Knox. "The Enchantments of Infrastructure." *Mobilities*
    7, no. 4 (2014): 521–36. https://doi.org/10.1080/17450101.2012.718935.

Helphand, Kenneth I. "The Bicycle Kodak." *Environmental Review* 4, no. 3 (1980):
    24–33. https://doi.org/10.2307/3984318.

Hendren, Sara. *What Can a Body Do? How We Meet the Built World.* New York:
    Riverhead Books, 2020.

Herlihy, David. *Bicycle: The History.* New Haven: Yale University Press, 2004.

Hoffman, Melody L. *Bike Lanes Are White Lanes: Bicycle Advocacy and Urban
    Planning.* Lincoln: University of Nebraska Press, 2016.

Horton, Dave, Paul Rosen, and Peter Cox, eds. *Cycling and Society.* Burlington, VT:
    Ashgate, 2007.

Huet, Natalie. "These Are the 10 Most Bike-Friendly Cities in the World (and 9 of
    Them Are in Europe)." *Euronews.* Accessed June 28, 2023. https://www.euronews
    .com/next/2023/06/20/these-are-the-top-10-bike-friendly-cities-in-the-world
    -and-9-of-them-are-in-europe.

Ingold, Tim. *The Perception of the Environment: Essays on Livelihood, Dwelling and
    Skill.* London: Routledge, 2000.

Jameson, Fredric. "Realism and Utopia in *The Wire*." *Criticism* 52, no. 3–4 (2010):
    359–72. https://muse.jhu.edu/article/447304.

Jamwal, Nidhi. "Why Firoza Came to Be Known as Mulund ki Cyclewali."
    The Better India, October 15, 2014. https://www.thebetterindia.com/15046
    /cyclewali-firoza-mumbai-cycling/.

John Abraham Architects. "The Carter Road Cycling Project." The Bombay
    Greenway, 2020. https://www.bombaygreenway.org/the-carter-road-cycling
    -project.

Jones, Phil. "Performing the City: A Body and a Bicycle Take on Birmingham, UK."
    Social & Cultural Geography 6, no. 6 (2006): 813–30. https://doi.org
    /10.1080/14649360500353046.

Joshi, Rutul. "Mobility Practices of the Urban Poor in Ahmedabad (India)." PhD
    diss., University of the West of England, Bristol, 2014.

Joshi, Rutul, and Yogi Joseph. "Invisible Cyclists and Disappearing Cycles: The

Challenges of Cycling Policies in Indian Cities." *Transfers* 5, no. 3 (2015): 23–40. https://doi.org/10.3167/TRANS.2015.050303.

Jungnickel, Kat. *Bikes and Bloomers: Victorian Women Inventors and Their Extraordinary Cycle Wear.* London: Goldsmiths Press, 2018.

Jungnickel, Katrina, and Rachel Aldred. "Cycling's Sensory Strategies: How Cyclists Mediate Their Exposure to the Urban Environment." *Mobilities* 9, no. 2 (2013): 238–55. https://doi.org/10.1080/17450101.2013.796772.

Kannan, Divya. "The Journey since 1947–III: Can the Bicycle Come Full Circle in India?" *The India Forum*, September 14, 2022. https://www.theindiaforum.in /article/journey-1947-can-bicycle-come-full-circle-india.

Kaviraj, Sudipta. "Filth and the Public Sphere: Concepts and Practices about Space in Calcutta." *Public Culture* 10, no. 1 (1997): 83–113. https://doi.org/10.1215 /08992363-10-1-83.

Khan, Naveeda. "Flaws in the Flow: Roads and Their Modernity in Pakistan." *Social Text* 24, no. 4 (2006): 87–113. https://doi.org/10.1215/01642472-2006-012.

Kidambi, Prashant. *The Making of an Indian Metropolis: Colonial Governance and Public Culture in Bombay, 1890–1920.* Burlington, VT: Ashgate, 2007.

Kidder, Jeffery. *Urban Flow: Bike Messengers and the City.* Ithaca: ILR Press, an imprint of Cornell University Press, 2011.

Krabbé, Tim. *The Rider.* Translated by Sam Garrett. New York: Bloomsbury, 2002.

Kuroda, Ken. "Shankar: Delivering Authenticity." In *Bombay Brokers*, edited by Lisa Björkman, 208–15. Durham, NC: Duke University Press, 2021.

Landis, Bruce W., Venkat R. Vattikuti, and Michael T. Brannick. "Real-Time Human Perceptions: Toward a Bicycle Level of Service." *Transportation Research Record: Journal of the Transportation Research Board* 1578, no. 1 (1997): 119–26. https://doi .org/10.3141/1578-15.

Larkin, Brian. "The Politics and Poetics of Infrastructure." *Annual Review of Anthropology* 42 (2013): 327–43. https://doi.org/10.1146/annurev-anthro -092412-155522.

———. *Signal and Noise: Media, Infrastructure, and Urban Culture in Nigeria.* Durham, NC: Duke University Press, 2008.

Lee, Doreen. "Absolute Traffic: Infrastructural Aptitude in Urban Indonesia." *International Journal of Urban and Regional Research* 39, no. 2 (2015): 234–50. https://doi.org/10.1111/1468-2427.12212.

Lino e Silva, Moisés. *Minoritarian Liberalism: A Travesti Life in a Brazilian Favela.* Chicago: University of Chicago Press, 2022.

Lowrie, Ian. "Dominic Boyer on the Anthropology of Infrastructure." *Platypus* (blog), March 3, 2014. https://blog.castac.org/2014/03/dominic-boyer-on-the -anthropology-of-infrastructure/.

Lugo, Adonia E. *Bicycle/Race: Transportation, Culture, and Resistance*. Portland, OR: Microcosm, 2018.

———. "Body-City-Machines: Human Infrastructure for Bicycling in Los Angeles." PhD diss., University of California, Irvine, 2013.

Lutz, Catherine. "The U.S. Car Colossus and the Production of Inequality." *American Ethnologist* 41, no. 2 (2014): 232–45. https://doi.org/10.1111/amet.12072.

Lutz, Catherine, and Anne Lutz Fernandez. *Carjacked: The Culture of the Automobile and Its Effect on Our Lives*. New York: Palgrave Macmillan, 2010.

Maini, Nidhi. "Dressed Up and on the Go: Women Cyclists in Modern Japan." *China Report* 56, no. 2 (2020): 259–81.

Mathur, Nita. "Shopping Malls, Credit Cards and Global Brands: Consumer Culture and Lifestyle of India's New Middle Class." *South Asia Research* 30, no. 3 (2010): 211–31. https://doi.org/10.1177/026272801003000301.

Meneses-Reyes, Rodrigo. "Law and Mobility: Ethnographical Accounts of the Regulation of the Segregated Cycle Facilities in Mexico City." *Mobilities* 10, no. 2 (2015): 230–48. https://doi.org/10.1080/17450101.2013.853388.

Menoret, Pascal. "Learning from Riyadh: Automobility, Joyriding, and Politics." *Comparative Studies of South Asia, Africa and the Middle East* 39, no. 1 (2019): 131–42.

Mhaske, Pandurang. "Mumbai Rides on Paver Blocks." *Mumbai Votes*, September 11, 2008. http://mumbaivotes.com/articles/3444/.

Millar, Kathleen. *Reclaiming the Discarded: Life and Labor on Rio's Garbage Dump*. Durham, NC: Duke University Press, 2018.

Miller, Daniel, and Sophie Woodward. "A Manifesto for the Study of Denim." UCL Anthropology. Accessed October 30, 2022. https://www.ucl.ac.uk/anthropology/people/academic-and-teaching-staff/daniel-miller/manifesto-study-denim.

Miller, Thaddeus R., and Amy Lubitow. "The Politics of Sustainability: Contested Urban Bikeway Development in Portland, Oregon." In *Incomplete Streets: Processes, Practices and Possibilities*, edited by Stephen Zavestoski and Julian Agyeman, 266–89. London: Routledge, 2015.

Mohan, Dinesh, and Geetam Tiwari. "Sustainable Transport Systems: Linkages between Environmental Issues, Public Transport, Non-Motorised Transport and Safety." *Economic and Political Weekly* 34, no. 25 (June 19–25, 1999): 1589–96. https://www.jstor.org/stable/4408103.

Monteiro, Fabiola. "Public Space: The Steps in the Right Direction." *Paper Planes*, July 31, 2020. https://www.joinpaperplanes.com/public-space-the-steps-right-direction/.

NACTO. *Urban Bikeway Design Guide*. National Association of City Transportation Officials. Accessed October 3, 2023. https://nacto.org/publication/urban-bikeway-design-guide/.

Nagle, Robin. *Picking Up: On the Streets and behind the Trucks with the Sanitation Workers of New York City*. New York: Farrar, Straus, and Giroux, 2013.

"Na mera, na hamara, yeh to ladkiyon ka bihar hai." NDTV, October 13, 2015. https://ndtv.in/videos/prime-time-not-mine-nor-ours-it-is-the-bihar-of-girls-386736.

Naraharisetty, Rohitha. "In the Gig Economy, Customers Are Complicit in Labor Exploitation." *The Swaddle*, August 20, 2021. https://theswaddle.com/swiggy-zomato-labor-exploitation/.

Naushad, Nashwa. "Vibrant Pune: City's Streets Transform into Vital Public Spaces." Institute for Transportation and Development Policy, August 31, 2017. https://www.itdp.org/2017/08/31/vibrant-pune-transforming-streets/.

Ng, Angie. "Top 10 Worst Cities for Cycling." We Love Cycling: Urban Cycling. Last modified January 27, 2017. https://www.welovecycling.com/wide/2017/01/27/top-10-worst-cities-cycling/.

Norton, Peter D. *Fighting Traffic: The Dawn of the Motor Age in the American City*. Cambridge, MA: MIT Press, 2008.

Oldenziel, Ruth, and Adri Albert de la Bruhèze. "Contested Spaces: Bicycle Lanes in Urban Europe, 1900–1995." *Transfers* 1, no. 2 (2011): 29–49. https://doi.org/10.3167/trans.2011.010203.

Paxson, Heather. *The Life of Cheese: Crafting Food and Value in America*. Berkeley: University of California Press, 2013.

Phadke, Shilpa, Sameera Khan, and Shilpa Ranade. *Why Loiter? Women and Risk on Mumbai Streets*. New Delhi: Penguin, 2011.

Pinch, Philip, and Suzanne Reimer. "Moto-mobilities: Geographies of the Motorcycle and Motorcyclists." *Mobilities* 7, no. 3 (2012): 439–57. https://doi.org/10.1080/17450101.2012.659466.

Poonam, Snigdha. *Dreamers: How Young Indians Are Changing the World*. Cambridge, MA: Harvard University Press, 2018.

Pucher, John, Geetam Tiwari, Zhong-Ren Peng, Rong Cao, and Yuan Gao. "Cycling in China and India." In *Cycling for Sustainable Cities*, edited by Ralph Buehler and John Pucher, 281–300. Cambridge, MA: MIT Press, 2021.

Pune Municipal Corporation. "Aundh Street Programme: From Road to 'Street.'" National Association of City Transportation Officials, September 2017. https://nacto.org/wp-content/uploads/2017/09/Pune.pdf.

Puranik, Radha. "Understanding Mumbai's Municipal Corporation." *Citizen Matters*, March 28, 2022. https://mumbai.citizenmatters.in/understanding-mumbais-municipal-corporation-30461.

Rademacher, Anne. *Building Green: Environmental Architects and the Struggle for Sustainability in Mumbai*. Oakland: University of California Press, 2017.

Ramakrishnan, Kavita, Kathleen O'Reilly, and Jessica Budds. "Between Decay and

Repair: Embodied Experiences of Infrastructure's Materiality." *Environment and Planning E: Nature and Space* 4, no. 3 (2020): 669–73. https://doi.org/10.1177/2514848620980597.

Rawson, Michael. *Eden on the Charles: The Making of Boston.* Cambridge, MA: Harvard University Press, 2010.

Reid, Carlton. *Roads Were Not Built for Cars: How Cyclists Were the First to Push for Good Roads and Became the Pioneers of Motoring.* Washington, DC: Island Press, 2015.

Rhoads, Edward J. M. "Cycles of Cathay: A History of the Bicycle in China." *Transfers* 2, no. 2 (Summer 2012): 95–120.

Roach, Mary. "Honk Honk BRIING BRIING (Look Out!) Make Way for the Bike Riders." *Bicycling*, June 19, 2013. https://www.bicycling.com/rides/a20012222/biking-mumbai-india/.

Roe, Dan. "Black Cyclists Are Stopped More Often than Whites, Police Data Shows." *Bicycling*, July 27, 2020. https://www.bicycling.com/culture/a33383540/cycling-while-black-police/.

Rosen, Jody. "The Bicycle as a Vehicle of Protest." *New Yorker*, June 10, 2020. https://www.newyorker.com/culture/cultural-comment/the-bicycle-as-a-vehicle-of-protest.

Rudd, Jean Porter. "My Wheel and I." *Outing Magazine* 25 (May 1895): 124–28.

Rudick, Roger. "SPUR Talk: Equity, Outreach, and the Oakland Bike Plan." *Streets Blog SF.* Last modified June 13, 2019. https://sf.streetsblog.org/2019/06/13/spur-talk-equity-outreach-and-the-oakland-bike-plan.

Sacco, Katherine. "Latent Commons in the City." Member Voices, *Fieldsights*, June 8, 2017. https://culanth.org/fieldsights/latent-commons-in-the-city.

Sadana, Rashmi. *The Moving City: Scenes from the Delhi Metro and the Social Life of Infrastructure.* Oakland: University of California Press, 2022.

Sadik-Khan, Janette, and Seth Solomonow. "Mean Streets: The Global Traffic Death Crisis." *Foreign Affairs*, March–April 2020. https://www.foreignaffairs.com/articles/world/2020-02-10/mean-streets.

———. *Streetfight: Handbook for an Urban Revolution.* New York: Penguin Books, 2016.

Sainath, Palagummi. "Where There Is a Wheel." *People's Archive of Rural India*, June 13, 2018. https://medium.com/@ruralindiaorg/where-there-is-a-wheel-b056ac1a4931.

Schwenkel, Christina. "Spectacular Infrastructure and Its Breakdown in Socialist Vietnam." *American Ethnologist* 42, no. 3 (2015): 520–34. https://doi.org/10.1111/amet.12145.

Scott, James C. *Seeing Like a State: How Certain Schemes to Improve the Human Condition Have Failed.* New Haven: Yale University Press, 1998.

Sennett, Richard. *The Craftsman.* New Haven: Yale University Press, 2008.

———. *Flesh and Stone: The Body and the City in Western Civilization.* New York: Norton, 1996.

Sethi, Aman. *A Free Man: A True Story of Life and Death in Delhi.* Noida, Uttar Pradesh: Random House, 2011.

Shakti: Sustainable Energy Foundation (SSEF). *Planning and Design Guideline for Cycle Infrastructure.* Delhi: SSEF, n.d.

Shamsie, Kamila. *Kartography.* Orlando, FL: Harcourt, 2004.

Sheller, Mimi. "Racialized Mobility Transitions in Philadelphia: Connecting Urban Sustainability and Transport Justice." *City & Society* 27, no. 1 (2015): 70–91. https://doi.org/10.1111/ciso.12049.

Sheller, Mimi, and John Urry. "The City and the Car." *International Journal of Urban and Regional Research* 24, no. 4 (2000): 737–57. https://doi.org/10.1111/1468 -2427.00276.

Simone, AbdouMaliq. "People as Infrastructure: Intersecting Fragments in Johannesburg." *Public Culture* 16, no. 3 (2004): 407–29.

Solomon, Harris. "Death Traps: Holes in Urban India." *Environment and Planning D: Society and Space* 39, no. 3 (2021): 423–40. https://doi.org/10.1177 /0263775821989700.

———. "Shifting Gears: Triage and Traffic in Urban India." *Medical Anthropology Quarterly* 31, no. 3 (2017): 349–64. https://doi.org/10.1111/maq.12367.

Sopranzetti, Claudio. *Owners of the Map: Motorcycle Taxi Drivers, Mobility, and Politics in Bangkok.* Oakland: University of California Press, 2018.

Spinney, Justin. "Cycling the City: Non-Place and the Sensory Construction of Meaning in a Mobile Practice." In *Cycling and Society*, edited by Dave Horton, Paul Rosen, and Peter Cox, 25–46. Hampshire, UK: Ashgate, 2007.

———. "A Place of Sense: A Kinaesthetic Ethnography of Cyclists on Mont Ventoux." *Environment and Planning D: Society and Space* 24, no. 5 (2006): 709–32. https://doi.org/10.1068/d66j.

———. *Understanding Urban Cycling: Exploring the Relationship between Mobility, Sustainability and Capital.* London: Routledge, 2020.

Sprinkle Consulting, Inc. *Bicycle Level of Service: Applied Model.* Tampa, FL: Sprinkle Consulting, 2007. https://nacto.org/docs/usdg/bicylce_Level_of _service_model_sprinkle_consulting.pdf.

Srivastava, Rahul, and Matias Echanove. "Tool-House Case Study: The urbz Office." urbz, May 21, 2012. https://urbz.net/articles/tool-house-case-study-urbz-office.

Srivastava, Sanjay. "The Meaning of the Sports Bicycle." *Kafila.* Last modified October 29, 2015. https://kafila.online/2015/10/29/the-meaning-of-the-sports -bicycle-sanjay-srivastava.

———. "National Identity, Kitchens, and Bedrooms: Gated Communities and

New Narratives of Space in India." In *The Global Middle Classes*, edited by Mark Leichty, Carla Freeman, and Rachel Heiman, 57–84. Santa Fe, NM: School of Advanced Research Press, 2012.

Stainova, Yana. "Enchantment as Method." *Anthropology and Humanism* 44, no. 2 (2019): 214–30. https://doi.org/10.1111/anhu.12251.

Stamatopoulou-Robbins, Sophia. *Waste Siege: The Life of Infrastructure in Palestine.* Stanford, CA: Stanford University Press, 2019.

Stehlin, John G. *Cyclescapes of the Unequal City: Bicycle Infrastructure and Uneven Development*. Minneapolis: University of Minnesota Press, 2019.

Stewart, Kathleen. *A Space on the Side of the Road: Cultural Poetics in an "Other" America*. Princeton: Princeton University Press, 1996.

Sulaiman, Sahra. "Equity 101: Bikes v. Bodies on Bikes." *Streets Blog LA*, September 28, 2016. https://la.streetsblog.org/2016/09/28/equity-101-bikes-v-bodies-on -bikes/.

Sur, Malini. "Ambient Air: Kolkata's Bicycle Politics and Post-carbon Futures." In *Disastrous Time: Beyond Environmental Crisis in Urbanizing Asia*, edited by Eli Elinoff and Tyson Vaughan, 65–82. Philadelphia: University of Pennsylvania Press, 2021.

———. "Cultures of Repair: Cargo-Cycles and Kinship in Kolkata." *Economic and Political Weekly* 55, no. 51 (2020): 34–39. https://www.epw.in/journal/2020/51 /review-urban-affairs/cultures-repair.html.

Tarfe, Abhishek. "The Custom Point Race." Velocrush, May 28, 2016. https:// velocrushindia.com/the-custom-point-race/.

Tate, Divya. "Retrospective—1992–2022." *Cycling Journal Podcast*, July 8, 2022. https://open.spotify.com/episode/3qfeit3sN67fqsahj2pl29.

Tiwari, Geetam. *Road Designs for Improving Traffic Flow: A Bicycle Master Plan for Delhi*. Report of the Transportation Research & Injury Prevention Programme, IIT New Delhi, 1999.

———. "Traffic Flow and Safety: Need for New Models for Heterogeneous Traffic." In *Injury Prevention and Control*, edited by Dinesh Mohan and Geetam Tiwari, 71–88. London: CRC Press, 2014.

Tiwari, Geetam, Anvita Arora, and Himani Jain. *Bicycling in Asia*. Report from the Interface for Cycling Expertise, I-CE, The Netherlands and Transport Research and Injury Prevention Programme, Indian Institute of Technology Delhi, 2008.

Tiwari, Geetam, and Nishant. *Travel to Work in India: Current Patterns and Future Concerns*. Report from the Transportation Research and Injury Prevention Programme, Indian Institute of Technology Delhi, 2018.

Torres-Barragán, Camilo Alfonso, Caitlin D. Cottrill, and Mark Beecroft. "Spatial

Inequalities and Media Representation of Cycling Safety in Bogotá, Colombia."
Transportation Research Interdisciplinary Perspectives 7 (2020): 1–11. https://doi
.org/10.1016/j.trip.2020.100208.

Trovalla, Ulrika, and Eric Trovalla. "Infrastructure Turned Suprastructure:
Unpredictable Materialities and Visions of a Nigerian Nation." *Journal of Material
Culture* 20, no. 1 (2015): 43–57.

Truitt, Allison, "On the Back of a Motorbike: Middle-Class Mobility in Ho Chi
Minh City, Vietnam." *American Ethnologist* 35, no. 1 (2008): 3–19. https://doi.org
/10.1111/j.1548-1425.2008.00002.x.

Tsing, Anna Lowenhaupt. *Mushroom at the End of the World: On the Possibility of Life
in Capitalist Ruins.* Princeton: Princeton University Press, 2015.

Tsui, Bonnie. *Why We Swim.* Chapel Hill, NC: Algonquin Books, 2020.

Untokening Collective. "Untokening 1.0—Principles of Mobility Justice." Untokening, November 11, 2017. http://www.untokening.org/updates/2017/11/11
/untokening-10-principles-of-mobility-justice.

Urry, John. *Sociology beyond Societies: Mobilities for the Twenty-First Century.*
London: Routledge, 2000.

———. "The 'System' of Automobility." *Theory, Culture and Society* 21, no. 4–5
(2004): 25–39. https://doi.org/10.1177/0263276404046059.

Vanderbilt, Tom. *Traffic: Why We Drive the Way We Do (and What It Says about Us).*
New York: Random House, 2008.

Visakha, Sneha. "Where Are Women Drivers? (with Dr. Sneha Annavarapu)." *The
Feminist City* (podcast), December 23, 2020. https://open.spotify.com
/episode/2bZRyNsnqGA3hfcSRSf5dO.

Vivanco, Luis. *Reconsidering the Bicycle: An Anthropological Perspective on a New
(Old) Thing.* London: Routledge, 2013.

Von Schnitzler, Antina. "Traveling Technologies: Infrastructure, Ethical Regimes,
and the Materiality of Politics in South Africa." *Cultural Anthropology* 28, no. 4
(2013): 670–93.

Wagh, Shweta, Hussain Indorewala, and Aaran Patel. "Mumbai's Coastal Road:
Making Land in a Drowning City." Scroll.in, August 31, 2020. https://scroll.in
/article/971791/mumbais-coastal-road-making-land-in-a-drowning-city.

Walljasper, Jay. "Ten Ways Bicycle-Friendly Streets Are Good for People Who Don't
Ride Bikes." AARP Livable Communities. Accessed October 20, 2021. https://
www.aarp.org/livable-communities/getting-around/info-2016/why-bicycling
-infrastructure-is-good-for-people-who-dont-ride-bikes.html.

Weinstein, Liza. *The Durable Slum: Dharavi and the Right to Stay Put in Globalizing
Mumbai.* Minneapolis: University of Minnesota Press, 2014.

Wilson, Kea. "On the ADA's 30th Anniversary, Remember: Bikes Are a Mobility

Assistive Device Too." *Streetsblog USA*, July 27, 2020. https://usa.streetsblog.
org/2020/07/27/on-the-adas-30th-anniversary-remember-bikes-are-a-mobility
-assistive-device-too/.

Wired. "The 20 Most Bike-Friendly Cities on the Planet, Ranked." June 17, 2019.
https://www.wired.com/story/most-bike-friendly-cities-2019-copenhagenize-
design-index/.

Zavestoski, Stephen, and Julian Agyeman, eds. *Incomplete Streets: Processes, Practices
and Possibilities*. London: Routledge, 2015.

Index

Page numbers in *italics* refer to illustration captions.

Padma Kaimal,

K. Sivaramakrishnan,

GLOBAL | and Anand A. Yang
SOUTH
ASIA | SERIES EDITORS

Global South Asia takes an interdisciplinary approach to the humanities
and social sciences in its exploration of how South Asia, through its global
influence, is and has been shaping the world.

Mumbai on Two Wheels: Cycling, Urban Space, and Sustainable Mobility,
   by Jonathan Shapiro Anjaria
Lahore Cinema: Between Realism and Fable, by Iftikhar Dadi
Adivasi Art and Activism: Curation in a Nationalist Age, by Alice Tilche
New Lives in Anand: Building a Muslim Hub in Western India,
   by Sanderien Verstappen
Mumbai Taximen: Autobiographies and Automobilities in India, by Tarini Bedi
Outcaste Bombay: City Making and the Politics of the Poor, by Juned Shaikh
The Ends of Kinship: Connecting Himalayan Lives between Nepal and New York,
   by Sienna Craig
Making Kantha, Making Home: Women at Work in Colonial Bengal, by Pika Ghosh
A Secular Need: Islamic Law and State Governance in Contemporary India,
   by Jeffery A. Redding
Making the Modern Slum: The Power of Capital in Colonial Bombay,
   by Sheetal Chhabria
History and Collective Memory in South Asia, 1200–2000, by Sumit Guha
*Climate Change and the Art of Devotion: Geoaesthetics in the Land of Krishna,
   1550–1850,* by Sugata Ray
Bhakti and Power: Debating India's Religion of the Heart, edited by John Stratton
   Hawley, Christian Lee Novetzke, and Swapna Sharma
*Marrying for a Future: Transnational Sri Lankan Tamil Marriages in the Shadow
   of War,* by Sidharthan Maunaguru
Gandhi's Search for the Perfect Diet: Eating with the World in Mind, by Nico Slate
*Mountain Temples and Temple Mountains: Architecture, Religion, and Nature in the
   Central Himalayas,* by Nachiket Chanchani
Creating the Universe: Depictions of the Cosmos in Himalayan Buddhism,
   by Eric Huntington
*Privileged Minorities: Syrian Christianity, Gender, and Minority Rights in Postcolonial
   India,* by Sonja Thomas